Urban Governance

D0071814

Historical Urban Studies

Series editors: Richard Rodger and Jean-Luc Pinol

Urban Governance

Britain and Beyond since 1750

Edited by

ROBERT J. MORRIS and
RICHARD H. TRAINOR

Ashgate

Aldershot • Burlington USA • Singapore • Sydney

JS
3025
.U733
2000

© Robert J. Morris, Richard H. Trainor and the contributors, 2000

All rights reserved. No part of this publication may be reproduced, stored in a retrieval system or transmitted in any form or by any means, electronic, mechanical, photocopying, recording, or otherwise without the prior permission of the publisher.

The authors have asserted their right under the Copyright, Designs and Patents Act, 1998, to be identified as the authors of this work.

Published by
Ashgate Publishing Limited
Gower House
Croft Road, Aldershot
Hants GU11 3HR
England

Ashgate Publishing Company
131 Main Street
Burlington
Vermont 05401
USA

Ashgate website: http://www.ashgate.com

British Library Cataloguing in Publication Data

Urban Governance: Britain and Beyond since 1750
  (Historical Urban Studies)
  1. Municipal government–Great Britain–History.
  2. Municipal government–History. 3. Cities and towns–
  Growth–Social aspects–History.
  I. Morris, R.J. (Robert John), 1943– . II. Trainor,
  Richard H. (Richard Hughes), 1948– .
  320.8'5'09

Library of Congress Catalog Card Number: 99–69568

ISBN 0 7546 0015 7

This book is printed on acid free paper

Typeset in Times Roman by Password, Norwich, UK
Printed and bound by Athenaeum Press, Ltd.,
Gateshead, Tyne & Wear.

Contents

Historical Urban Studies
General Editors' Preface

Density and proximity of buildings and people are two of the defining characteristics of the urban dimension. It is these which identify a place as uniquely urban, though the threshold for such pressure points varies from place to place. What is considered an important cluster in one context may not be considered as urban elsewhere. A third defining characteristic is functionality – the commercial or strategic position of a town or city which conveys an advantage. Over time, these functional advantages may diminish, or the balance of advantage may change within a hierarchy of towns. To understand how the relative importance of towns shifts over time and space is to grasp a set of relationships which is fundamental to the study of urban history.

Towns and cities are products of history, yet have themselves helped to shape history. As the proportion of urban-dwellers has increased, so the urban dimension has proved a legitimate unit of analysis through which to understand the spectrum of human experience and to explore the cumulative memory of past generations. Though obscured by layers of economic, social and political change, the study of the urban milieu provides insights into the functioning of human relationships and, if urban historians themselves are not directly concerned with current policy studies, few contemporary concerns can be understood without reference to the historical development of towns and cities.

This longer historical perspective is essential to an understanding of social processes. Crime, housing conditions and property values, health and education, discrimination and deviance, and the formulation of regulations and social policies to deal with them were, and remain, amongst the perennial preoccupations of towns and cities – no historical period has a monopoly of these concerns. They recur in successive generations, albeit in varying mixtures and strengths; the details may differ but the central forces of class, power and authority in the city remain. If this was the case for different periods, so it was for different geographical entities and cultures. Both scientific knowledge and technical information were available across Europe and showed little respect for frontiers. Yet despite common concerns and access to broadly similar knowledge, different solutions to urban problems were proposed and adopted by towns and cities in different parts of Europe. This comparative dimension informs urban historians as to which were systematic factors and which were of a purely local nature: general and particular forces can be distinguished.

These analytical frameworks, considered in a comparative context, inform the books in this series.

Jean-Luc Pinol
Richard Rodger

Université des sciences humaines de Strasbourg
University of Leicester

Preface

Richard H. Trainor and Robert J. Morris

The chapters in this book are part of a renaissance, and a refocusing, of urban history in Britain, with implications for the study of the subject in other countries as well as in the UK.

The book's origins lie in a conference on the theme of 'Urban Governance' held at the University of Leeds by the Urban History Group in March 1998: the chapters are revised versions of some of the papers given on that occasion.[1] The Leeds conference was the fifth in a new series of annual residential meetings held by the Group, which has resumed the pattern that flourished from the late 1960s to the mid-1980s, initially under the leadership of H.J. Dyos.[2] The current series of conferences represents an increasingly successful attempt by the Urban History Group to attract and energise a new generation of urban historians in the same way that, in an earlier phase, the organisation inspired predecessors who joined the profession in the two decades commencing in the mid-1960s. Like the journal *Urban History*,[3] then, and the forthcoming *Cambridge Urban History of Britain*,[4] the current conferences of the Urban History Group both reflect and contribute to a new lease of life for the subject in Britain. Happily this renaissance, like the initial phase, has not been conceived in narrowly British terms, as the contents of the current volume indicate. By attracting conference participants and authors based in and/or studying other countries, the new phase of urban history in Britain has linked itself effectively to a similar renewal of the subject elsewhere, evident for example in the American-based Urban History Association and the biennial international conferences of urban history.

This volume's theme of 'urban governance' encapsulates the way in which the new phase of urban history in Britain both builds on and goes beyond the approach of former decades. 'Governance' encompasses the municipal sphere on which so much valuable earlier work focused. However, reflecting increasing concern with 'civil society',[5] the concept also stretches into other arenas which attract the attention of ever more urban historians, notably the non-municipal arms of local government, voluntary institutions, and the organisations of professional and business life. Also, this volume indicates the ways in which urban history, including the study of municipal affairs, has become increasingly concerned with the connections *among* spheres of urban activity. Moreover, some of the chapters contained here deal, as the subject increasingly does, with topics such as ritual and culture,

and with issues such as identity, power and class, which transcend particular
types of institution and, in many ways, formal institutional life itself.

The book's first three chapters set the scene for those that follow. Robert
Morris begins by exploring the concept of governance and relating it to the
last two centuries of urbanisation. Then, investigating how urban historians
can use concepts derived from political science to study governance, Mike
Goldsmith and John Garrard demonstrate how the local élites of the late
twentieth century differ from their Victorian predecessors. Finally, Richard
Trainor's chapter directs attention to the voluntary sphere as well as to
local government, preferring an emphasis on adaptation to one on decline
in the analysis of long-term changes in urban governance.

The next three chapters apply recent perspectives in urban history to the
study of local government, refusing to take for granted the identity, efficacy
and timing of key leaders and policies. Employing systematic quantitative
analysis in his study of Victorian municipalities, Robert Millward explains
why different types of town had varied in their patterns of municipal spending
and undermines any simple link between expenditure and improvements in
public health. In a chapter which challenges the traditional preoccupation
with elected élites in local government, Irene Maver's case study of Glasgow
indicates the importance of municipal civil servants, despite major changes
in the political context, in determining the nature and impact of the policies
pursued in governing a major industrial city. Then Michèle Dagenais explores
the limits of activity by local government, explaining why Canadian cities
differed from their British counterparts in the timing of direct municipal
provision of services.

Chapters 7, 8 and 9 shed new light on agencies of governance which were
not, at least initially, entirely municipal. The importance of overlapping
jurisdictions, and of earlier patterns of recruitment and powers, emerges from
Ann Day's analysis of Portsea's improvement commissioners, who only
slowly and partially adopted the public health agenda of subsequent decades
and authorities. The significance of central as well as local authorities features
in her story, as it does in Chris Williams's study of the reform of Sheffield's
police force, which (again like Day's) discourages a simple 'teleological'
(or 'Whig') approach to the analysis of local governance. Also, like many
other authors in the book, Williams stresses the difficulty as well as the
necessity of acquiring legitimacy in local governance. Tim Willis's study of
health care in Sheffield before 1948 emphasises the variety of agencies,
statutory and otherwise, which were involved: they do not appear so different
from the policy networks operating in the 1990s. He also notes the importance
of ideology to the policies adopted.

These ambiguities characterise the studies of the smoke pollution problem
in Chapters 10 and 11. Geneviéve Massard-Guilbaud shows that the legal
framework itself, and the political technicalities which surrounded it, provide

only part of the explanation for the chequered history of the regulation of industrial pollution in urban France in the nineteenth and early twentieth centuries. A similar perspective on governance underpins Jean Adams's study of smoke abatement in mid-nineteenth century Stockport. She also uses the conceptual framework of 'non-decisions' to explain why, despite interference from London, regulaticn of the problem was delayed and ineffective.

The following two chapters, which touch on local government only in passing, indicate the importance of other urban institutions to the overall pattern of governance. Donna Loftus demonstrates the importance of voluntary bodies which promoted industrial conciliation, noting their increasingly complex ties to statutory organisations. Similarly, Campbell Lloyd's study of medical élites in Glasgow and Edinburgh shows how the interactions of medical academics and medical licensing bodies, with each other and with local government, affected not only the legitimacy of the local medical establishment but also the pattern of professional life and medical care more generally.

Chapters 14, 15 and 16 indicate the utility, in understanding urban governance, of standing back from the mêlée of conflicting institutions. Casting new light on a problem usually analysed only with reference to public health, Julie Rugg's study of graveyards demonstrates how the inhabitants of early nineteenth-century towns had to choose the types of agencies through which to deliver this basic service. As with so many aspects of urban governance, the choice (local, secular, usually non-profit organisations) was by no means predetermined. Meanwhile, Simon Gunn's investigation of ritual shows its importance to the civic culture of large cities not simply as co-ordinating disparate activities but also as a projection of authority and continuity which made power visible. Finally, Narayani Gupta's exploration of the management of public space in nineteenth- and twentieth-century Delhi points to the importance for governance not only of political frameworks but also of deep-seated cultural assumptions, including the perceptions of ordinary urban-dwellers themselves. Gupta's study – taking urban governance not only outside Britain but also beyond the framework of formal institutional life – exemplifies many of the innovative aspects not only of this collection but also of recent urban history more generally.

Notes

1. The organisers of that conference included Professor Richard Rodger (University of Leicester), Professor Colin Pooley (University of Lancaster) and Dr John Garrard (University of Salford). Like other meetings in the resumed series, the conference was held back-to-back with the annual conference of the Group's original parent body, the Economic History Society, whose conference organiser, Professor John Chartres (University of Leeds), also contributed greatly. Crucial assistance with the current volume has been provided by Mrs Lorna Aitken of the Department of Economic and Social

History, University of Edinburgh, and Mrs Maureen Galbraith, Department of Economic and Social History, University of Glasgow. Information on the Group can be obtained from Professor Rodger at the Department of Economic and Social History, University of Leicester, Leicester LE1 7RH.

2. For important collections of essays arising out of the initial phase of the Urban History Group, see H.J. Dyos (ed.), *The Study of Urban History* (London: 1968) and D. Fraser and A. Sutcliffe (eds), *The Pursuit of Urban History* (London: 1983). Earlier conferences in the second series were held at the Universities of Nottingham (1994, on culture), Edinburgh (1995, on élites), Lancaster (1996, on space) and Sussex (1997, on civil society).

3. Edited by Richard Rodger and published by Cambridge University Press since 1992, the journal is a direct successor to the *Urban History Yearbook* (1974–91, published by Leicester University Press). Both periodicals have had close associations with the Group. For instance, *Urban History* has published special numbers based on recent conferences: on culture, S. Nenadic (ed.), (vol. 22, 1998) and on civil society (vol. 25, 1998).

4. In three volumes, on the medieval, early modern and modern periods, edited respectively by Professors David Palliser (University of Hull), Peter Clark (University of Leicester) and Martin Daunton (University of Cambridge).

5. See the essays by R.J. Morris, G. Morton and M. Gorsky in *Urban History* (vol. 25, 1998), pp. 289–301, 348–67, 302–22.

Contributors

Jean Adams is part-time lecturer in Politics and History at the University of Salford.

Michèle Dagenais is Associate Professor in the Department of History at the Université de Montréal.

Ann Day is a Research Associate in the History Research Centre at the University of Portsmouth.

John Garrard is Senior Lecturer in Urban History at the University of Salford, specialising in the study of nineteenth-century cities.

Mike Goldsmith is Pro Vice Chancellor and Professor of Government and Politics at the University of Salford and author and editor of several books and articles on comparative local government.

Simon Gunn is Principal Lecturer in History in the School of Cultural Studies at Leeds Metropolitan University.

Narayani Gupta is Professor in the Department of History and Culture, Jamia Millia Islamia, New Delhi.

Campbell F. Lloyd is a Research Associate in the Wellcome Unit for the History of Medicine at the University of Glasgow.

Donna Loftus, who completed a PhD on social economy in mid-nineteenth century England, is a Research Associate working on Victorian auto-biography in the History Research Centre at the University of Portsmouth.

Geneviève Massard-Guilbaud is lecturer in Modern History at Blaise-Pascal University, Clermont-Ferrand, France.

Irene Maver is a lecturer in Scottish History at the University of Glasgow, and author of *Glasgow* (Edinburgh University Press, 2000).

Robert Millward is Professor of Economic History at the University of Manchester.

Robert J. Morris is Professor of Economic and Social History in the Department of Economic and Social History at the University of Edinburgh.

Julie Rugg is a member of the Cemetery Research Group at the University of York.

Richard H. Trainor is Vice-Principal, and Professor of Social History in the Department of Economic and Social History, at the University of Glasgow.

Chris Williams is a Research Fellow in the European Centre for the Study of Policing at the Open University.

Tim Willis was a research student in the Department of History at Sheffield Hallam University, and is now a Research Associate in the Department of Geography at the University of Portsmouth.

CHAPTER ONE

Governance: two centuries of urban growth

Robert J. Morris

At the heart of this book is a set of topics which have long attracted the attention of urbanists and urban historians, the growth and 'reform' of urban local government,[1] centre-local relationships,[2] public health and pollution,[3] local government finance,[4] the nature of local social élites[5] and of participation in local government.[6] Approaching these topics through the concept of governance not only brings a series of new questions to this familiar ground but also extends the scope of enquiry for the historian seeking to understand the towns and cities of Britain in a period of rapid growth and change. Such an approach has also led to a discussion that has set British experience against the experience of other places that were deeply influenced by British practice and values, such as India, or by the processes of industrialisation and growth, such as France, or by all these, such as Canada.

Questions of governance must be central to a variety of enquiries into the nature of the urban place. Governance as a concept gains its power from the questions posed, questions about the ordering of order, and about the organisation and legitimisation of authority. At the heart of governance are the sets of institutions and procedures through which a political system operates. In other words, the patterns and processes which create and organise authority, provide access to resources, provide for the delivery of services, and generate and deliver policy. These questions concern the interaction of government and society in a way which recognises that governance is not limited to actions of 'the state' and that the boundary between state and civil society is permeable and blurred.[7]

As Goldsmith and Garrard show, the debate over governance arose in the context of the 1980s which saw considerable changes and growing tension in the relationship between the state and the market. Most noticeable was the privatisation of a wide range of state-owned industrial corporations followed by the return to profit-seeking ownership of a number of the 'natural monopolies' which nineteenth-century urban élites had taken into public ownership. This was accompanied by the growth of public–private partnerships. Initially these were directed towards urban regeneration in projects such as the London Docklands Redevelopment Corporation established in 1981.[8] There was a growing recognition that policy was generated and services delivered in the context of a network of state, local state, voluntary and private (i.e. profit-orientated) agencies. By the end of the decade there was an increase in the use within the state sector, of mechanisms borrowed from the world of business, such as market testing, contracting out, the use of performance indicators, the delivery of resources through a process of competition between state agencies for limited funds and other devices designed to mimic the discipline of profit-seeking, branch plant accountancy and the scrutiny of the stock market.[9]

This tension of state and market and the associated changes were accompanied by the growing power of a variety of supranational organisations. Some, like the European Union and World Trade Organisation, derived their authority from nation states, but gathered increasing autonomy. Others were based upon the creation and increasing efficiency of global markets for capital and commodities. Legal entities, notably multinational companies gained power over employment and investment in the localities in a way which was difficult for the state to direct, structure or control.[10]

Debate arose in the 1970s and 1980s from a sense that political administrative systems had reached a point of diminishing returns. The growth of the state sector was perceived to be delivering neither increases in welfare nor in economic growth. Many social systems seemed to be becoming ungovernable in the sense that the political system was unable to deliver 'consent'. Where pluralist political systems existed, electorates rejected parties identified with the expansion of the state. In other political systems, black markets expanded and productivity in the formal economy stagnated. Indeed, political theorists reflecting on this period related the success of some political systems and the failure of others not only to the existence of a pluralist political system but also to the dominance of market relationships and to the breadth of civil society. Civil Society in this context referred to social relationships and institutions which were free both of the prescriptive direction of the state and of the family and community. In any Darwinian struggle of social systems, the winner in terms of war, economic competition, and welfare delivered to citizens was the system which included major limits on the power of the state.[11]

This sense of ungovernability and the limits of politics and administration was linked to a growth in three aspects of social and economic interaction: its complexity and diversity; the dynamic character of both technology and socio-economic relationships (or speed of change); and the increase in interdependence which could entail huge losses from quite minor failures but at the same time increased the potential gains from co-operation. These changes led to a recognition that the patterns and processes which had delivered 'policy' and organised authority needed to be questioned and extended. Centre–local relationships and hierarchies of authority were replaced or perhaps supplemented by networks and partnerships. Policy-makers sought to 'steer' rather than control social and economic relationships. The power and influence of information and argument were recognised as well as the partially autonomous power of media with a bewildering sense of global unity in terms of apparent knowability, implied agency and moral responsibility.

This debate was both analytical and formative. It was designed to understand what was happening but also to direct decision-takers and policy-makers. The historian alerted by these debates can plunder them for questions and will also wish to remind the political scientist that many of the patterns identified with the post-1970s period were not new. Partnerships and networks, varied patterns of service delivery, diminishing returns to government and ungovernability can all be identified in the case studies in this collection. The historian's contribution must be tempered and informed by a recognition of the very different nature of the dynamics of state and society in the nineteenth-century urban industrial economy.

First the urban élites were coherent, integrated and based in the locality. The political, the social and the capital-owning élites were coherent and integrated because of common membership, because of family links and intermarriage. They met at church and chapel, public meetings, public and private social occasions. They were often divided by party and religion but developed codes and conventions for negotiating such differences.[12] The resident owner-manager was the dominant form of organization for local capital.[13] Local government included major and minor owners of local capital. Indeed the successful management of a business was considered by many as an essential qualification for being elected as a local councillor.[14] Élite is used here to refer to those social groups identified with a concentration of power. In some localities, as the study of Portsea/Portsmouth indicates, this might not involve especially high social status. In other places the participation of the high-status élite fluctuated in response to challenges from lower-status groups.[15]

Especially distinctive in the nineteenth century was the intensely self-referential nature of the urban place. The newspaper, the trade directory and the structure of voluntary societies predominantly referred to the urban place. Units of local government were created for the town as were parliamentary constituencies. This self-referential culture concealed important links and networks between towns and between town and country. Networks of cousins, of religious congregations and voluntary societies linked towns, and linked provincial town to metropolis. Labour, capital and commodity markets meant that Manchester, Birmingham, Leeds and the rest waited anxiously for news of the London capital market, skilled artisans supported a tramping system to sustain labour mobility, and prices in the cotton plantations of the United States were part of the economic fortunes of Lancashire towns.[16] Nevertheless, the nineteenth century saw nothing to equate to the wilful destruction of urban identity in the local government reforms of the 1970s, or in the national and global restructuring of media in the last half of the twentieth century.

The most important difference lay in the relationship of state and market. The late twentieth-century changes in governance originated in bureaucratic failures. The nineteenth century was responding to market failure – pollution, public health, poverty, education and public order were all issues which when left to market forces generated increasing negative externalities, sometimes in the dramatic form of epidemic and riot but usually in the persistent dangers of disease, disorder, premature death and alienation. These failures were related to three features of social and economic relationships. The first was a major inequality of income which may indeed have increased in the early nineteenth century. Such inequalities lay behind features of working-class housing and the employment of children which attracted growing concern and attention during the century.[17] The second feature was the absence or imperfection of representative elements in government which blocked a universal identity with state authority at either a local or national level. Finally, urban growth itself was already by the 1830s producing aspects of the complexity and interdependence associated with the post-1970s debate. The density and complexity of the city meant that the externalities generated by housing and health were magnified. The natural monopolies of water and gas were a product of the piped technology required by the urban place and this was one of many urban patterns which drew in the involvement of local state agencies.

Many of these case studies were located in a period which experienced the beginning of a protracted expansion in the power and resources of the state, and during that period of expansion itself with the consolidation of the hierarchical centre–local relationships involved.

What, then were the major directions of change in the nature of governance in the period covered by the chapters in this collection?

First, there was simply more of it at all levels. The state, both central and local, generated a greater variety of agencies with more tasks, powers and resources. The same happened within civil society. Voluntary associations were not new in the 1780s, but in the 70 years which followed they increased in number and variety.[18] Even at the level of the individual, the governance of self became more elaborate and disciplined in terms of manners, etiquette and self-governance.

Within the state and within civil society there was an important shift in the basis for claiming legitimacy. State agencies moved towards more systematic control by representative processes. These processes were very far from democracy. It was property or some limited form of citizenship which was represented in a variety of electoral processes. Self-electing municipal corporations which drew legitimacy from their charters were replaced by corporations which were regularly tested by representative elections. As new agencies were created – improvement commissioners, poor law boards and school boards – they were selected by representative elections. Even in civil society, there was a move towards the subscriber democracy form of voluntary society in which committees and officers were chosen by the votes of subscription-paying members at annual general meetings.[19] Earlier associations had tended to have closed or self-selecting membership based upon the lodge or the trust. New members required to be proposed and accepted rather than simply joining by paying a subscription.

The focus was increasingly upon the urban place. When the eighteenth century had taken collective action, the emphasis tended to be upon the county association. The towns were gathering places for the county at the assize, the assembly or the race meeting.[20] When Daniel Defoe visited the cloth market at Leeds at the start of the century, he was watching the town as the organising centre for the economic activity of the countryside. When the cloth halls were built in mid-century, the owners of stands were the clothiers from the surrounding villages. The Leeds General Infirmary founded just after mid-century gathered its subscriptions from surrounding county families as well as from the local élite.[21] On the other hand, the Leeds Public Dispensary, founded in the early nineteenth century, was a town organisation dominated by subscribers from the town.[22] This focus upon the town and the self-referential nature of the urban place were dominant parts of the governance and self-perception of urban communities. Throughout the period there was a tendency for the many supra-urban structures which existed to be partly hidden from public comment. In the public domain of courtroom and newspaper nothing could be more local than the magistrates, both county and borough, but they were appointed by the Home Secretary and, in most places, until the 1830s and 1840s, were heavily dependent upon units of the regular army for main force backing. Such organisations increased with the growing complexity and integration of urban industrial society. The legislative authority required for local improvements in paving and drainage, for canals, turnpikes and railways was a matter for the Private Bill Committee of the House of Commons. In the manufacturing areas key elements of capital were locally owned but regulated by the Factory Inspectorate, a body created in 1833 and controlled with bureaucratic precision through a hierarchy based in London.[23] By the 1860s, most railways were controlled by large national companies operating under Board of Trade Regulations. The provision of schooling was intensely local, operated by voluntary societies and, after 1870–72, by locally elected, local rate-raising school boards but under those same acts of the 1870s, they were to be inspected by hierarchies based in London and Edinburgh.

Within the structures of nineteenth-century local government there were dynamic and apparently contradictory patterns. After the creation of representative government in the reforms that followed the Municipal Corporations Act of 1835, the new municipal corporation gathered many functions about itself, especially those of police and improvement commission. Boundaries were extended as part of an imperfect spatial rationalisation designed to mass the reserves of government resources with the aim of increased efficiency and effectiveness. Running counter to this trend of unifying the structures of local government was a fragmentation which responded to the socio-cultural divisions within urban society. The Poor Law boards remained on the edge of urban government.[24] Education was so divisive that it required its own representative agency designed to accommodate the clash of religious sectarian interests.

The growing number of agencies of governance were, in essence, collective agencies. They were designed to deal with problems and achieve objectives which were impossible within the allocative mechanisms of the family and the market. As such these agencies needed to attract trust from and be accorded legitimacy by diverse groups and individuals, most of whom had an imperfect knowledge of each other and differed in their interests and social values. Legitimacy and support were claimed in a number of ways. A culture which provided information and debate within a public sphere evolved in the late eighteenth and early nineteenth centuries. Accounts were published and audited. In the voluntary sector subscription lists were published. The meetings of local government bodies and their committees were held in public, and the debates and speeches reported often quasi-verbatim in the local newspaper press. Public meetings were called, held and reported with a ritualised format of open debate and tolerance. The manner in which contentious public issues were settled moved from the disorder of riot and suppression to the more ordered form of public meeting and petition.[25] The legitimacy of these debates and meetings was based upon their openness to all sides in an argument and the representative nature of the participants. The second source of legitimacy came from the increasing use of bureaucratic forms in which individual actions were bound by rules and regulations, and were recorded to ensure scrutiny and consistency.[26] An important element in the hierarchical structure of such bureaucracies was the paid officials, many of whom possessed specialist and professional forms of knowledge which justified their decisions and power. Emerging from these structures was a culture in which knowledge, information and argument gained an impact in debate, decision and the allocation of power and legitimacy. 'Communicative rationality' or the authority of a good argument, in the phrase of Habermas, was not the only or even the dominant form in nineteenth-century governance but it was a form which gained increasing authority.[27]

These chapters show the variety of ways in which the ordering of order could be produced and in which policies and services could be delivered. The major options were as follows:

1 Institutions based upon representative elections and taxation delivered services with a unified space or territory.

   (a) A subset of this category asserted central or imperial authority through prefects or colonial officials. Representatives were used as a base for consultation and not as the direct source of authority. In Britain there were a growing number of boards and inspectors who worked within the territorial remits of region and locality.

2 There were specialist territorial institutions such as school boards and Poor Law boards with their own particular structure of representative election and bureaucratic and professional support.

   (a) There were an increasing number of regulatory approval-giving, authority-giving bodies, which legitimated and reproduced knowledge and expertise (like the Scottish universities). The nineteenth century saw a growing number of charter bodies which attributed authority to those who operated in the local and urban environment, such as lawyers, medical men and engineers. Some such as Northern Lights provided services, in this case maintaining lighthouses in Scotland.

3 Services might be delivered through co-operation between state and 'voluntary bodies', as in the example of medical services.

4 There were many voluntary non profit making bodies such as mechanics institutions, public dispensaries and charities for the relief of the poor.

5 Some voluntary organisations, such as some of the cemetery companies and bath companies, sought limited profits. Five per cent philanthropy was not only concerned with London housing.

6 At the other extreme of this continuum, the delivery of gas and water and much transport was made by companies operating for profit, but this was done in such a way that the authority of the urban was required, notably in matters of way leave for the 'natural monopolies'.

Local government was and still is a crucial element of urban governance. The question, 'Whose authority?' still has familiar answers in terms of the class composition of elected bodies, but the question also needs to be posed in terms of central and local state, in terms of elected representatives and officials, in terms of professional versus political authority. Local government was a form of authority which derived from the complex compulsions and legitimacies of 'the state'. In theory the British derived their 'legitimacy' of government from the notion either of 'consent' (Locke) or of 'utility' (Bentham). In practice by the mid-eighteenth century, British urban authority came from three sources, previous charters (usually a seventeenth-century one renewing earlier grants), other legal agreements, or from Parliament in Westminster. By the late eighteenth century all 'new' forms of state authority came from Parliament rather than directly from the Crown.

There was a paradox in this relationship. Despite the assertive ambition of the localities in Britain to be self-referential, despite the frequently made contrast between the centralized nature of the French state and the local nature of the British state, the legitimacy of state power in legal fact and theory derived from Parliament or, to be accurate, the Crown in Parliament. This total dependence of the locality upon the centre was evident every time a local élite required some form of legislation.[28] This dependence was mediated by the networks of political patronage and influence which operated through the aristocratic families and, by the mid-nineteenth century, through the political parties.

Within localities, the agencies of the local and central state were not the only locations of authority and legitimacy. Ownership of capital in land, commerce and manufacturing was accepted as a qualification to claim legitimate authority within state agencies and civil society. This authority claimed legitimacy not only from the simple ownership of capital but from a link between responsibility and privilege which was asserted across the public sphere.

Consent to this government was organised not just by the implied threat of force behind each Act of Parliament but also by the organisation of consent through ritual, through politics and ideology. In an important chapter Gunn pays attention to some of the very visible forms of urban ritual, and in doing so leaves many questions. The state was much more than the aggregation of those agencies which had a monopoly of legitimate force.

During the period covered by these chapters, two recent and increasingly important sources of authority and legitimacy emerged. Many of the activities of government rapidly created and expanded a key form of authority – the bureaucracy. Members of these bureaucracies were bearers of skill and knowledge, organisers of information. The most numerous records of local government do not involve the grand events of elections and council chamber debates but the countless records of demands, receipts and permissions, lamp rates, improvement rates, pavement rates and, above all, building permits. Behind these slips of paper were officials patiently filling columns in rate books and financial accounts. They were joined by the Town Clerk, the Manager of the Gas Works and a Medical Officer of Health. These people derived their authority from complex bodies of specialist knowledge whilst the clerk in the rates office derived authority from the organisation of a more basic set of information, the account book entry and the tiny slips of paper that recorded and acknowledged payment or which calculated and reminded citizens and property owners of the sums which were due. Authority derived from the records themselves and the Act of Parliament which legitimated them.

In one case study after another, scientific and professional knowledge played an influential part in the creation and implementation of policy. Any shift in authority from moral worth and social status towards the rational knowledge of bureaucracies, professionals and experts was imperfect and contested. This imperfection lay in the nature of that knowledge as well as its implementation. In the 1850s and 1860s it was not self-evident that the dictates of the public health propagandists would produce the results anticipated. Indeed in several places ill-placed sewage and water supply systems only made matters worse. Even in the 1920s, as the example of Sheffield indicates, the apparently self-evident logic of the benefits of smallpox vaccination was contested. Even in this case it was not simply a matter of the ethical liberal argument for individual freedom of choice versus scientific logic. From the point of view of the local working-class politician energies directed towards the painful process of vaccination might well have produced better results if directed towards improving housing and the incomes of the poor. Specialist legitimacy had to be fought for. The contest over bodies for anatomy classes in the 1830s was one aspect of this.[29] Contests over the prestigious and voluntary posts as surgeon and physician in the local voluntary hospitals involved social as well as professional qualifications. Campbell Lloyd shows that the agencies which attributed professional status were an important part of urban governance. These contests were given a central place in George Eliot's novel *Middlemarch*. Smoke and industrial pollution were other issues in which incomplete scientific logic played a part. Such logic involved not only the analysis of the problem but equally importantly the proposal of solutions. Despite the very different authority structures in Stockport and Clermont-Ferrand the outcome was equally indecisive throughout the nineteenth century. The centrally appointed prefect, decision-taker, transmitter of power, resolver of contradictions was in general weak in the face of the manufacturers' local knowledge and interest. Lord Redesdale, aristocratic power broker, might force smoke clauses upon the locality with the authority of Parliament and the expert witnesses of its select committees, but masterly inactivity in the locality created a crude but effective implementation gap which placed the issue once more off the agenda. The legitimacy of the public meeting or the pressure group campaign came to depend upon the quality of its information. The Anti Corn Law League used a torrent of 'facts' as well as moral and political argument. When Edward Baines defended the educational record of the manufacturing districts, he filled his writing with tables and figures, most gathered from the new cultural products of census and parliamentary report.[30]

The capacity to produce 'knowledge' was enhanced and greatly influenced by the powerful resources of government with its enquiries, committees and reports. 'Communicative rationality' gained increasing agency, legitimacy and authority independent of the status and authority of the individual and institution doing the communicating, but that influence was contested and by no means decisive.

How effective was this multi-centred protean structure of governance? How indeed should its effectiveness be judged? Historians have abandoned any simple concept of 'social control' as a useful way of understanding policy and social action in an industrial society. Such a concept implied a sense of coherent and co-ordinated action on the part of élites and a lack of autonomy and agency by subordinate groups which did not accord with the evidence. Indeed it was not clear what sort of evidence was appropriate for an often ill-defined concept.[31] The literature on governance has introduced a concept of 'steering' by policy-makers which recognizes the interaction and multi-centred nature of sources of power and initiative. Certainly the urban élites of the industrial city system had a variety of projects towards which they tried to steer other social groups. The resulting relationship was much more one of bargaining than control. Such projects might involve the ordered educated populations sought by urban middle-class élites in the nineteenth century, the imperial authority of India or the 'booster' growth in population, capital and real estate values of the North American town. Judgements on the effectiveness of authority and power must recognise that the agencies and relationships which projected power were diffuse, multi-centred and networked. 'Steering', the promotion of projects, involved bargaining, interaction and co-operation in an increasingly complex and interdependent society. From this feature came the development of a variety of practices designed to foster trust within these patterns of co-operation: open discussion; representative agencies; the publication and public discussion of information and argument; and the presentation of scientific and professional argument and expertise as an objective source of authority, autonomous of social status and interest.

The major strands of urban theory all suggest that urban growth and urbanisation in themselves provided incentives for an increase in governance. The concept of modern urbanization as size, density and complexity raises many questions of order and co-ordination.[32] Considered as a biological entity the urban place would rapidly evolve into a perpetual traffic jam dispersed by high death rates created by disease and violence. The density of the urban place was a perfect environment in which water-borne and droplet infection could prosper. The apparent lack of social discipline in secondary social relationships was equally suitable for immorality and violence. This process would only be accelerated by the alienation and anomie experienced by individuals. This is perhaps a caricature of some aspects of urban theory and of one strand of the cultural interpretations of the urban. It is also an account of an event which never happened. Human beings rapidly learnt to live in the growing city without the trauma which theory and cultural introspection predicted. The reflexive aspects of the structures and cultures of human society were and are nowhere more clearly exemplified than in the urban place. Within two or three generations industrial urban society had reversed the unfavourable urban death rates of the nineteenth century to a point where the rapidly urbanising areas of Africa in the twentieth century are likely to have a more favourable demographic regime than the countryside.

Weber's concept of the urban place as a market and a fort paid direct attention to the nature of urban authority and its organisation.[33] The organization of authority was both integral to the nature of urbanism and essential to the co-ordination of the many activities, elements and experiences that make up the urban. Although the work of anthropologists has been principally directed at early forms of urbanisation, their questions need to be directed at the urban industrial system.[34] Governance was involved with the creation of 'meanings'. This has appeared in two forms. First in the development of ritual, ceremony and myth. As Gunn shows, such ritual developed in a fairly coherent way over the nineteenth century. In India, 'meanings' were imposed and contested creating considerable discontinuities. New meanings were also involved in the creation of knowledge and in the contest between scientific and professional knowledge, and ethical, religious and political interest and assertion.

Conclusions derived from an initial series of chapters must be tentative but several directions of change have already been identified. The contrast between the British case studies and those of France, Canada and India suggests the manner in which context influenced the agenda and outcomes of governance. As Dagenais shows, Canadian urban government was initiated in a context which emphasised the interests of real estate. British urban policy-makers had little need to encourage urban growth in order to sustain the value of their real estate. The need was to control some of the results of such growth, notably in public health. Millward's figures do show that the historian's emphasis on public health was justified by the resource allocation of local authorities. It should be remembered that other aspects of governance would not show up in spending figures such as building regulations where the cost would fall upon the builders, property owners and rent payers not the local authority. In North America, fire and the development of urban real estate dominated. In India, the need to impose the authority and ensure spatial security of the colonial government had a prominent place along with the objective of integrating Indian economic activity with imperial trade patterns.

The patterns of governance outlined in these chapters show the variety of structures within which services were delivered. The delivery of the same service took place in many different ways. The orderly and socially acceptable disposal of the dead was at once a universal requirement but also one which had particular urban aspects of health and decency in large dense settlements. Rugg's study showed that burial of the dead changed in response to the pressures of urban growth but could be delivered in a variety of ways ranging from old parish religious institutional based structures to commercial or modified commercial structures. The common feature for success and acceptability was some form of local identity with the urban place. Many aspects of the patterns of governance outlined between 1750 and 1950 reflect the patterns identified in the 1980s and 1990s. Partnerships were involved in the delivery of health and hospital services. Partnership was also involved in working-class education and, by mid-century, in further education. Voluntary schools gained and accepted a growing amount of state finance and regulation from the 1830s onwards. The blurred boundary between state and civil society was also involved in the Wage Conciliation Boards. In effect the state provided the framework for self-regulation through the partnership of two major interests, labour and capital. Within all these patterns the growing but contested importance of scientific and professional knowledge and expertise appeared in study after study. Those who seek to understand the 'order' of British towns and cities between 1750 and 1950 must identify multiple sources and patterns of power and authority involved in the creation and implementation of policy, and in the social 'steering' attempted by élites and other interest groups.

Notes

1. J. Redlich and F.W. Hirst, *Local Government in England* (1903); Brian Keith-Lucas, *English Local Government in the Nineteenth and Twentieth Centuries* (1977); Derek Fraser, *Power and Authority in the Victorian City* (Oxford: 1979).
2. Christine Bellamy, *Administering Central-Local Relations, 1871–1919: The Local Government Board in its Fiscal and Cultural Context* (Manchester: 1988); E.P. Hennock, 'The Creation of an Urban Local Government System in England and Wales', in *Stadteordnungen des 19. Jahrhunderts* (Cologne and Vienna: 1984).
3. Anthony S. Wohl, *Endangered Lives: Public Health in Victorian Britain* (London: 1983); Anne Hardy, *The Epidemic Streets: Infectious Disease and*

the Rise of Preventive Medicine, 1856–1900 (Oxford: 1993).

4. Robert Millward and Sally Sheard, 'The Urban Fiscal Problem, 1870–1914: Government Expenditure and Finance in England and Wales', *Economic History Review*, 48 (1995) pp. 531–5; E.P. Hennock, Finance and Politics in urban local government in England, 1835–1900, *Historical Journal*, 6 (1963), pp. 212–25.

5. R.J. Morris, *Class, Sect and Party: The Making of the British Middle Class: Leeds, 1820–50* (Manchester: 1990); Stana Nenadic, 'The Structure, Values and Influence of the Scottish Urban Middle Class: Glasgow, 1800–1870', PhD thesis, University of Glasgow, 1986; 'The Victorian Middle Classes', in W. Hamish Fraser and Irene Maver (eds), *Glasgow, Vol. II: 1830–1912* (Manchester: 1996), pp. 265–99; R.H. Trainor, 'Authority and Social Structure in an Industrial Area: A Study of Three Black Country Towns, 1840–1890', DPhil thesis, University of Oxford, 1981; R.H. Trainor, *Black Country Elites: The Exercise of Authority in an Industrialized Area, 1830–1900* (Oxford: 1993).

6. John Garrard, *Leadership and Power in Victorian Industrial Towns, 1830–1880* (Manchester: 1983).

7. Jan Kooiman (ed.), *Modern Governance: New Government – Society Interactions* (London: 1993); Graeme Morton, 'Civil Society, Municipal Government and the State: Enshrinement, Empowerment and Legitimacy: Scotland, 1800–1929', *Urban History*, 25 (1998), pp. 348–67; and Chapter 2 by Mike Goldsmith and John Garrard in this volume.

8. Sue Brownhill, *Developing London's Docklands* (London: 1990); Docklands Consultative Committee, *The Docklands Experiment: A Critical Review of Eight Years of the London Docklands Development Corporation* (London: 1990).

9. Kooiman, *Modern Governance*, especially the introduction and chapter by Kooiman, pp. 1–8 and 35–49.

10. Doreen Massey, *Spatial Divisions of Labour: Social Structures and the Geography of Production* (London: 1984).

11. Francis Fukyama, *The End of History and the Last Man* (London: 1992); Ernest Gellner, *Conditions of Liberty: Civil Society and its Rivals* (London: 1994); Jon A. Hall (ed.), *Civil Society: Theory, History, Comparison* (Cambridge: 1994); Robert D. Putnam, *Making Democracy Work: Civic Traditions in Modern Italy* (Princeton, NJ: 1993).

12. Morris, *Class, Sect and Party*, pp. 264–79.

13. Sidney Pollard, *The Genesis of Modern Management* (London: 1965); François Crouzet, *The First Industrialists: The Problem of Origins* (Cambridge: 1985).

14. Garrard, *Leadership and Power* p. 24.

15. E.P. Hennock, *Fit and Proper Persons: Ideal and Reality in Nineteenth Century Urban Government* (London: 1973).

16. Leonore Davidoff and Catherine Hall, *Family Fortunes: Men and Women of the English Middle Class, 1780–1850* (London: 1987); Humphrey R. Southall, 'The Tramping Artizan Revisits: Labour Mobility and Economic Distress in Early Victorian England', *Economic History Review*, 44 (1991), pp. 272–96.

17. Richard G. Rodger, 'The Invisible Hand: Market Forces, Housing and the Urban Form in Victorian Cities', in Derek Fraser and Anthony Sutcliffe (eds), *The Pursuit of Urban History* (London: 1983) pp. 190–211; R.J. Morris, 'The State, Elite and the Market: The "visible hand" in the British Industrial System', in Herman Diederiks, Paul Hohenberg and Michael Wagenaar (eds), *Economic Policy in Europe since the Later Middle Ages: The Visible Hand and the Fortune of Cities* (Leicester: 1992), pp.177–99.

18. R.J. Morris, 'Clubs, Societies and Associations', in F.M.L. Thompson (ed.), *The Cambridge Social History of Britain, 1750–195*, vol. 3 (Cambridge: 1990), pp. 395–443.
19. Derek Fraser (ed.), *Municipal Reform and the Industrial City*, (Leicester: 1982); R.J. Morris, 'Voluntary Societies and British Urban Elites, 1780–1870: An Analysis', *Historical Journal*, 24 (1982), pp. 95–118.
20. Francis Hill, *Georgian Lincoln* (Cambridge: 1966).
21. Daniel Defoe, *A Tour through the Whole Island of Great Britain* (London: 1928), (Everyman edition), pp. 204–5; S.T. Anning, *The General Infirmary at Leeds*, 2 vols (Edinburgh: 1963).
22. *Leeds Mercury*, 11 January 1840.
23. Robert Gray, *The Factory Question and Industrial England, 1830–1860* (Cambridge: 1996); John R. Kellett, *The Impact of Railways on Victorian Cities* (London: 1969).
24. For one spectacular example of boundary extension in this context see Irene Maver, 'Glasgow's Civic Government', in W. Hamish Fraser and Irene Maver (eds), *Glasgow, vol. II, 1830–1912* (Manchester: 1996); M.A. Crowther, *The Workhouse System, 1834–1929* (London: 1981).
25. Charles Tilly, *Popular Contention in Great Britain, 1758–1834* (Cambridge, MA: 1995).
26. Max Weber, in *Economy and Society*, (edited by Guenther Roth and Claus Wittich), vol. 2 (Berkeley, CA: 1978), pp. 941–1006.
27. Kooiman, *Modern Governance*, p. 109; Anthony Giddens, *The Consequences of Modernity* (Oxford: 1990).
28. Garrard, *Leadership and Power*, p. 101.
29. Ruth Richardson, *Death, Dissection and the Destitute* (London: 1987).
30. Edward Baines, jr, *On the Social, Educational and Religious State of the Manufacturing Districts* (London: 1843).
31. Gareth Stedman Jones, 'Class Expression versus Social Control', in Stedman Jones, *Languages of Class: Studies in English Working Class History, 1832–1982* (Cambridge: 1983), pp. 76–89; Michael Ignatieff, 'Total Institutions and the Working Classes: A Review Essay', *History Workshop*, 15 (1983), pp.167–73; Peter Mandler (ed.), *The Uses of Charity: The Poor on Relief in the Nineteenth Century Metropolis* (Philadelphia: 1990), especially the introduction by Mandler and the chapter on London by Ellen Ross.
32. Louis Wirth, 'Urbanism as a Way of Life', in Louis Wirth, *On Cities and Social Life*, ed. Albert J. Reiss, jr (Chicago: 1964).
33. Max Weber, *The City*, translated and edited by Don Martindale and Gertrud Neuwirth (New York: 1958).
34. Joseph Rykwert, *The Idea of a Town* (Princeton, NJ: 1988); Paul Wheatley, 'What the Greatness of a City Is Said to Be', *Pacific Viewpoint*, 4 (1963), pp. 163–89 and Paul Wheatley, 'Archaeology and the Chinese City', *World Archaeology*, 2 (1970), pp. 159–85.

CHAPTER TWO

Urban governance: some reflections

Mike Goldsmith and John Garrard

Urban governance is all the rage in the political science literature. One can hardly turn the pages of a journal without finding an article which refers to the subject, its latest incarnation and developments – as well advice on how to do things better. This chapter reviews the topic in the light of some traditional concerns of urban historians and seeks to illustrate the ways in which modern urban governance differs from that more familiar to many urban historians.

The current preoccupation with governance is a reflection of changes in the relationship between the state and the market which have taken place in most developed countries over the last 20 years, but especially in countries such as Britain, the USA, Australia and New Zealand. Much of the 1980s in Britain and since has seen the central–local government relationship change, first under the various Conservative regimes – changes which themselves led to the use of local governance as a phrase to describe local political systems in the UK – and more recently again under the Blair Government. In Europe, North America, and further afield, similar changes in intergovernmental relationships have taken place – but often in an opposite direction, with a process of decentralisation taking place in countries like the USA, France, Spain, Belgium and Italy in contrast to what most commentators have seen as a process of centralisation occurring in Britain. What that recent experience means is that, as Newton and Karran noted in the mid-1980s, British local government is now very much *sui generis*, reflecting a penetration of the locality by the centre in a fashion unknown almost anywhere else in the Western world.[1]

Bearing that in mind, what do we mean by this phrase 'urban governance'? It is important that we start with a simple definition. The word 'governance' is in danger of following several other concepts used by political scientists, such as corporatist, globalisation, postmodern, in taking on the characteristics of a Heinz product in having 57 varieties of definition. Essentially the word 'governance' is used to describe the set of institutions, rules and procedures by which a political system is governed. In relation to cities or localities it has come into fashion following the increased fragmentation of local institutions in countries like the UK during the 1980s and 1990s. These changes have brought into play a whole range of new local institutions, many of them non-elected, but which are responsible for a whole range of local-level services and the like. Indeed, as a reviewer of a recent collection of essays pointed out[2] (perhaps rightly berating the authors represented in the collection for ignoring this phenomenon in a discussion of local democracy), such quangos account for a considerable amount of public expenditure. But in addition there is a third characteristic associated with the growth of such institutions – namely, the development of local-level partnerships, coalitions and networks based on a process of networking, often having to operate under sets of rules and procedures laid down by central government. As Bennington points out,[3] local or urban governance suggests the following:

> a broadening of the notion of local government beyond its traditional role in the (re)distribution and the delivery of statutory services into a wider role of 'governing' all aspects of the local community – providing political leadership in civil society rather than a bureaucratic public administration

To this might be added the involvement of a wider range of actors in the business of governing the local community, and the development of partnerships and joint ventures by the local authority with other public, private, voluntary and grassroots organisations.[4] Bennington usefully suggests four dimensions to the concept. First, there is the idea of moving downwards from the local authority to the grassroots – a process which involves developing and articulating the voices of the grassroots community, building the capacity of local interest groups, forming coalitions and negotiating solutions to problems. In this sense, municipal governments are engaged in building civic capacity amongst the local population. Second, there is a movement from local governments outwards to other agencies, a process involving a whole series of joint ventures, coalitions, and building networks and partnerships with other organisations, many of which are often orchestrated by the local authority. Third, there is movement inwards within the local authority, a movement which involves the provision of strategic direction, vision and leadership within the local authority as an organisation, coupled with greater internal delegation – from council to officers and from the top of the bureaucracy downwards. Fourth, there is movement upwards to central and European government and other public arenas, movement which sees the municipality and its leader performing representational, protective and promotional roles, working more closely with central government and with the various directorates of the European Commission, as well as regional and local governments drawn from other countries.

Yet, some of these key features of contemporary urban governance will be familiar to the urban historian. Nineteenth-century urban government in Britain would meet the requirements of a fragmented system almost *par excellence*, certainly in the middle of the century, notwithstanding the development of municipal boroughs after 1835. Before then, authority was very much dispersed amongst a variety of bodies – parish authorities responsible for poor relief; magistrates with responsibility for some governmental functions; borough reeves, police or improvement commissioners and others. After the 1835 Act, while things improved somewhat, borough powers were frequently shared between the new borough council and the foregoing bodies, and later with such bodies as the Board of Guardians and the Education Board.[5] In this context it is doubtful whether Britain has ever had a system of local government as distinct to local governance, if by the former we mean a single unit responsible for all local affairs.

Nor is local governance in this sense unique to the UK, as anyone remotely familiar with the USA can easily testify – one has only to reflect on Wood's classic study of New York government, aptly named *1400 Governments*.[6] The impact of the reform movement in American cities also brought with it similar features – a growth in non-elected bodies responsible for particular activities, with a multitude of bodies, elected and appointed, generally responsible for a single activity.[7] Many Canadian cities are not too dissimilar in the features they contain.[8]

If nineteenth-century UK cities had a system of urban governance, then what is different about the present day, and how have these changes come about? How have many other countries avoided a similar kind of fragmentation? Hopefully, by an analysis of these types of questions, we can throw some light on the issue of urban governance in a way which is both interesting and helpful.

At the risk of producing a caricature, let us begin by looking at nineteenth-century local politics in Britain. The one thing they were is local, with penetrations by the centre often bitterly resisted, and with most developments depending on local initiative, such as the use of locally initiated improvement legislation or through the adoption through by-laws of national permissive legislation, or increasingly from 1871 Provisional Orders from the Local Government Board.[9] Furthermore, local politics reflected local interests, which themselves engaged in local affairs. Economic activities were largely local – or at best regional – even though trade was international, as critics of the modern concept of globalisation remind us.[10] Capital was local – tied to local business and manufacturing industry – and élite were local and integrated – economic, social and political élite substantially overlapped.[11] Indeed, local élites were often active in local affairs out of a sense of public duty (*noblesse oblige?*), and did not depend on their political activity for social or economic status – rather the other way round. The most distinguished could sometimes be persuaded to enter the uncertain pleasures of Parliament – at least in part to safeguard local interests. At the same time the media and most charities were distinctly local until almost the end of the century.

As the century progressed, there was increasing central–national level concern at the failure of the municipal level to tackle some major problems – pauperism, public health, education in particular – but even here localities retained a great deal of local discretion in terms of the way they dealt with affairs. And the great reforms of the 1880s, with the creation of multi-purpose authorities, effectively confirmed local government as the major provider of local services, with (compared with today) extensive local autonomy – a model to be admired and copied around the world. This model also reflected a kind of political settlement between centre and locality – in Bulpitt's[12] terms a distinction between the centre's concerns for 'high politics' with the locality looking after 'low politics' relatively unconstrained or overseen – for example, by comparison with France, Denmark and Norway which depended on state officials (prefects) to oversee and approve the activities of local governments. In Britain localities were trusted to keep low politics off the national agenda – a real 'sewerage without tears' view. Nevertheless, for most locally initiated developments one national body remained crucial, namely Parliament and, most particularly, the Private Bill Committees. These latter could often have a destructive impact on improvement bills, especially if these were seen as affecting property interests.

The problem with this caricature and its almost 'golden era of local government' overtones is that it is an oversimplification and did not last long. Single-purpose bodies continued to exist or were invented again, and the first steps were taken towards an emerging welfare state. Political parties took on a greater form of organisation, especially with the emergence of the Labour Party after the First World War. Partisanship – and the often bitterly divisive form it took – changed British local politics in the 1920s and 1930s,[13] colouring them in a fashion not often found previously, and notwithstanding nineteenth century experience of partisan conflict. For most of the interim, British local politics remained much more confrontational than in other countries, where (as in Scandinavia) co-operative/corporatist styles of politics are more common. At the same time, British local politics has reflected national patterns to a far greater extent than elsewhere, notably in the USA.[14] Yet British local politics have failed to penetrate the national stage in the same way that they do in for example France and the USA; nor have parties adopted the extensive clientelistic practices and nature to be found in Southern European countries or the way in which such practices characterised the 'unreformed' party-dominated cities of the Midwest and North East United States.[15] So the development of an adversarial party culture in Britain, which persisted until the early 1980s when hung councils appeared on a widespread basis,[16] linked to a tradition in which territorial politics outside the periphery did not play a major part on the UK political stage, created an environment where confrontation would result when one of the main parties came to power nationally with a desire to rewrite the political agenda, as happened in 1979 with the Conservatives. The battles between centre and locality, so prevalent in Britain in the 1980s, reflected the fact that one party, the Conservatives, dominated the national stage, and another party, Labour, dominated the local – especially urban – setting.[17]

Of itself, this partisan difference would not have been so problematic – for example many Conservative counties resisted the introduction of comprehensive education in the 1960s. What was different was the scale of change sought by the Thatcher government – the rolling back of the state, privatisation, reduced public expenditure, an attack on vested corporate interests not regarded favourably by the party and leader in power. In a system where the centre delivers little, rolling back the state would mean an attack on local government, the primary service-producing and service delivery agency. That the party of the locality was also the party of the welfare state only added spice to events; equally important was the weakness of the same party in opposition in Parliament. Thus many of the left in local government saw it as their duty to oppose Thatcher.[18] This acrimonious struggle could only have one winner – the centre, given the weak constitutional/legal position of local government in the UK as compared with many of its counterparts elsewhere. In a context where local government appeared largely unwilling to change and follow the new priorities set by the central government, one way in which change could be induced was through the introduction of new structures at the local level – largely on a one-off basis, to tackle some of the problems and to produce new changes of direction – so Training and Enterprise Councils, Urban Development Corporations, housing action trusts and health trusts all followed.[19] Add to this privatisation – perhaps more correctly changes in regulatory regimes (contracting out; changes in transport ownership, limits on taxing and expenditure, both current and capital) – and by the end of the 1980s Britain had a much weakened system of local government in comparison with its counterparts in much of Western Europe – and one which was much more centralised than it had been a decade earlier.

But the move to a more fragmented system of local service delivery was not simply a partisan reaction to local opposition to central government policies. It can also be seen in part as a reflection of a broader ideological change about the nature of large organisations, the role of government generally, and the relationship between the state and the market. The simplest expression of this change is the Osborne and Gaebler[20] fashionable phrase – steering not rowing – or in British terms those of Nick Ridley[21] – enabling not doing. Here, in a reflection of public choice theories[22] about the nature of (particularly local) government, governments were to set broad strategic frameworks, devise systems in which other (particularly private sector) agents would deliver a limited range of public goods and services. At the same time this would change the perception of the individual in society from that of citizen to that of consumer: a change which implies that consumer rights in effect replace citizen (voice or participation) rights. Seen at its most extreme in New Zealand (and in some Australian states – Victoria, for example, abolished all local government for a short while in the mid-1980s), echoed in parts of Reagan's America, such changes were also strongly driven by the Thatcher and indeed by the Major governments in Britain.[23]

Some writers, especially those of a more sociological bent[24] interpret these changes as a move from a Fordist mode of production to a post-Fordist or postmodernist form – 'lean and mean' organisations, adopting just-in-time methods, small, orientated towards niche markets, in contrast to the large overly bureaucratised Fordist manufacturing plants/industries, some of which have disappeared from the UK scene over the last 20 years. If changes of this type were occurring in the private sector, then surely they could be applied to the public sector – regardless of whether or not such distinctions were valid in either sector. Again acceptance of this kind of perspective would influence governments' thinking about institutional and policy arrangements – just as the big business model had influenced the Heath government in the early 1970s at the time of local government reform in 1972.[25] So then part of the move towards governance can be understood as following from a changing ideology and interpretation of the 'most appropriate' forms of local institutions – again perhaps summarised by a shift from a representative system of local government to a responsive and responsible system of local governance, and again reflected in the idea of the 'New Public Management' of the 1990s.[26]

But two other changes over the last 50 to 100 years ensure that the nature of urban governance in the late twentieth century is different from its counterpart in the late nineteenth. First, there is the fragmentation of local élites – no longer is social, economic and political power concentrated in the hands of a few. Today, by contrast, power is split up and divided out – albeit still amongst the few. Partisan political élite must seek the support of business/economic élites in the process of coalition building at the local level, whilst social position no longer carries the same weight in local politics it did in the nineteenth century. The building of what Stone calls regimes,[27] or what Rhodes would call policy communities,[28] based on extensive networks and networking, is another characteristic of the new urban governance. Whether it be for City Challenge, European funding, Olympic bids or European City of Culture status, urban governance today is characterised by this process of networking and of partnership building.[29] But it could be argued that the nineteenth-century urban leadership did similar things. The point is that today's partnerships are of a different nature from those of the nineteenth century. The political élite is a partisan one (far more so than its nineteenth-century counterpart) whereas the economic élite no longer comprises the owners of local enterprises but far more the managerial representatives of national or multinational companies or else retired business people, often from similar companies, with few remaining links to the world of business. Nor is capital, the source of funding for developments, local any longer but certainly national or multi-national. This century has seen the financial sector in Britain change from being local/regional to regional/national and now to international/global; indeed probably as much of the British banking system is either foreign owned or shared with foreign owners as it is British owned, but then the nature of financial services has also changed. The consequence for present day systems of urban governance is clear – not only is the nature of the local regime/élite different from its nineteenth-century counterpart, but it is dependent on external support (financial and more generally) if it is to be able to succeed.[30] Compare this with the period between 1945 and 1980 when local government was 'king' of the urban welfare service delivery system (education, housing, public transport, social services), when public utilities delivered gas, water, sewerage and electricity, and when central government accepted a major responsibility for economic development and for dealing with regional imbalances. Today British local governments do far less, and have to do it in partnership with a wide range of other partners.

The nature of these other partners is worth a brief sidetrack. First, in most cases partners are representatives of organisations/sectors, rather than individual entrepreneurs or wealthy philanthropists. Second, despite the Thatcher/Major governments' attempt to bring 'big business' back into local affairs, few big business people are actually to be found. There are some exceptions (the North West Business Leadership Team, of which the Duke of Westminster is chair and which includes companies such as ICI, BNFL and British Aerospace is an example), but rather it is sector representatives or professional managers, who may have come from either the public or the private sector, or else these participants are retired business people. Third, the last 20 years has seen the increasing involvement of the third, not-for-profit or voluntary, sector in local affairs and, increasingly, in local service delivery – care for the elderly or child care being but two examples. In the housing field one can also point to the rise of housing associations as the major provider of housing for rent, for example, whilst the environmental arena represents another growth area of similar activity. And again one comes across the representatives of the voluntary sector – managers of the lobbying pressure groups, not-for-profit organisations, environmental groups concerned with promoting sustainability – all seeking to influence public policy and expenditure, not least at the local level. In other words one could argue that there now exists a new political class, often technically based (the so-called professionals)[31] who dominate local politics – often more so than the politicians (though many of these are now effectively professional as well) all of whom, if only because of the rules of the game, find themselves obliged to work in partnership with other bodies. These professionals network together, frequently break bread together, and spend considerable time in each other's company settling issues of the day. Training and Enterprise Councils, Business Links, Chambers of Commerce, the Confederation of British Industry, Age Concern, partnership for this, partnership for that – all bodies with which the average city politician now has to deal, as he or she seeks to secure some extra leverage making it possible to put together a more persuasive bid for money – either from central government or from Brussels. And, of course, the skills of these participants are unevenly distributed, mobilisation of bias exists and opportunities for corrupt practices grow.

The last themes we wish to reflect upon are those of globalisation and European integration.[32] Neither of these concerns mattered much to the average nineteenth-century city politician, though his business success may well have depended on international trade. His twentieth-century counterpart has to be at home welcoming Japanese would-be investors, or dealing with European Commission bureaucrats on the streets and in the corridors of Brussels. The last 20 years, as I have suggested, have seen the local political agenda change significantly. Economic well-being has always been an issue for urban governments in Britain, though perhaps less so than in the USA, and for much of the post-war period, with notable exceptions, city governments did not have to give it a high priority – they concentrated instead on social development and the regulation of land use. But the processes of global change, especially in terms of their impact on the older industrial areas of Britain and Europe, have forced many cities to focus attention on economic regeneration and to follow policies of economic boosterism more generally associated with countries like the USA, Canada and Australia. Cities compete to maintain or improve their position in the world urban hierarchy – and to do so again involves networking, partnership and working with a range of other institutions.

In the context of the European Union (EU) and the associated integration processes, urban and regional governments have become increasingly involved on the European stage. Whilst this is not universally true, there are some which are extremely active and heavily committed to European partnerships. Thus Birmingham, Glasgow, Sheffield and Manchester are as active, if not more so, as cities such as Barcelona and Bordeaux, or regions like Wallonia, Alsace-Lorraine or Nord Pas du Calais. In large part this is a reflection of eligibility for EU funding – especially the structural funds – and it is also a result of the EU adopting the subsidiarity principle in 1992, pushing things down to the lowest possible level at which they can be conducted. But some British cities – Glasgow, Birmingham and Manchester for example – were active on the EU stage before 1992, seeing Europe as a means of replacing some of the lost government funding suffered under the Thatcher years. Political leaders, chief executives and their staff from cities like these are as at home on the European stage as they are in their own backyard. They use Europe as a way of exchanging experiences, building coalitions with which to lobby, perhaps building political careers on a wider stage – membership of the Committee of the Regions or leader of one of the pan-European lobbying groups, for example. The networks are bigger, the world of governance wider and they take with them representatives of business, higher education and the voluntary sector – yet another partnership. But, perhaps more importantly, the process of EU-wide regulation and direction in areas such as the environment, consumer affairs, transport and public contracts increasingly brings local governments and other agencies into contact with the wider European scene. This largely unresearched area represents another of the major changes which local governance has faced in recent years.[33]

In conclusion, if some of the features of modern urban governance – fragmentation of political authority, the spread of non-elected institutions; lack of co-ordination between them; possible opportunities for corrupt practice, political patronage and lack of accountability – all sound familiar to the urban historian (especially one of the nineteenth century), there are significant differences as well. Local élites are more fragmented, more partisan, perhaps less accountable, yet may also comprise a new political class. The resources they can draw upon are largely external to the locality or city; indeed, many of the members of local coalitions, networks or partnerships may themselves be effectively non-local. Finally, the kinds of stage on which such local coalitions have to play are not only local but also national and increasingly international, as cities and localities compete to retain or improve their status in a process of adaptation brought about by processes of change which are today increasingly global rather than regional or national in scope.

Notes

1. K. Newton and T. Karran, *The Politics of Local Expenditure* (London: Macmillan, 1985), p. 122.
2. M.R. Jones, reviewing D. King and G. Stoker (eds), 'Re-thinking Local Democracy', *Government and Policy*, 16, (1996), pp. 248–9.
3. J. Bennington, 'On Local Governance', paper presented at Economic and Social Research Council (ESRC) Conference on Local Governance, Exeter (1994).
4. For other attempts at defining 'governance' see, *inter alia*, G. Stoker, 'Gov-

ernance as Theory: Five Propositions', paper presented to the conference *Enjeux Des Debats sur La Gouvernance* (University of Lausanne, November, 1996); G. Stoker and D. Pyper, 'Understanding Governance', Special Issue of *Public Policy and Administration*, 12, (1997), pp. 1–4, (see also the contributions by Rod Rhodes and Guy Peters in the same issue) and J. Kooiman (ed.), *Modern Governance* (London: Sage, 1993).

5. See, for example, D. Fraser, *Urban Politics in Victorian England* (Leicester: Leicester University Press, 1997); D. Fraser, *Power and Authority in the Victorian City* (Oxford: Blackwell, 1979); J.A. Garrard, *Leadership and Power in Victorian Industrial Towns* (Manchester: Manchester University Press, 1983).

6. R.C. Woods, *1400 Governments* (New York: Doubleday, 1964).

7. See for example J.C. Bollens, *The Metropolis: Its People and Politics* (New York: Harper and Row, 1975); and T.R. Dye and B. Hawkins (eds), *Politics in the Metropolis*, (2nd edition) (New York: Merrill, 1971).

8. See, for example, D. Higgins, *Urban Canada* (Toronto: Macmillan, 1977); D. DelGuidice and S.M. Zacks, 'The 101 Governments of Metro Toronto', in L. Feldman and M. Goldrich, *Politics and Government of Urban Canada* (Toronto: Methuen, 1969), pp. 219–31; and W. Magnusson and A. Sancton (eds), *City Politics in Canada* (Toronto: University of Toronto Press, 1983).

9. On the strength of local autonomy versus central government impingement see *inter alia*, C. Bellamy, *Administering Central–Local Relations: the Local Government Board in its Fiscal and Cultural Context* (Manchester: Manchester University Press, 1988); J. Prest, *Liberty and Locality: Parliament, Permissive Legislation and Ratepayers: Democracies in the Mid-Nineteenth Century* (Oxford: Clarendon Press, 1990).

10. P. Hirst and G. Thompson, *Globalization in Question* (London: Polity, 1996). See also A. Scott (ed.), *The Limits of Globalization* (London: Routledge, 1997).

11. Garrard, *Leadership and Power*; R.H. Trainor, *Black Country Elites: The Exercise of Authority in an Industrialised Area, 1830–1900* (Oxford: Clarendon Press, 1993); E.P. Hennock, *Fit and Proper Persons* (London: Edward Arnold, 1973); J.M. Lee, *Social Leaders and Public Persons* (Oxford: Clarendon Press, 1963). As an example of where such an overlap did not exist or where economic leaders exhibited little interest in municipal affairs see M.J. Daunton, *Coal Metropolis* (Leicester: Leicester University Press, 1977).

12. J. Bulpitt, *Territory and Power in the United Kingdom* (Manchester: Manchester University Press, 1983).

13. See, for example, K. Young, *Local Politics and the Rise of Party* (Leicester: Leicester University Press, 1975); G.W. Jones, *Borough Politics* (London: Macmillan, 1969); M.J. Daunton (ed.), *Councillors and Tenants: Local Authority Housing in English Cities, 1919–1939* (Leicester: Leicester University Press, 1984); T. Adams, 'Labour and the Erosion of Local Peculiarity', *Journal of Regional Studies*, 10, (1990), pp. 23–47.

14. See in particular on Britain, J. Gyford, S. Leach and C. Game, *The Changing Politics of Local Government* (London: Unwin Hyman, 1989); and their earlier 1986 work for the Widdicombe Committee 'The Conduct of Local Authority Business', report of the Committee of Enquiry into the conduct of Local Authority Business, Research Volume 1. See also J. Gyford and M. James, *National Parties and Local Politics* (London: Allen and Unwin, 1983); and K. Young and M. Davies, *The Politics of Local Government since Widdicombe* (London: Joseph Rowntree Foundation, 1990). For a brief discussion of other countries' experience see M. Goldsmith and K. Newton, 'Local Government Abroad', in *Widdicombe 1986*, Research Volume 4, and H. Wolman and M.

Goldsmith, *Urban Politics: A Comparative Approach* (Oxford: Basil Blackwell, 1992), pp. 139–45.

15. For a specific comparison of the USA and the UK see H. Wolman and M. Goldsmith, *Urban Politics and Policy: A Comparative Approach* (Oxford: Blackwell, 1992); and for a comparison also involving France and Canada see M. Keating, *Comparative Urban Politics* (Cheltenham: Edward Elgar, 1992). The original study of the effects of party politics in the USA is L. Steffens, *The Shame of the Cities* (New York: Hay and Wang, 1903), (1957 edition), but on machine politics the classic study remains H. Gosnell, *Machine Politics* (Chicago: Chicago University Press, 1937). On the impact of reform see S. Welsh and T. Bledsoe, *Urban Reform and its Consequences* (Chicago: Chicago University Press, 1988).

16. On the politics of hung councils in this period see S. Leach and J. Stewart, *The Politics of Hung Councils* (London: Macmillan, 1992). More recent figures on the number of hung councils can be found in C. Ralling and M. Thrasher, *Local Elections in Britain* (London: Routledge, 1997).

17. This period has been extensively researched and discussed. For an overview see G. Stoker, *The Politics of Local Government* (London: Macmillan, 1992), (2nd edition). See also A. Cochrane, *Whatever Happened to Local Government?* (Milton Keynes: Open University Press, 1993).

18. As an example of this opposition see M. Parkinson, *Liverpool on the Brink* (Hermitage, Berks: Policy Journals, 1985); and S. Lansley, S. Goss and C. Wolmar, *Councils in Conflict* (London: Macmillan, 1989).

19. On the rise of non-elected bodies see Stoker, *Politics*, ch. 3; H. Davis, *Quangos and Local Government: A Changing World* (London: Frank Cass, 1996), and A. Greer and P. Hoggett, 'Quangos and Local Government', in L. Pratchett and D. Wilson (eds), *Local Democracy and Local Government* (London: Macmillan, 1996).

20. D. Osborne and T. Gaebler, *Re-Inventing Government: How the Entrepreneurial Spirit is Transforming the Public Sector* (Reading, MA: Addison-Wesley, 1992).

21. N. Ridley, *The Local Right: Enabling Not Providing* (London: Centre for Policy Studies, 1988).

22. The public choice literature is too vast to be summarised here. A prize-winning British text which reviews the literature is P. Dunleavy, *Democracy, Bureaucracy and Public Choice: Economic Explanations in Political Science* (Hemel Hempstead: Harvester Wheatsheaf, 1991). Probably the most frequently cited work of relevance to the local government field is C. Tiebout, 'A Pure Theory of Local Expenditures', *Journal of Political Economy*, 64 (1956), pp. 416–24.

23. On New Zealand see, for example, J. Boston, J. Martin, J. Pallor. and P. Walsh (eds), *Reshaping the State: New Zealand's Bureaucratic Revolution* (Oxford: Oxford University Press, 1991); and on Australia see M. Jones, *Transforming Local Government* (St Leonards, NSW: Allen and Unwin, 1993); and for a comparative study see F. Castles, R. Gerritson and J. Vowles (eds), *The Great Experiment: Labour Parties and Public Policy Transformation in Australia and New Zealand* (St Leonards, NSW: Allen and Unwin, 1996).

24. See for example B. Jessop, 'Towards a Schumpeterian Workfare State? Preliminary Remarks on Post-Fordist Political Economy', *Studies in Political Economy*, 40 (1993), pp. 7–40; E.W. Soja, 'Los Angeles 1965–1992: The Six Geographies of Urban Restructuring' in A. Scott, E.W. Soja and R. Weinstein (eds), *Los Angeles: Geographical Essays* (Berkeley: University of California

Press, 1994). See also M. Davis, *City of Quartz: Excavating the Future in Los Angeles* (London: Verso, 1990) and the interesting collection edited by S. Watson and K. Gibson, *Postmodern Cities and Spaces* (London: Basil Blackwell, 1995). For other views about the nature of the postmodern city, see for example G. Stoker, 'Creating a Local Government for a Post-Fordist Society: The Thatcherite Project?', in J. Stewart and G. Stoker (eds), *The Future of Local Government* (London: Macmillan, 1989); G. Stoker, 'Regulation Theory, Local Government and the Transition from Fordism', in D. King and J. Pierre (eds), *Challenges to Local Government* (London: Sage, 1990); and G. Stoker and K. Mossberger, 'The Post-Fordist Local State: The Dynamics of its Development', in J. Stewart and G. Stoker (eds), *Local Government in the Nineties* (London: Macmillan, 1995), pp. 210–227. Examples of Painter's rather dense contributions can be found at J. Painter, (1991): 'Regulation Theory and Local Government', in J. Stewart and G. Stoker, *The Future of Local Government* (London: Macmillan, 1989), and in J. Painter, 'Regulation Theory, Post-Fordism and Urban Politics', in D. Judge, G. Stoker and H. Wolman, *Theories of Urban Politics* (London: Sage, 1995), pp. 276–95. This latter book is an excellent review of current theoretical approaches.

25. Typical of this kind of thinking was the Bains' Committee Report of 1972: *The New Local Authorities: Management and Structure* (London: HMSO, 1972).

26. On the introduction of 'New Public Management' ideas into local government see, for example, L. Pratchett and M. Wingfield, 'The Demise of the Public Sector Ethos', in L. Pratchett and D. Wilson (eds), *Local Democracy and Local Government* (London: Macmillan, 1996); S. Leach, J. Stewart and K. Walsh, *The Changing Organisation and Management of Local Government* (London: Macmillan, 1994).

27. C. Stone, *Regime Politics: Governing Atlanta, 1946–1988* (Kansas: Kansas University Press, 1989). See also S. Elkin, *City and Regime in the American Republic* (Chicago: Chicago University Press, 1987).

28. Rhodes's writing in this area is extensive. For its application to Britain in the 1980s see R.A.W. Rhodes, *The National World of Local Government* (London: Macmillan, 1986); and R.A.W. Rhodes, *Beyond Westminster and White-hall* (London: Unwin Hyman, 1988). More recently see, R.A.W. Rhodes, *Policy Networks*, (Milton Keynes: Open University Press, 1996).

29. For an example of British studies in this area see the work of A. Harding, 'Public-Private Partnerships in the UK', in J. Pierre (ed.), *Partnership in Urban Governance: An International Perspective*, (Basingstoke: Macmillan, 1997); A. Harding, 'The Rise of Growth Coalitions, UK style?', *Environment and Planning C: Government and Policy*, 9, (1991).

30. See, *inter alia*, A. Harding, 'Public-Private partnerships in the UK', J. Pierre (ed.), *Partnership in Urban Governance: An International Perspective*, (Basingstoke: Macmillan, 1997); A. Harding, 'Is there a new Community Power and why should we need one?', *International Journal of Urban and Regional Research*, 20, (1996).

31. On this line of argument see H. Perkin, *The Rise of Professional Society: England Since 1880* (London: Routledge, 1990). See also M. Laffin, *Professionalism and Policy: The Role of the Professions in the Central-Local Relationship* (Aldershot: Gower, 1986).

32. On globalisation and its impact on local government see A. Harding and P. LeGales, 'Globalisation and Urban Politics', in A. Scott (ed.), *The Limits of Globalization* (London: Routledge, 1997), pp. 181–201; P. LeGales, 'Urban Governance and Globalisation: the Fading Charm of European Cities', paper

presented to ISA World Congress (Montreal, July 1998); and M. Goldsmith, 'Urban Change and Local Politics in Europe', paper presented to ISA World Congress, (Montreal, July 1998). On the European Union and local government see, *inter alia*, M. Goldsmith and K.K. Klaussen (eds), *European Integration and Local Government* (Cheltenham: Edward Elgar, 1997); M. Goldsmith, 'British Local Government in the European Union', in J. Bradbury and J. Mawson (eds), *British Regionalism and Devolution* (London: Jessica Kingsley, 1997), pp. 215–34, P. John and J. Bennington, 'Local Democracy and the EU', *Research Report no. 6* (London: Commission for Local Democracy, 1994); C. Jeffrey (ed.), *The Regional Dimension of the EU* (London: Frank Cass, 1996).
33. In addition to Goldsmith and Claussen 'Sub National Partnerships and European Integration', in J. Bradley and J. Mawson (eds) *British Regionalism and Devolution* (London: Jessica Kingsley, 1997), pp. 235–53; see *inter alia* P. Bongers, *Local Government and 1992* (Harlow: Longman, 1992); P. John, *The Europeanisation of British Local Government* (Luton: LGMB, 1994); P. John, 'Centralisation, Decentralisation and the European Union: The Dynamics of Triadic Relationships', *Public Administration*, 74 (1996), pp. 293–312; and S. Martin and G. Pearce, 'The Impact of Europe on Local Government: Regional Partnerships in Local Economic Development', in P. Dunleavy and J. Stanyer (eds), *Contemporary Political Studies* (Belfast: PSA, 1994).

CHAPTER THREE

The 'decline' of British urban governance since 1850: a reassessment*

Richard H. Trainor

Introduction: a tale of two Lord Provosts

Contrasts between the civic careers of two Lord Provosts of Glasgow epitomise the apparent 'decline' in British urban governance since the middle of the nineteenth century. Sir James Lumsden, born in 1808, was the son of a well-to-do Glasgow wholesale stationer, who was one of the early Lord Provosts of the reformed city and the first chairman of the Clydesdale Bank. His son, educated at the Grammar School of Glasgow and at Glasgow University, soon diversified his own business interests into prominent positions both in banking and in railway promotion, notably as chairman of the Glasgow and Southwestern Railway Company. When the younger Lumsden was proposed for the office of Lord Provost in 1866, the broad range of his business involvements was praised; it was said that he was a 'gentleman of large practical experience ... at the head of a large mercantile firm in Glasgow'. Lumsden's public activities were not confined to the Council: he was a leading member of Glasgow's Merchants' House and a deputy lord lieutenant for two counties; he also played a major part in two great local philanthropic institutions, the Royal Infirmary and the Glasgow Benevolent Society. In addition, he was a believer in civic unity: taking up the Lord Provostship, Lumsden voiced a 'determination to know neither sect nor party'. Among his achievements as Lord Provost, Lumsden played a prominent part in a great non-sectarian, non-partisan occasion: laying the foundation stone in 1868 for the new site of the University of Glasgow. Lumsden entertained the Prince and Princess of Wales to lunch in his own home on the day, and was subsequently knighted. In short, Lumsden was a member of the city's social élite whose economic and social prominence spilled over into an illustrious, diverse career in civic life.[1]

The second example, Pat Lally, Lord Provost in the later 1990s, appears to be a different sort of civic figure altogether. Born without significant social advantages in Glasgow in the late 1920s, Lally had the benefit neither of an élite secondary education nor of university experience. Lally was also quite unlike Lumsden in having devoted the bulk of his career to the Council, having been first elected as early as 1966. Lally's municipal career was exceptionally turbulent, with periods in positions of influence alternating frequently with intervals on the backbenches. In particular, Lally and his allies battled noisily with the faction of Councillor Jean McFadden – a university lecturer – his rival for the positions of Council Leader and Lord Provost. Lally was dogged by controversy, notably when he was associated with the removal of commissioned murals from the city's new concert hall and when he refused to discontinue his annual hospitality at the Edinburgh Military Tattoo. Most spectacularly, in early 1998 Lally became the focus of national attention when a Labour Party investigation into alleged 'sleaze' led to an attempt to force him from his party membership and the Provost's chair. Thus Lally would appear to be a 'public person' rather than a 'social leader', to use J.M. Lee's well-known distinction, with narrowly focused civic interests which have had mixed results for the city and its people.[2]

The nature and value of the 'decline' thesis

The transition from Lumsden to Lally fits in with a venerable tradition of commentary on British urban local government – and, more broadly, on the governance of cities and towns. As early as the 1850s, only two decades after municipal reform, observers lamented the social standing and the calibre of councillors. By 1869 a parliamentary select committee highlighted the reluctance of well-off men to participate in local government.[3] G.C. Brodrick's 1875 critique was typical of many, before and since, which have linked inappropriate social position with inadequate public skills. According to Brodrick, the local government of towns was 'almost entirely in the hands of shopkeepers and struggling professional men, engaged in many callings and with few hours to spare for public business'.[4] By 1902, looking back on two-thirds of a century of municipal reform, Ostrogorski castigated the 'decline of the intellectual and, to some extent, moral standard of the personnel of the town councils'.[5] Similar attitudes have surfaced frequently in this century. For instance, Neville Chamberlain, writing privately about local government while at the Ministry of Health in 1926, suggested that 'in too many cases one sees important offices held by men who are not quite of the class, calibre and standard one would like to see there'.[6] More specifically, in 1938 Lady Simon, a member of a Manchester family with an illustrious civic past, noted that whereas in 1838 more than half the members of the City Council were merchants and manufacturers, 100 years later fewer than one-seventh of the councillors were drawn from these occupations. For her an acceleration in long-shifting patterns of residence by the well-to-do was critical: 'The city became the place they worked in by day and abandoned in the evening'.[7] These criticisms have become even more strident since the Second World War. Thus that doyenne of the civil service, Dame Evelyn Sharp, argued in the 1960s that too few businessmen, and too many retired people and 'housewives', served on councils.[8] In the decades since, as the reputation of councils has sunk lower, hostile analyses of this kind have become a commonplace of British public discourse.

The concept of 'decline' has also attracted historians and contemporary social scientists who have studied urban governance. Many historians, noting the significant numbers of top businessmen and professionals who served as councillors in the decade or two following the Municipal Reform Act, have called attention to a falling off from about the 1870s of social rank and – it would seem – of ability and achievement. For example, F.M.L. Thompson, observing that many wealthy provincial manufacturers and merchants moved their homes into the countryside in the later Victorian period, suggests that 'Leadership of the work-town then passed by default to those who lived there all the time: the local builders, traders, shopkeepers, perhaps the resident doctors and solicitors, all of whom were in the middling to lower end of the middle class'. He includes in this grouping the increasingly powerful municipal bureaucrats. According to Thompson, a 'fractured' upper middle class having achieved only 'a small taste of what might have been', 'the small shopkeepers, tradesmen and businessmen, abetted by the growing number of white-collar workers, virtually took control of the cities in the course of the fifty years before 1914'.[9] Similar analyses can be found in historical accounts by scholars such as W.A. Robson and Donald Read.[10]

For these historians, and others of a similar persuasion, such phenomena and their ramifications were not confined to local government narrowly defined. For example, in a very nuanced recent analysis, John Garrard has noted the 'decline' after 1880 of the 'urban squires' who had played very prominent roles in the first decades after municipal reform as they attempted to supplement their private power with public authority. The latter declined as these urban notables became decreasingly represented on councils, over the agenda of which they had less and less control. In the late Victorian period these upper middle-class 'squires' were better represented in voluntary societies, but this role was subject to state inroads and was increasingly institutionalised. In both local government and philanthropy, Garrard argues, influence increasingly had to be shared with the lower echelons of the middle class and the working class.[11] A much more negative version of this broad approach to governance can be found in W.D. Rubinstein's recent insistence, writing from the perspective of the interwar period and of London-based leaders, on the collapse of the provincial élites starting about 1880.[12] To varying extents, therefore, many scholars see local governance between the mid-nineteenth century and 1914 as a process of decline in social level, competence, political legitimacy and policy outputs.

After 1914, many scholars believe, urban governance went from bad to worse in these respects. For Robson, local government – whose powers had already been under pressure from central government before the First World War – found itself increasingly hemmed in thereafter.[13] In the interwar years, intensified flight by the bourgeoisie from their homes in the towns, reliance by public corporations on managers without roots in localities and the rise of Labour strength on many councils – these factors further depressed the social level, and arguably the effectiveness, of local élites. For Thompson, 'The loss of interest in municipal government by the city fathers ... became almost total after the First World War'.[14] In Wales, according to D.W. Howell and C. Baber, middle-class élites lost confidence as a long period of Labour dominance began. According to Mike Savage, the movement of Preston's élites to the countryside provided an opportunity for Labour activists whose own residential stability enhanced their political effectiveness. Similarly, Ross McKibbin argues that as built-up areas expanded much more rapidly than population, an extreme separation between work and home often developed for the upper middle class, inhibiting its civic interventions. Even in localities where the residual lower middle class kept control of local government in the face of the Labour challenge, it was – according to Savage – often defensive and parochial. Similarly, John Walton argues that in the North-West 'Urban local government ... passed almost completely into the hands of a secondary élite of shopkeepers, tradesmen and a few managers'; the results were 'penny-pinching local government policies'.[15]

From these perspectives, 'decline' accelerated dramatically after the Second World War. A powerful central state eroded the powers of local government; the voluntary sector shrank; the prosperous middle class resided even less frequently in urban areas; municipal matters became increasingly technical and time-consuming; the Labour Party consolidated its local government strength; and the grip of party tightened more generally over municipal affairs.[16] For example, David Cannadine suggests in his study of Colchester that 1945 was 'a great watershed, witnessing the disappearance from town councils of real "social leaders", who have since devoted their attention exclusively to business or private philanthropy'.[17] Many scholars have noted that worsening partisan bitterness accelerated the detachment of the prosperous from local élite activities: in Banbury in the 1950s, Margaret Stacey reported, differences between Labour and Conservative were too deep-seated even to be discussed politely.[18] In the

1960s, many political scientists noted that voter turnout in local elections was low and that those who voted seemed concerned only with registering a verdict on the national government of the day. Public commitment to the system of local government seemed in decline, and there was growing confusion about the qualities desired in councillors.[19] Neatly encapsulating the negative view taken by analysts of the more recent period is the title of a collection published in 1985: *Half a Century of Municipal Decline*. And scholars believe that the situation continues to worsen, particularly due to the increasing powers of unelected 'quangos' and the increasing prominence of council 'sleaze'. As Ken Young and Nirmala Rao wrote in 1997, 'today's local authorities are less widely trusted, respected, or thought important than was the case thirty years ago'.[20]

To some extent this familiar picture is the result of the projection on to local governance of the myth of the 'golden age' – a process under way well before 1835. Yet there is substance as well as shadow in the 'decline' thesis. The Victorian system of local governance was under considerable financial, political and social pressure in the early twentieth century;[21] its interwar counterpart had many practical and political difficulties, and few would dispute that in the 1990s governance of towns and cities experienced serious financial and political troubles. Even Pat Lally's loyalists might have admitted that Glasgow's urban governance has recently been more troubled than its counterpart of 150 or even, perhaps, 50 years ago. Likewise, these trends are related, albeit in complex ways, to major shifts in the social composition of local leaders – increasingly distinguishing such 'public persons', particularly in local government, from the top economic and social figures of their areas.[22] None the less, the re-examination which follows will suggest that this prevalent emphasis on 'decline' is both exaggerated and blinkered. An emphasis on adaptation and diversification is a more fruitful way of understanding changes in urban governance, especially if we discard the implication in much of the literature that high social status and political quiescence are signs of health in the running of towns and cities. Adhering to 'decline' as a conceptual framework risks overlooking the many ways in which the considerable shifts in structure, personnel, substance and style which have occurred in urban governance during the last century and a half have enhanced as well as undermined the process.

The persisting effectiveness of urban élites to 1914

With reference to the Victorian and Edwardian periods, the 'decline' interpretation begins on the wrong foot by overestimating the social substance of the early and mid-Victorian decades. In most towns there was at most a brief period during which the wealthiest economic figures predominated in local government – though in the many localities where this phase occurred it could have lasting beneficial effects as a precedent to inspire later service by the well-to-do and/or the talented.[23] By the 1870s, contemporaries had largely adjusted their 'ideal' of local government to encompass some real diversity of social rank, where this was understood to include people of middle-middle as well as upper middle-class status – i.e. the whole of the substantial middle class.[24] These local government leaders were, on the whole, politically effective as well as socially comfortable; despite frequent ratepayers' revolts, the prosperous usually gained re-election and got their way on key policy decisions.[25] Moreover, these notables – who were often powerful figures in voluntary, business and private life as well – reinforced their authority from other spheres of activity. As R.J. Morris has pointed out, such involvement – notably in voluntary societies – might enhance the élite's prominence and influence inside the middle class even when its impact on the population as a whole was more problematical.[26] As a result, the complex mix of altruistic and selfish incentives for the prosperous to remain active in the civic affairs of a still locally focused society continued to be powerful.[27]

Nor does scepticism about social decline in urban governance up to the 1880s entail acceptance of a significant falling-off between the 1880s and 1914. As work on the Black Country, Lancashire and Norwich has shown, 'gentrification' affected far fewer businessmen, caused those who were affected to move much smaller distances from urban localities, and prompted much less change in their urban loyalties, than is often supposed.[28] Partly as a result, there were still many very well-off, if sometimes not the wealthiest, economic figures on the councils of most towns in the years leading up to 1914. Several leading businessmen served, for example, on the councils of Bristol, Colchester, Glasgow, Leeds, Nottingham and West Bromwich in the 1890s.[29] Admittedly, the councils – often larger in absolute terms by the turn of the century than they were in the 1850s – had a smaller proportion of upper middle-class people by the end of the period than at its start. However, if attention is broadened to encompass social substance – including all those groups likely to side with economic leaders against small property owners – the argument for decline is not strong. Indeed the aggregate substantial wealth of these élites, and of the urban provincial middle classes more generally, helps to diminish the implications for social leadership of the lesser income and wealth levels of provincial towns and cities compared with the metropolis. Leaving aside the many very well-off middle-class citizens of a provincial city such as Glasgow, even smallish Black Country towns had at least a few figures of great wealth – suitable as intermediaries for regional and national élites – combined with a much larger number of individuals of moderate affluence, people well adapted to respected and influential leadership within the towns.[30] Likewise, the argument for significantly declining social rank by urban élites is less convincing if consideration is extended to the leaders of voluntary organisations (such as hospitals and cultural institutes) and of business-related civic organisations (such as chambers of commerce) as well as to aldermen and councillors. As Garrard points out, by 1914 there were still many individuals who combined high socio-economic rank with a substantial public presence and were influentially active in a number of major public spheres.[31] Although some of these surviving civic giants were increasingly diverted to less intensive public roles, mayoralties and presidencies of voluntary associations had significant social impact both through public ritual and major contributions of prestige, cash and land.[32] Thus the great economic figures evolved a useful division of labour with the still substantial but less well-off middle-ranking manufacturers, substantial professional people and commercial figures who made up the majority of late Victorian civic leaders.[33]

Meanwhile, the increasing religious and partisan as well as social diversity of élites increased their legitimacy – especially in relation to the middle class as a whole (a significant minority in most towns by end of the century) but also in relation to the mass of the population. Earlier on, acceptance of a role for a lower middle-class minority of leaders had helped to neutralise the ratepayers' movements of the third quarter of the century. From the 1870s, the entry of a minority of workingmen and trade union organisers enhanced the élite's right to govern in an increasingly democratic age. The acceptance of other types of minorities – especially Primitive Methods and the Independent Labour Party – had a similar effect. Increasing diversity, of course, brought dangers of greater disunity within the élites. Yet, the worst excesses of partisanship and sectarianism faded from the local elections and subscribers' meetings through which the élites were recruited.[34] Social tensions were more intractable, but civic leaders of all social origins shared many of the prevailing social assumptions of the day, including the need to rescue and if possible improve the social 'residuum'. Meanwhile, the increasingly diverse élites were held together by a pattern in which the lion's shares of top leadership positions in major civic institutions went to the better-off, who often were influentially active in more than one organisation. A classic case was Glasgow's wealthy Lord Provost, Sir David Richmond who launched the successful campaign for the reconstruction of the city's leading voluntary hospital, the Royal Infirmary.[35] By contrast, activists from socially humble groups were better represented – in another instance of division of labour – among auxiliary élite groups such as Sunday School teachers, election workers and members of charity fund-raising committees.

Did the greater complexity of the élites, and the increasing stridency of rivals outside civic institutions, limit the élites' effectiveness? Garrard would emphasise that well-off leaders increasingly had to yield prominence and influence to activists of humble rank. Also, wealthy businessmen increasingly had to negotiate, notably with trade union councillors, on municipal issues such as the 'trade union rate', and with working men's hospital governors on criteria for admission to voluntary hospitals. In addition, the impact of individuals, diluted by the waning coherence and impact of 'urban squire' families, was increasingly mediated through institutions, thereby potentially 'deforming the gift', to use Stedman Jones's phrase.[36] Yet while mediation diminished the identification of particular individuals with civic initiatives, this effect was not drastic in medium- and small-sized towns.[37] Also, a more institutional approach diverted resentments to intermediate figures such as hospital waiting-room supervisors and rate collectors. Moreover, returning to the more important issue of the collective impact of urban élites, by the end of Victoria's reign – in the Black Country, in Glasgow and many other urban areas – although élites had to bargain with a broader cross-section of society than six decades earlier, their decisions were much more generally accepted than in the 1830s. In part the consequence of greater institutional power, this better controlled state of affairs also resulted from leaders who – more often than in the early and mid-Victorian periods – offered a decent minimum of services, made them available less unfairly (after concessions on gas pricing, for example), delivered them in more acceptable forms (as in taking increasing account of workers' preferences in cultural and recreational efforts) and provided them in less abrasive ways (reflected for instance in greater tact on public platforms). Such concessions were very useful politically yet remained more at the margins than at the core of local social power: the upper middle-class figures who stayed active usually continued to have significant impact on key decisions, even in local government; projects were more often modified than dropped, as in the many public park initiatives of the late nineteenth century.[38]

The influence of these well-off élites was buttressed by the increasing civic emphasis of their activities – a trend found in Helen Meller's Bristol as well as in the West Midlands and Glasgow. As the local press reveals, the élite increasingly relegated unpleasant aspects of urban life to the edge of their own and the public's attention. Civic ritual overlooked the contentious spheres of religion and politics and the more coercive arenas of poor relief, industrial relations and law and order while emphasising those spheres characterised more by consensus between leaders and ordinary residents: local government and philanthropy. Non-partisan, non-denominational, socially inclusive ceremonies in the 1880s such as the stone-layings of West Bromwich Institute or of Glasgow's City Chambers contrasted sharply with the much more restrictive events of the early nineteenth century such as the opening of West Bromwich's Christ Church in the late 1820s or the many Glasgow events of that period which gave pride of place to the established Church of Scotland. The Institute's opening featured a parade a mile and a half long which included working-class adults and children as well as élite members from various towns. As the mayor, Reuben Farley, suggested, it was hoped that the Institute would 'unite together in bonds of sympathy and good feeling all who come under ... (its) influence'.[39] Ritual, like the new style and substance of policy, helped to glorify top leaders, including those active only outside the municipal sphere.

Thus the exercise of urban authority was arguably more effective in the late nineteenth and early twentieth centuries than in the early nineteenth century and perhaps even than in the 1850s when wealthy leaders were most prominent. There was little or no 'decline' – even though, and partly because, élites were more diverse and perhaps less autonomous. What is remarkable is not so much the difficulties as the persistence, resilience and flexibility of these élites.

How far was this equilibrium undermined by increasing limits on authority imposed from outside the towns? Undoubtedly, urban élites had less impact outside their localities than within their boundaries.[40] Yet while the centralising forces in Britain as a whole were strengthening by the early years of the twentieth century, so too were countervailing forces, especially the district and regional organisations such as chambers of commerce which provided effective instruments for the best-off leaders of towns and cities in their dealings with central government. Urban MPs, who were increasingly locally focused and locally recruited, were also useful mediators.[41] Moreover, at least up to 1914, there was much continued scope for local initiatives, and for local discretion concerning the extent to which, and the manner by which, central policies would be adopted. Furthermore, localities on the whole took advantage of these opportunities in the period down to 1914, both municipally (regarding optional as well as compulsory services) and in terms of philanthropic effort, which arguably peaked just before the First World War.[42] Thus, for the period before 1914 the case for 'decline' of urban governance is not made, either in terms of the social substance of urban élites or of their political and policy effectiveness.

Limits to decline c. 1914–80

What of the period between 1914 and 1939? Although the interwar years required far more extensive adaptation by middle-class urban élites than did the Victorian and Edwardian years, perceptions of decline in the 1920s and 1930s have been exaggerated. While central government exercised more administrative control after 1918 than before the First World War, there was still considerable scope for local government initiative, as Birmingham Council demonstrated with its bank, airport and orchestra.[43] Local government bureaucrats continued to increase their influence, but this helped councils deal with Whitehall and still left councillors with much important committee work to perform. Writing in 1934, J.B. Priestley could still plausibly call England the 'country of local government'.[44]

Likewise, despite increased suburbanisation the social profile of interwar urban élites declined less than is often assumed, especially taking into account the knock-on social effects of the rapidly rising proportion of Labour councillors. With regard to local government itself, in towns such as Birmingham, Colchester, and Wolverhampton the post-war downturn came mainly from the 1930s; even then it was not drastic, notably in Norwich. Admittedly, leading industrialists were under-represented in Northampton, and in Wolverhampton manufacturers were fewer among those who entered the council between 1929 and 1945 than during the preceding decade. But in Birmingham the manufacturers were still the largest group on the council, the 'pivot of the civic life of the city' in Asa Briggs's phrase, and in Colchester the real detachment of social leaders from local government came after 1938.[45] Meanwhile, with respect to the private sphere of urban governance, during the interwar years the substantial echelons of the middle class, male as well as female, remained numerously active in the leadership of philanthropic organisations and such business-orientated civic bodies as chambers of commerce.[46] As late as the 1920s, churches and chapels, too, retained considerable vitality overall.[47] Admittedly, cracks had begun to emerge in the dominance of the voluntary sector by the well-off middle class. In Banbury, for example, the increasingly numerous physically mobile members of the middle class often spurned the leadership styles of native élites. However, while the heavy 'overlapping' of the leaders of key institutions had declined from its Victorian heyday, sectarian complications within the middle class mattered less in the interwar years as organisations such as Rotary helped to bridge the church–chapel divide.[48]

Partly because of these continuities in patterns of leadership, partly because only the top echelons of the middle class fled to the countryside before the 1930s, the interwar years witnessed a further flourishing of an urban civic pageantry attracting broad public attention. In Colchester the oyster festival was already 'grand, public [and] consensual' before 1914, but the interwar period was the time when it was 'perpetuated, consolidated and extended'. Likewise, in Northampton attendance at that town's festival was both a response to the losses of the war and a reaction to post-war social strains, especially those most common in the middle class.

Similarly, mayors set up relief funds to cope with the end of full employment in towns such as Northampton and Norwich.[49] Admittedly, in this newly democratic system the substantial middle-class élite's position was less secure and – particularly where Labour flourished – more restricted than hitherto. The legitimacy of the urban social system was considerably more contested than before 1914. Also, controversy surrounds the public health and relief records of local authorities, and Edinburgh provides an example of the selfishness of a local authority dominated (as many councils were) by propertied interests.[50] None the less, well-off leaders in towns such as Leeds and (at least before 1933) in Norwich continued to produce civic improvements of considerable utility and even grandeur.[51]

While the deterioration in the position of substantial middle-class élites worsened after 1945, and while the post-war period saw intensified worries about local governance more generally, the argument for a sharp decline is again difficult to sustain, at least for the first 30 years of the post-war period. The councillors and officials of local government retained considerable discretion at least into the 1960s: indeed for municipal élites the period 1945–80 may have been the most powerful ever as local institutions remained central to the implementation of national policies.[52] With regard to social composition, a significant minority even of Labour councillors were non-manual in a town such as Banbury; more generally the middle class predominated in terms of numbers of councillors both in counties and in county boroughs.[53] Wealthy members were unusual in towns like Wolverhampton, but the correlation between social position and competence was even looser by the 1950s than it had been during the previous century.[54] As Sutcliffe and Smith wrote of Birmingham at the end of the 1960s, 'The Council certainly contained fewer big industrialists, and the proportion of white-collar workers and professionals rose in both party groups, but there was still no shortage of able and devoted committee chairmen'. In so far as councillors had failed fully to keep pace with the growing complexity of local government, the slack was taken up by an increasingly numerous and well-known cadre of local professional civil servants.[55] With regard to the voluntary sphere, the churches enjoyed a prolonged pause in their decline during the 1950s, while the voluntary social services retained a major role during that heyday of the welfare state.[56] Even in the 1960s, if politics attracted fewer activists than before, voluntary associations remained very well subscribed especially by the better-off.[57] Likewise, there remained, in that decade, strong links between councillors and the leaders of major voluntary associations, even though individual societies tended to be led either by Labour or by the Conservatives.[58]

With regard to the public, voter turnout in local government contests in the 1950s and 1960s was much lower than in parliamentary elections.

However, this may have reflected not so much alienation as the satisfaction with local services reported by two-thirds of those surveyed in 1957 combined with the declining novelty of the democratic nature of the electoral system by the 1950s.[59] Also, those who bothered to vote – in an electoral system much more inclusive with regard to class and gender than its earlier counterpart – had an impact on policy as well as on party: the spending levels of individual councils during the period correlate well with patterns of party control.[60] In addition, in the changed social atmosphere of the post-war period the decreasing presence of the truly wealthy on councils may have been more of a boost than a handicap to their legitimacy.[61] In any event, while local government, and local élite institutions and ritual more generally, were of decreasing interest to the public at large, the population enjoyed services much superior in quantity, efficiency and dignity of delivery to those they would have experienced in the interwar period, let alone the Victorian years. As late as 1969 George Jones could plausibly pronounce a generally positive verdict on the local political system, judging its lack of agitation in Wolverhampton a 'tribute to the responsiveness of the Council to the needs of the people'.[62]

A broader context for the decline of urban governance in the 1980s and 1990s

Thus it seems that the historical reality of *acute* decline in the social standing, links to the voluntary sector, perceived efficiency and – above all – the legitimacy of local government is largely confined to the last quarter century or so – the period in which the major landmarks are Peter Walker's massive reorganisation of local government in 1974, Dennis Healey's initiation of tough financial discipline on local authorities and the Thatcher government's introduction of uniform business rates and abolition of the Greater London Council (GLC). As John Davis argues, after 1979 the Conservatives brought out the anti-local government potential of the statutory framework set up in 1945.[63] The Thatcherites, whose abolition of the GLC showed that all localities were subservient to the government, accelerated a decline in council autonomy which had begun in earnest only from the 1960s.[64] In addition, local government became characterised by especially large units and significant splintering of authority *vis-à-vis* quangos; these factors in turn rapidly undermined the legitimacy of councils.[65] Likewise, the Thatcher government's denigration of 'society' may have combined with its preference for the voluntary sector to place charities, from the perspective of a large segment of the population, under an ideological cloud. Rapid falls in church attendance and political party membership suggested an even more general unravelling of the urban institutional framework.

Yet there are reasons to suppose that the widespread condemnation of British urban government – and, more generally, of British urban governance – even for the last two decades is a judgement slightly exaggerated and overly precise. With the marked exception of the scattered riots of the early 1980s, law and order has not broken down in British towns and cities – in part because of the continuing vitality, in England and Wales, of voluntary service by local notables as Justices of the Peace. Many voluntary societies continue to flourish despite declines in uniformed youth groups and in organised religion comparable to those found in other countries. Nor is British local government – or charity – at all corrupt by the standards of many parts of the world (or of Britain's own urban past). What newspapers in the UK call 'sleaze' is often no more than the noisy rivalries arising from normal political ambition operating through strong party machines. In fact, many of the problems of urban government are shared with, and in many respects derived from, those of central government and of the political system and its political culture as a whole. In the context of advanced Western nations generally, the vitality of the United Kingdom's governance is limited by especially strong doses of political centralisation, party discipline and formal accountability. Certainly urban governance now often lacks the talented leaders and the legitimacy of the century and a third preceding the 1970s. But this unfortunate, if often exaggerated, situation is shared with the national level in which voter turnout and respect for politicians and key private institutions have fallen substantially during the last quarter of the twentieth century.[66] Thus the deterioration of urban governance in recent years is an aspect of a general crisis in governance in the UK and, to a lesser extent, other Western countries – unusually bad in Britain in part because national leaders appear to have forgotten one of the key features of their country's modern history: that vigorous, effective local governance can make a major contribution to a harmonious and efficient society.

It is time to discard the language of 'decline' in the analysis of British urban governance, even for this most recent period. What should be substituted – and is beginning to be, as many of the other papers in this volume indicate – is a more subtle conceptual framework. This approach drops 'Whig' history and 'Tory' history alike, analysing instead how patterns of urban governance are shaped by, and themselves help to shape, local social systems which in turn interact with national and international forces.

Somewhat surprisingly, the apparently contrasting careers of the two local leaders with which this chapter began can be reconciled with an emphasis on adaptation rather than decline. James Lumsden was not a civic paragon who attained popular success as a matter of course: he lacked his father's common touch, his election as Lord Provost was hotly contested and he backed away from Liberalism (the city's consuming partisan passion of the day) in the latter stages of his career.[67] Thus his civic record embodied some of the difficulties of the 'social leader' approach, just as his successes – like those of Victorian urban governance more generally – owed much to adaptation (notably with regard to sectarianism) to an increasingly complex social and political environment. Meanwhile, for all its turmoil, Pat Lally's career demonstrated in many respects a successful adjustment to a political culture much more populistic and party-dominated than that of Lumsden's day. Lally's political style – combining a simple, direct personal approach with energetic use of the partisan power and the civic symbols of office – evidently served his popularity well with the rank and file of a city famed, in his era, for allegiance to the Labour Party, friendliness and lavish hospitality. In these ways, Lally's role as an elected 'public person' rather than a well-off 'social leader' was probably more an asset than a liability to his standing both in his own party and with the general public. Moreover, like many 'public persons' in late twentieth-century local government, Lally forged a working relationship with his city's economic and social élites through spirited promotion of the locality in cultural and general civic endeavours as well as in strictly municipal affairs. In particular, Lally contributed significantly to the broadly based campaigns that culminated in Glasgow's designations as European City of Culture in 1990 and UK City of Architecture and Design in 1999.[68] Furthermore, Lally's subsequent, apparently disastrous fall from political grace was short-lived, in part because it was as much the result of central as of local opposition to the Lord Provost. In 1998 the Court of Session intervened on Lally's behalf to thwart the national Labour Party's attempts to sustain his suspension from the party and to remove him from office. Lally served out his term with considerable panache, notably when he conferred a civic award on the Princess Royal during her visit to Glasgow in January 1999. Having decided not to heed calls to stand again for the Council's leadership, Lally received tributes from fellow councillors at the last formal meeting of his term.[69] This was not a complete revival of Lally's personal influence, and the Lord Provost's difficulties prior to his restoration indicated the many respects in which, during the last 25 years, urban governance has declined substantially not only in local esteem but also in power *vis-à-vis* national forces. Yet the eleventh-hour victory of Pat Lally – the ultimate survivor of Glasgow's social system – suggests that the long-term resilience and adaptability of British urban governance are by no means fully played out.

Notes

* I wish to acknowledge the research assistance of Dr Mark Freeman in the

preparation of this chapter.

1. *Biographical Sketches of the Honourable the Lord Provosts of Glasgow* (Glasgow: J. Tweed, 1883), pp. 241–60, with quotations from p. 241 and p. 245. Cf. I. Maver 'Glasgow's Civic Government', in W.H. Fraser and I. Maver (eds), *Glasgow Vol II 1830–1912* (Manchester: 1996), pp. 441–85

2. *Who's Who in Scotland 1998* (Irvine: Carrick Media, 1998), p. 262; *The Herald*, 9 Feb. 1999, p. 7; J.M. Lee, *Social Leaders and Public Persons: A Study of County Government in Cheshire since 1888* (Oxford: 1963).

3. E.P. Hennock, *Fit and Proper Persons: Ideal and Reality in Nineteenth Century Urban Government* (London: 1973), p. 312; D. Read, *The English Provinces: A Study in Influence* (London: 1964), p. 237. Cf. R.H. Trainor, *Black Country Elites: The Exercise of Authority in an Industrialised Area 1830–1900* (Oxford: 1993), p. 287 for similar laments in an 1878 enquiry into Poor Law guardians.

4. Quoted in Hennock, *Fit and Proper Persons*, p. 319. Cf. list of late nineteenth century complaints in G.W. Jones, *Borough Politics: A Study of the Wolverhampton Town Council, 1888–1964* (London: 1969), pp. 149–50.

5. Osregorski, *Democracy and The Organisation of Political Parties*, vol. 1, p. 490, quoted by L.J. Sharpe, 'Elected Representatives in Local Government', *British Journal of Sociology*, 13 (1962), p. 209, n. 11.

6. Quoted by J. Davis, 'Central Government and the Towns, 1840–1950', *Cambridge Urban History of Britain Volume 3: 1840–1950* (Cambridge: forthcoming), from PRO HLG 8/111, 11 June 1926.

7. Quoted in Read, *English Provinces*, p. 238; Cf. B. Robson, 'Coming Full Circle: London versus the Rest 1890–1980', in G. Gordon (ed.), *Regional Cities in the UK 1890–1980* (London: 1986), pp. 227–8; K. Chorley, *Manchester Made Them* (London: 1950).

8. Sharpe, 'Elected Representatives', pp. 201–3; Read, *English Provinces*, pp. 240–41.

9. F.M.L. Thompson 'Town and City', in F.M.L. Thompson (ed.), *The Cambridge Social History of Britain 1750–1950*, 3 vols (Cambridge: 1990), vol. 1, pp. 47, 66.

10. Robson, 'Coming Full Circle', pp. 220–21; Read, *English Provinces*, pp. 233–5, 237–9.

11. 'Urban Elites, 1850–1914: The Rule and Decline of a New Squirearchy?', *Albion*, 27 (1995), pp. 583–621.

12. 'Britain's Elites in the Interwar Period', in A.J. Kidd and D. Nicholls (eds), *The Making of the British Middle Class? Studies of Regional and Cultural Diversity since the Eighteenth Century* (Stroud: 1998), pp. 198–200.

13. Robson, 'Coming Full Circle', p. 221 ff.

14. Thompson, 'Town and City', p. 72.

15. J.K. Walton, 'The North-west', n Thompson (ed.) *Cambridge Social History* vol. 1 (see note 9), pp. 410–11; Howell Baber, 'Wales', Thompson (ed.), *Cambridge Social History*, vol. 1 (see note 9), p. 350; M. Savage, 'Urban History and Social Class: Two Paradigms', *Social History*, 20 (1993), pp. 73–6 and *idem*, *The Dynamics of Working-Class Politics: The Labour Movement in Preston 1880* (Cambridge: Cambridge University Press, 1870), p. 113.

16. Davis, 'Central Government and the Towns', K. Young & N. Rao, *Local Government since 1945* (Oxford: 1997), pp. 2, 127; Robson, 'Coming Full Circle', p. 227; A. Sutcliffe, 'The "Midland Metropolis": Birmingham 1890 – 1980', in Gordon, *Regional Cities* (see note 7), pp. 32–3; Jones, *Borough Politics*, pp. 62–3, 97–8, 119.

17. D. Cannadine, 'The Transformation of Civic Ritual in Modern Britain: The

Colchester Oyster Feast', *Past and Present*, 94 (1982), pp. 125–6.

18. M. Stacey, *Tradition and Change: A Study of Banbury* (Oxford: 1960), p. 54. Cf. Read, *English Provinces*, p. 260 on the discouragement to the able inherent in the 'petty party system' and Chapter 2 by Goldsmith and Garrard (in this volume), which notes the growing distinction between partisan and economic élites.

19. Robson, 'Coming Full Circle', pp. 227–8; A. Sutcliffe and R. Smith, *History of Birmingham Volume III 1939–1970* (London: 1974), p. 95, n. 2, drawing on D. Butler and D. Stokes, *Political Change in Britain* (London: 1969); J. Harris, 'Society and the State in Twentieth-Century Britain', in Thompson (ed.), *Cambridge Social History*, vol. 3, (see note 9), p. 111; *Hennock, Fit and Proper Persons*, pp. 335–48.

20. Young and Rao, *Local Government*, p. 306.

21. Cf. A. Offer, *Property and Politics 1870–1914* (Cambridge: 1981); M.J. Daunton, *Coal Metropolis: Cardiff 1870–1914* (Leicester: 1977).

22. See, for example, A.H. Birch, *Small-Town Politics: A Study of Political Life in Glossop* (Oxford: 1959), p. 38; R.V. Clements, *Local Notables and the City Council* (London: 1969), ch. 8.

23. D. Fraser, *Power and Authority in the Victorian City* (Oxford: 1979), pp. 158–9. Cf. Read, *English Provinces*, p. 237.

24. As used in this chapter, 'upper middle class' refers to large industrialists and other leading business and professional people; 'middle middle class' to middling manufacturers, managers and substantial dealers, and professionals; 'lower middle class' to white collar employees and small (but employing) retailers and craftsmen. Cf. Trainor, *Black Country Elites*, pp. 387–9.

25. Hennock, *Fit and Proper Persons*, pp. 314–16; Trainor, *Black Country Elites*, pp. 242–3, 254–8 and 'The Élite' (hereafter referred to as 'Glasgow's Élite') in Fraser and Maver, *Glasgow vol. II* (see note 1), pp. 239–42, 257; and N.J. Morgan and R.H. Trainor, 'The Dominant Classes', in W.H. Fraser and Morris (eds), *People and Society in Scotland, ii: 1830–1914* (Edinburgh: 1990), 128–9. Compare J. Garrard, *Leadership and Power in Victorian Industrial Towns 1830–80* (Manchester: 1983), which focuses on towns with unusually strong surviving populistic institutions and – especially in the case of Rochdale, with its Pioneers – exceptionally strong countervailing working-class élites.

26. R.J. Morris, 'Clubs, societies and associations', in Thompson (ed.) *Cambridge Social History* (see note 9), pp. 406 ff and *Class, Sect and Party: The Making of the British Middle Class: Leeds, 1820–50* (Manchester: 1990). Cf. F.K. Prochaska, 'Philanthropy', in Thompson (ed.), *Cambridge Social History* (see note 9), p. 359; Trainor, *Black Country Elites*, p. 317 and ch. 8, *passim*; P. Shapely, 'Charity Status and Leadership: Charitable Service and the Manchester Man, *Journal of Social History*, 32 (1998), pp. 151–77.

27. On motives see Trainor, *Black Country Elites*, pp. 103–11.

28. Trainor, 'The Gentrification of Victorian and Edwardian Industrialists', in A.L. Beier et al. (eds), *The First Modern Society* (Cambridge: 1989), pp. 167–97; A.C. Howe, *The Cotton Masters 1830–1860* (Oxford: 1984), pp. 29–32, 252–4; B. Doyle, 'The Structure of Élite Power in the Early Twentieth Century City: Norwich, 1900–35', *Urban History*, 24 (1997), pp. 182–3.

29. Trainor, 'Urban Elites in Victorian Britain', *Urban History Yearbook* (Leicester: 1985), p. 5 and 'Glasgow's Elite', p. 255; G. Crossick, 'Urban Society and the Petite Bourgeoisie in Nineteenth-Century Britain' in D. Fraser and A. Sutcliffe (eds), *The Pursuit of Urban History* (London: 1983), p. 315 n. 32; E. S. Griffith, *The Modern Development of City Government*, vol. 1, (London:

1927), pp. 186–7; H. Meller, *Leisure and the Changing City, 1870–1914* (London: 1976), p. 87; Cannadine, 'Colchester', p. 115; R.A. Church, *Economic and Social Change in Nottingham 1815–1900* (London: 1966), pp. 370–73; Hennock, *Fit and Proper Persons*, p. 227; Garrard, 'The History of Local Political Power: Some Suggestions for Analysis', *Political Studies*, 25 (1977), pp. 257–9. Cf. A.J. Kidd, 'Introduction: The Middle Class', in A. J. Kidd and K.W. Roberts (eds), *City, Class and Culture* (Manchester: 1985), pp. 12–15.

30. Trainor, *Black Country Elites*, pp. 62–81. For a recent study challenging the scarcity of provincial, compared with metropolitan, wealth see: T. Nicholas, 'Wealth Making in Nineteenth and Early Twentieth Century Britain: Industry v. Commerce and Finance', *Business History*, 41 (1999), pp. 16–36.

31. Garrard, 'Urban Elites', p. 609. A.J. Kidd, 'Charity Organisation and the Unemployed in Manchester c.1870–1914', *Social History*, 9 (1984), p. 54. Cf. S. Yeo, *Religion and Voluntary Organisations in Crisis* (London: 1976), pp. 227–8, 300, with an emphasis on decline.

32. Trainor, *Black Country Elites*, pp. 280–81, 318–20, 359–60

33. A similar division of labour – rather than an 'aping' of aristocratic styles – developed, in those towns and cities with significant aristocratic presences, between the wealthiest businessmen and the peerage. Cf. D. Cannadine (ed.), *Patricians, Power and Politics in Nineteenth Century Towns* (Leicester: 1982), including Trainor, 'Peers on an Industrial Frontier: the Earls of Dartmouth and Dudley in the Black Country c.1810 to 1914'.

34. Trainor, 'Urban Elites', p. 7 and *Black Country Elites*, pp. 188–92, 222–30; Fraser, *Power and Authority*, pp. 41, 49, 57, 77; G. Sutherland, *Policy-Making in Elementary Education 1870–1895* (London: 1973), pp. 68–70; Meller, *Leisure*, pp. 77–9, 84, 122, 126; Cannadine, 'Colchester', p. 116; R. Newton, *Victorian Exeter 1837–1914* (Leicester: 1968), pp. 102–6, 183–4, 213–38; Garrard, *Leadership*, p. 107.

35. Trainor, 'Glasgow's Elite', p. 236.

36. G. Stedman Jones, *Outcast London* (Harmondsworth: 1976), pp. 251–2. Cf. Garrard, 'Urban Elites', pp. 602 and *passim*.

37. Trainor, *Black Country Elites*, p. 351, 365; P. Joyce, *Work, Society and Politics: The Culture of the Factory in Later Victorian England* (Brighton: 1980), p. 170.

38. Trainor, 'Urban Elites', pp. 10–12 and *Black Country Elites*, pp. 354–7, 376–7. Cf. Garrard, 'Urban Elites', which notes the continued presence of some wealthy people even on councils and suggests that urban squires countered decreasing impact outside borders with increased impact (including the retention of flamboyant styles) inside them until 1914, tending to defuse class tensions.

39. *Free Press* (West Bromwich), 9 August 1884; Trainor, 'Glasgow's Elite', pp. 246–50 and *Black Country Elites*, pp. 368–70; Meller, *Leisure*, pp. 14–15 and *passim*.

40. Cf. Garrard, 'Urban Elites', pp. 597–8.

41. E. Gordon and R. Trainor, 'Employers and Policymaking: Scotland and Northern Ireland, c.1880–1939', in S. Connolly et al. (eds), *Conflict, Identity and Economic Development: Ireland and Scotland, 1600–1939* (Preston: 1995), pp. 254–67; Trainor, *Black Country Elites*, pp. 222–30 and 'Glasgow's Elite', pp. 251–2.

42. P.J. Waller, *Town, City and Nation: England 1850–1914* (Oxford: 1983), p. 22; Davis, 'Central Government'; Fraser, *Power and Authority*, pp. 157 ff; P. Thane, 'Government and Society in England and Wales, 1750–1914', in

Thomson (ed.), *Cambridge Social History* vol. 3 (see note 9), p. 36; Doyle, 'Structure of Élite Power', p. 192.

43. A. Briggs, *History of Birmingham Volume II: Borough and City 1865–1938* (London: 1952), pp. 269–71; K.B. Smellie, *A History of Local Government* (2nd edn, London: 1949), pp. 117–18.

44. J. B. Priestley, *English Journey* (London: 1994 edn), p. 32. Cf. Davis, 'Central Government' and Hennock, *Fit and Proper Persons*, pp. 335–8.

45. Briggs, *Birmingham*, p. 277; M. Dickie, 'Town Patriotism in Northampton, 1918–1939: An Invented Tradition?', *Midland History*, 17 (1992), p. 114; Jones, *Borough Politics*, p. 368; Cannadine, 'Colchester', p. 123; Doyle, 'Structure of Elite Power', p. 196.

46. Read, *English Provinces*, pp. 238–9; Jones, *Borough Politics*, p. 130; Thane, 'Government and Society', pp. 83–4.

47. J. Obelkevich, 'Religion', in Thompson (ed.), *Cambridge Social History*, vol. 3 (see note 9), pp. 348–9.

48. R.I. McKibbin, *Classes and Cultures: England 1918–1951* (Oxford: 1998) pp. 81–2, 96; Stacey, *Tradition and Change*, pp. 88–9 and *passim*.

49. Cannadine, 'Colchester', p. 108; Dickie, 'Northampton', p. 129; Doyle, 'Structure of Elite Power', p. 193.

50. V. Berridge, 'Health and Medicine', in Thomson (ed.), *Cambridge Social History*, vol. 3, (see note 9), pp. 226–7; D. McCrone and B. Elliott, *Property and Power in a City: The Sociological Significance of Landlordism* (Basingstoke: 1989).

51. M. Bateman, 'Leeds: A Study in Regional Supremacy', in Gordon, *Regional Cities*, (see note 7), pp. 105–7; Doyle, 'Structure of Elite Power', pp. 183, 191, 195, 197. For similar vigour in Blackpool see J.K. Walton, *Blackpool* (Edinburgh: 1998).

52. Young and Rao, *Local Government*, pp. 129, 300–301; R.A.W. Rhodes, *Control and Power in Central/Local Government Relations* (Farnborough: 1981). For the latter argument, see Chapter 2 by Goldsmith and Garrard in this volume and N. Hayes, *Consensus and Controversy: City Politics in Nottingham 1945–1966* (Liverpool: 1996), pp. 9–10.

53. Stacey et al., *Power, Persistence and Change: A Second Study of Banbury* (Oxford: 1975), p. 159; Sharpe, 'Elected Representatives', pp. 190–91, 196–7.

54. Jones, *Borough Politics*, pp. 93–4, 153 and *passim*, modifying Sharpe, 'Elected Representatives'. For worries concerning the pre-1914 link between social standing and local government achievement see M.J. Daunton, *Coal Metropolis: Cardiff 1870–1914* (Leicester: 1977) and L.J. Jones, 'Public Pursuit of Private Profit? Liberal Businessmen and Municipal Politics in Birmingham, 1865–1900', *Business History*, 25 (1983), pp. 240–59.

55. *Birmingham*, p. 475; Read, *English Provinces*, p. 222; Stacey, *Power, Persistence and Change*, p. 50. For the technical problems of councillors see: Sharpe, 'Elected Representatives', p. 203; Hennock, *Fit and Proper Persons*, p. 335 ff; and P.J. Waller, *Democracy and Sectarianism: A Political and Social History of Liverpool 1868–1939* (Liverpool: 1981), pp. 354–5.

56. Morris, 'Clubs, Societies and Associations', pp. 422–3; R. Crossman, 'The Role of the Volunteer in the Modern Social Service', in A.H. Halsey (ed), *Traditions of Social Policy* (Oxford: 1976), pp. 259 ff.

57. Stacey, *Power, Persistence and Change*, pp. 50–1

58. Jones, *Borough Politics*, p. 127ff, 135–7, 147.

59. Read, *English Provinces*, p. 241.

60. L.J. Sharpe and K. Newton, *Does Politics Matter? The Determinants of Pub-*

lic Policy (Oxford: 1984), p. 202.

61. In Glossop, for example: Birch, *Small-Town Politics*, p. 187.
62. Jones, *Borough Politics*, p. 348.
63. Davis, 'Central Government and the Towns'.
64. Young and Rao, *Local Government*, pp. 130–31, 301. On the GLC see Robson, 'Coming Full Circle', p. 229.
65. For this argument, see Chapter 2 by Goldsmith and Garrard in this volume.
66. For these broader problems see D. Kavanagh, 'Political Culture in Great Britain: The Decline of the Civic Culture', in G.A. Almond (ed.), *The Civic Culture Revisited* (Boston, MA: 1980), pp. 124–76.
67. *Lord Provosts of Glasgow* (see note 1), pp. 241–60.
68. *The Herald*, 9 February 1999.
69. *The Herald*, 30 June 1998; *Scotland on Sunday*, 31 January 1999; *The Herald*, 31 January 1999 & 24 April 1999. Shortly thereafter Lally was succeeded by his close ally, Alex Mosson (*The Herald*, 18 May 1999).

CHAPTER FOUR

Urban government, finance and public health in Victorian Britain[*]

Robert Millward

Introduction

The focus of this chapter is the great expansion of the urban infrastructure in Victorian Britain. The story is well known with urban areas witnessing a huge number of new waterworks, sewer systems, gasworks and bridges and, towards the end, electricity stations, tramways and schools. Even the railways made a big impact on the urban infrastructure as buildings were cleared and subsequently factories and houses clustered round the new track.[1] The political dimensions of this story for town councils and their elected representatives have received much attention from historians,[2] as have the administrative and policy issues for central government, featuring major personalities like Chadwick and Simon.

The economic dimensions of the urban story have, however, had much less attention and they are crucially linked to a major theme of this book: the institutional and organisational options facing local councillors and officials. What, in particular, were the economic forces affecting the scope of urban government with respect to both municipal services and regulation of the private sector? Some of the arguments developed here derive from studies currently under way (with colleagues at Manchester) of a sample of 36 towns in England and Wales using data from the Local Taxation Returns and the reports of the Registrar-General on mortality.[3] There are three specific questions which are now addressed:

1 How can we broadly conceptualise the way the infrastructure was expanded? Was it simply an increase of services collectively supplied and consumed and financed by local taxes? Or were the more complex configurations (such as Leeds Corporation explicitly subsidising water supplies from gas profits) indicative of other strategies?

2 What were the alternatives to municipal provision? Was municipal provision of water and gas in Oldham a response to similar forces which prompted Newcastle to rely on private electricity and water supplies, and Eastbourne and Bournemouth to rely more generally on the private sector?

3 What can we say about success and impact; did regulation have more impact than municipal provision?

The size of the expansion of the urban infrastructure, 1870–1914

As the first nation to shift to factory work, Britain witnessed unprecedented economic and social problems. By the middle of the nineteenth century, Britain's major towns were congested cesspits of disease and rising mortality.[4] In his magisterial study of 'City Growth' Williamson has tended to play down the special problems of early Victorian Britain, arguing that Belgium, France, Holland, Germany and other continental European countries were soon to experience the same urban problems whilst the growth of cities was actually less than that in Third World countries since 1950.[5] However, the decline in the share of agriculture in employment and national income in Britain, by 1840, was very large, was unprecedented and was unrepeated. That is, when other countries achieved real income levels equivalent to Britain in 1840, the share of agriculture in their economies was considerably higher,[6] and the concomitant urbanisation problems so much less. Although many features of the classic period of the British industrial revolution, 1770–1840, are disputed, in particular whether living standards improved, the shift in the urban/rural balance is not a matter of dispute. Neither is there much doubt that the investment rate in the urban infrastructure over that period fell well short of that in other parts of the economy, as Williamson himself shows.[7] Finally, the political culture in early nineteenth-century Britain was inimical to central government intervention in aid of local problems.[8] Substantial increases in national income per head might have ushered in different attitudes but before the 1840s it is not clear that any such increase had occurred.

In this light the second half of the nineteenth century is seen as something of a catch-up. From the 1870s we find infrastructure expansion at local level, including housing, was accounting for about one-third of all investment in the UK and amounted to £40 million at 1900 prices. This figure includes local government capital works programmes, housing (which was mainly private sector), and all other private sector agencies like gas companies, schools, hospitals, water companies and private electricity generating stations. By the early 1900s the total had risen to nearly £100 million, that is about 40 per cent of all UK investment. Even when housing is excluded the volume of investment is nearly as much as the whole of manufacturing industry in a country which was supposedly the workshop of the world. Of this total, local government was the fastest growing element (Figure 4.1) and was then accounting for practically all public investment in Britain.

The strains which the urban expansion was imposing on town council budgets are best shown by some estimates for the sample of towns. In the last quarter of the century, expansion of town populations seem to carry few economies of scale. A rise of, say 10 per cent in a town's population resulted in a 30 per cent increase in town council expenditures on public health, police, roads etc., unless the population explosion was accompanied by an equivalent extension of town boundaries (which was not common) and even then expenditures would rise by at least 10 per cent.[9]

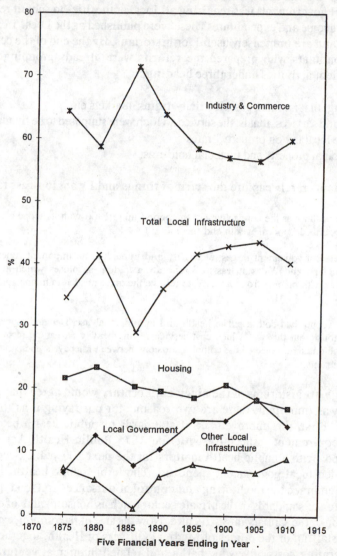

Figure 4.1 Shares of UK investment 1870–1910 (average annual percentage)

Source: C. H. Feinstein, *National Income, Expenditure and Output of the United Kingdom, 1855–1965* (London: Cambridge University Press, 1972), app. tables 39 and 40, and C. H. Feinstein and S. Pollard (eds), *Studies in Capital Formation in the United Kingdom, 1750–1920* (Oxford: Clarendon Press, 1988), app. tables II and IX.

Public health as a core activity

How can the increase in the urban infrastructure be characterised? From the 1870s the newly established Local Government Board (a department of central government) was requiring all local authorities to submit returns of their income and expenditure. These were published as the Local Taxation Returns and are immensely useful for historians. By the end of the century the accountants who prepared the returns were already grouping local government activities under three headings:

- trading, that is water, gas, electricity, trams, markets etc.,
- rate fund services, that is, the services which were supposed to be financed by the local tax on property, 'rates',
- municipal property and financial holdings.

Accountants rarely capture the spirit of things and I want to stress rather:

1 Public health was the core activity in the period up to 1900 with its scope closely circumscribed by local wealth and income.

2 Municipal involvement in gas, electricity and trams had an important function (in England and Wales at least) of generating trading surpluses which acted, together with income from property, to relieve the taxes needed to finance public health.

3 Water supply had both a public health and an industrial use. Demand increased enormously but this was a high cost service relying heavily on natural resources and the outcome reflected the complex tensions between ratepayers, industrialists and citizens.

Although all historians of the nineteenth century would agree that public health was important, there are two reasons for portraying it as the core activity. First, the improvement of standards of public health became a legal requirement, especially with the 1875 Public Health Act which governed British public health matters for the next 100 years. Second, it dominated local government spending. The term 'public health' is here used to embrace the monitoring and control of nuisances and food quality, regulation of standards in the private sector (such as housing) and, of course, provision of the sanitary infrastructure. Now the size of the running expenses on the staffing of the offices of Medical Officers of Health, together with the operating costs of sewers, baths and related municipal ventures was quite modest.[10]

However, current expenditure trends are misleading in that public health in the nineteenth century was a very capital-expensive activity as new sewers, waterworks and street improvements were instigated. By the

1880s, as Table 4.1 shows, capital expenditure out of loans (which accounted for most of the investment undertaken) for sewers, hospitals, commons, baths, parks and workhouses was accounting, with water supply, for about one-quarter of the total investment of all local authorities in England and Wales. This is an underestimate because expenditures which appear in summary accounts[11] (also see Table 4.1) as roads or streets, often had a public health dimension. Our scrutiny of the Local Taxation Returns now makes it clear that spending on paving, flood channels, street improvements and maintenance had a strong health dimension in the pre-motor era and was reflected in the placement of many of these items in the local authorities' 'sanitary account'. Our estimates for the sample of towns are given in Table 4.2, whilst Figure 4.2 illustrates how sanitation and water, properly measured, dominated the capital works programmes of local authorities until electricity and trams entered the picture towards the turn of the century.

Finally we should note in this context that water investment was of the same order of magnitude as sanitation by the 1870s but undoubtedly exceeded it in the earlier part of the century. This was a mixed blessing,[12] since middle-class expenditures on water closets, sinks etc., together with heavy demands from industry, clogged up drainage systems equipped for less hectic times and worsened the health problem. Much of the early investment in water favoured manufacturing interests especially in the textile belt such that we find soft water for Wakefield and Manchester was given precedence over local hard, pure water supplies.

Table 4.1 Annual average expenditure out of loans by local authorities in England and Wales, 1883–1913 (£ millions)

	1883 to 1885	1886 to 1890	1891 to 1895	1896 to 1900	1901 to 1905	1906 to 1910	1911 to 1913
Education	1.3	1.0	1.3	2.2	2.4	2.7	3.0
Public hlth.#	1.2	1.7	2.4	3.7	5.3	3.5	1.6
Roads	2.2	1.5	1.3	2.1	5.2	2.2	1.8
Other services	1.8	1.5	3.3	3.4	4.0	3.4	5.4
Sub-total	6.5	5.7	8.3	11.4	17.9	11.7	11.8
Water	1.2	1.7	1.5	2.3	10.3*	2.8	2.3
Gas	0.5	0.3	0.5	0.8	1.1	0.5	0.4
Electricity	0	0	0.3	1.5	3.8	1.6	1.4
Tramways^	0	0	0.1	1.0	4.2	2.9	0.8
Rest+	0.9	0.6	0.5	1.1	1.5	5.9*	1.2
Trading total	2.9	2.6	2.9	6.7	20.9	13.7	6.1
Grand total	**9.4**	**8.3**	**11.2**	**18.1**	**38.8**	**25.4**	**17.9**

Notes
Sewerage, workhouses, hospitals, commons, parks.
* Reflects establishment of Metropolitan Water Board and Port of London Authority respectively.
^ Entry is actually 'transport services'.
+ Harbours, docks, piers etc.

Source: Data refer to financial years ending in the year quoted and are taken from B.R. Mitchell, *British Historical Statistics* (Cambridge: 1988).

Table 4.2 Municipal capital expenditure by function, 1870–1913 (annual average expenditure per town in £'000; sample of 36 towns in England and Wales)

	1871 to 1875[1]	1876 to 1880[1]	1881 to 1885	1886 to 1890	1891 to 1895	1896 to 1900	1901 to 1905	1906 to 1910	1911 to 1913
Sewers	0.9	2.0	3.0[2]	3.7	8.5	8.8	11.2	8.1	5.0
Streets	na	na	11.2[2]	6.9	7.3	16.1	23.5	10.7	8.8
Water	5.7	9.4	17.7[2]	14.3	14.8	10.9	24.4	18.2	16.4
Other	na	na	5.4[2]	6.7	12.2	38.8	32.3	9.9	10.3
Total sanitation & water	na	na	37.2[2]	31.7	42.8	74.7	91.4	46.9	40.5
Education	0	0	0.1	0.2	1.0	0.9	6.4	9.9	9.3
Other services	na	na	8.3	8.3	14.8	31.0	27.5	13.3	11.0
Gas	0.1	3.4	3.5	3.4	4.0	5.2	9.1	3.3	2.8
Electr.	0	0	0	0	0	4.3	29.7	10.4	8.3
Tramways	0	0	0	0	0	3.1	33.1	6.3	4.1
Other trading	na	na	0.3	0.7	26.63	5.0	11.0	11.1	2.3
Grand total	na	na	49.4	44.3	89.2[3]	124.2	208.2	101.2	78.3

Notes

General: The figures for sanitation were estimated independently of the others (see Bell and Millward (1998 [see endnote 3]) and the overall totals therefore need to be read with caution.

1) The figures for the 1870s are estimates and the entries for sewers include parks, baths, refuse and hospitals.

2) The entries for water and sanitation relate to 1884 and 1885.

3) Includes loan by Manchester Corporation for Ship Canal.

Source: Annual Local Taxation Returns for England and Wales.

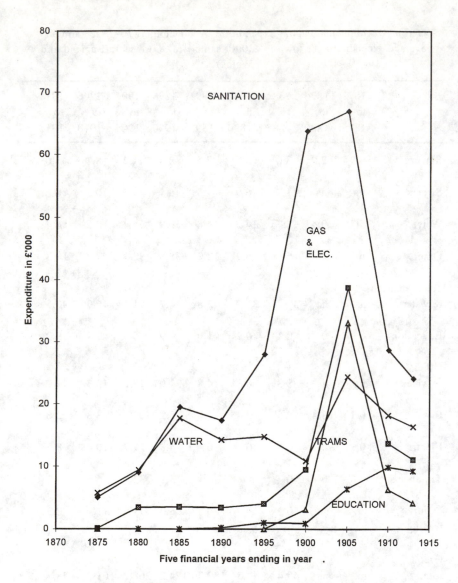

Figure 4.2 Municipal capital expenditure, 1870–1913 (annual average expenditure
per town; sample of 36 towns in England and Wales)

Source: Local Taxation Returns. 1870s figures are estimates and the last observation
relates to 1911–13.

Institutional options

The story of how these programmes were financed has often been told in terms of the rise in rates, in ratepayers' revolts and with intervention from the central government largely delayed until the twentieth century.[13] This is clearly part of the story, for all local authorities were committed to financing the expansion of policing, public health and education in the second half of the nineteenth century. They did not leave local citizens to contract and pay for these services themselves. Instead the local authorities levied taxes in the form of rates which constituted an important item of local authority income. They did not even subcontract the provision of these services to private agents, as Chadwick had suggested, with his idea of a roving town improvements company. Rather, they supplied the services 'in-house'.

However, this is not the full story because as well as rate income there were other options. Indeed when it came to services like trams, water supply, gas and electricity, where tariffs, fares and meter charges had traditionally been levied, a divergence of practice arose. Some towns left the provision of services to the private sector. Others municipalised. In making this decision, it is clear that town councillors were conscious of the revenues which such traded services might generate to reduce the burden of the rates.

To appreciate this issue fully we should note that the capital programmes for public health generated loan charges in the form, each year, of interest payments and repayment of principal on the loans raised. These annual charges, when added to staffing, fuel and the other running costs of policing, education and public health were what local government had to cover each year from income, that is, rates and other sources. The wealth of a town could well affect the level and quality of service. Moreover the costs of supplying services also varied across towns, in part because of differences in wages etc., but also because of differences in the sheer volume of resources needed in towns of differing population densities. Policing, health, and education were all expensive to deliver in the growing congested towns of industrial Britain. Finally, we should note that there were many local residents who did not pay rates directly, quite apart from users or beneficiaries (of trams, water supplies, street cleansing, health services etc.) who did not even reside locally.

This bears directly on the choice as to which body would provide trading services like gas, markets, water supply, electricity, trams and harbours. A key element of the municipalisation programme (in England and Wales at least) was that property income and trading profits were often used to supplement and relieve rate income.[14] Moreover, getting access to these profits was a prime mover in the very act of municipalisation, given that there were no prospects of levying a local profits or sales tax. There are plenty of examples of explicit rate relief and of declarations of its importance. Joseph Chamberlain classically advised that unless a council had substantial property income ('estates') other revenue sources would have to be found to relieve rates.[15] Emile Garcke, a well-known opponent of municipal trading and managing director of British Electric Traction, a large private electricity company, told a parliamentary select committee in 1903 that most municipal electrical undertakings were being run for profit to ease municipal finances.[16] In addition, by the early 1900s, the Local Government Board was insisting that transfers from trading activities be recorded in the accounts. For some towns (Leeds, for example) the amounts were quite large but there were marked differences across towns. Gross profits in the last quarter of the century in our sample of 36 towns were equal to about 50 per cent of rate income. After deducting loan charges this falls to 25 per cent and we should acknowledge that a good part of this actually came from property holdings like docks and racecourses.[17] Nevertheless the act of municipalisation tells us a lot about motives and agencies, especially when we look at its incidence and the role of the private sector.

The public interest in how the trading services were provided stemmed from two matters. First, economies of scale pervaded electricity generation and distribution, gasworks and gas distribution and tramways so that private sector provision often led to local monopolies.[18] Second, there were standards of service (like water quality) which could not be left solely to the market. A regulatory framework was established in parliamentary legislation from the 1840s onwards (such as the 1847 Waterworks Clauses Acts plus individual acts for each town). There is little doubt that arm's length regulation of private companies is a sophisticated form of public control which requires much stronger monitoring and control systems than existed in the nineteenth century and the weakness of parliamentary control has often been invoked, if only implicitly, to explain municipal trading activities. However, I still stress the role of rate relief in England and Wales for several reasons.

There were many towns reliant on private companies and, for such towns, arm's-length regulation and other pressures were presumably felt to be enough. Private provision flourished early in the century when councils were frequently dominated by leaders who were owners of the water and gas suppliers. The rising representation on elected town councils of rate-paying owners of small property undermined this but private companies, by the time of the First World War, still accounted for about 60 per cent of gas supplies and about one-third of trams and electricity. The differing proportions partly reflect the fact that a gas company was more expensive to buy out since there was no legislation like the 1870 Tramways Act and the 1882

Electric Lighting Act which gave compulsory purchase rights to town councils. Private companies also continued where town councils had alternative income sources and where therefore the need to expropriate trading surpluses was less. Hence the quite striking continuing presence of private gas companies in the ports (Liverpool, Bristol, Southampton, Hull etc.) where dockland property yielded a useful income. Leeds and Birmingham are good counter-examples since they had little property income and therefore ventured extensively into municipal trading. Private utilities also flourished where the local rates base was strong from the presence of wealthy inhabitants and where public health problems were much less (Eastbourne, Bournemouth). Finally, we should recognise that the act of municipalisation was administratively costly (required a special Act early on) and conversely would suit only certain kinds of local government structures, particularly the big provincial towns where utility operations were especially cost-effective. Thus scantily populated rural areas straddling several local government boundaries were left to the private sector as were many small towns. So, of course, was London with its disastrous hotchpotch of authorities.

Two puzzles remain. In Scotland trading surpluses were not used in this way and, indeed, there were tablets of stone outlawing such practices. In any case, says Fraser,[19] rates in Scotland fell on the tenant as well as the landlord (in contrast to England and Wales) so there was less need to mulct the service user in the same way. If it was not rate relief, what was it? Scholars like Fraser[20] and Maver[21] writing about Glasgow are implicitly saying arm's-length regulation of the private sector was weak. The main difficulty in evaluating the Scottish case is that there has been little assessment of what was happening in the private sector. Comparisons between Glasgow and other towns are needed.

Water supply is another intriguing area. Gross trading profits were high but after deducting loan charges, water supply generally made a financial loss. Data on loan charges and net profits for individual municipal trading sectors do not appear in the Local Taxation Returns until the turn of the century, but it is then clear from both the national picture (Table 4.3) and estimates for the sample towns (Table 4.4) that water supplies were a financial liability. Water revenues came, of course, not from direct residential user charges but from water rates and metered industrial users. By Edwardian times 80 per cent of water supplies were in municipal hands. Explanations of this have often invoked the poor quality of service from the private companies[22] or the alleged unwillingness of private companies to engage in the required long-term investments (or 'short-termism').[23] All of this is difficult to reconcile with the huge private investment occurring in the railways with bridges, tunnels and track spreading into the remote parts of Wales, Scotland and Cornwall. What was so special about water?

My own speculation is that the spread of water supplies was indeed perceived to be inadequate but that the reason for this was the price controls which actually did work in this industry. Quite unlike manufacturing industry, gas supply, railway operations and electricity generation and distribution, water supply was subject to hugely diminishing returns. Very costly projects tapping the water resources of Wales for Birmingham, the Lake District and the Pennines for Manchester and Loch Katrine for Glasgow are only the more grandiose examples of an industry heavily reliant on natural resources. The pressure from town council health requirements plus manufacturing demands for water meant that price increases would be limited. Hence the outcome was low meter rents and generous compensation schemes for manufacturers affected by local reservoir developments. It also led eventually to cheap water for residents, that is, water 'rates', which precluded water undertakings earning any net profit.

Table 4.3 Financial performance of trading activities of all local authorities in Britain, 1883–1913 (£ million)

	Water	Gas	Elect.	Trans-port	Docks, piers, etc.	Total
1883[1]						
Oper. costs	0.8	2.6	n.a.	n.a.	1.1	n.a.
Gr. profit	0.8	0.6	n.a.	n.a.	n.a.	n.a.
Revenue	1.6	3.2	n.a.	n.a.	n.a.	n.a.
1894						
Oper. costs	1.1[1]	4.6	0.1[2]	0.1[1]	1.8	7.7[3]
Gr. profit	1.7[1]	1.4	n.a.	0.1[1]	n.a.	n.a.
Revenue	2.8[1]	6.0	n.a.	0.2[1]	n.a.	n.a.
1903						
T. costs	5.4	8.4	2.2	4.1	4.4	24.5
Net profit	-0.4	0.6	0	0.5	n.a.	0.7[4]
Revenue	5.0	9.0	2.2	4.6	n.a.	25.2[4]
1908						
T. costs	9.1	9.2	3.9	8.2	5.3	35.7
Net profit	-0.4	0.5	0.1	0.9	n.a.	1.1[4]
Revenue	8.7	9.7	4.0	9.1	n.a.	36.8[4]
1913						
T. costs	10.1	10.1	5.4	10.6	9.7	45.9
Net profit	-0.6	0.8	0.1	0.6	-0.3[5]	0.6[5]
Revenue	9.5	10.9	5.5	11.2	9.4[5]	46.5[5]

Notes
1) Excludes Scotland.
2) Excludes England and Wales.
3) Excludes water supply and transport in Scotland and electricity in England and Wales.
4) Excludes net profits of docks.
5) Excludes net profit of docks in Scotland.

Definitions: Revenue includes all receipts, grants, tolls and fees. Oper. costs comprise annual labour, fuel, maintenance and other operating costs. T. costs comprise operating costs plus annual loan charges. Gr. profit is revenue less operating costs as defined above. Net profit is revenue less total costs as defined above. Before 1903 the cost figures for England and Wales in our source (Mitchell 1988) exclude loan charges as do the data for Scotland before 1893. The post-1902 data do not identify loan charges separately.

Source: B.R. Mitchell, *British Historical Statistics* (Cambridge: 1988), pp. 609–29.

Table 4.4 Average annual trading profits per town council 1896–1913 (sample of 36 towns in England and Wales: £'000)

	1896–1900	1901–03	1904–10	1911–13
Water: Profits	20.28	21.35	28.36	32.53
Loan Charges	n.a.	n.a.	31.34[1]	31.88
Gas: Profits	10.69	12.24	14.7[1]	15.54
Loan Charges	n.a.	n.a.	11.26[1]	12.38
Electricity profits	0.75	8.58	16.99	20.16
Loan Charges	n.a.	n.a.	15.44	19.05
Trams: Profits	0.71	12.14	18.03	18.20
Loan Charges	n.a.	n.a.	14.10	15.73
Market Profits	3.15	3.32	3.04	4.05
Cemetery Profits	-0.04	-1.65	0.02	0.76
Harbour Profits	-0.25	0.27	0.97	3.44
Estates Profits	14.62	15.12	15.50	17.08
Total Profits	49.96	71.35	100.03[2]	113.85[2]
Loan Charges	n.a.	n.a.	73.72	88.86

Notes
1) Excludes Sunderland, 1906.
2) Excludes Thetford, 1908–12.

Sources and definitions:
The source is Local Government Board, Annual Local Taxation Returns, 1871–1913. Entries are unweighted averages of the 36 towns and therefore columns do not necessarily add up. Profits data are gross trading profits. Profits of electricity, trams, cemeteries and harbours were non-existent or zero before 1896. Loan charges include interest and principal repaid but relevant aggregate data are not available for the years before 1904. Data refer to the financial years of town councils ending in the year quoted.

The growth and impact of public health spending

Let me now return to the core activity, public health. What did determine spending levels? Towns with only small estates and few trading activities (such as many of the small southern towns like Hastings) would not have difficulties if they had a strong rates base or few public health problems. Otherwise they would be in trouble. We have looked at this issue for the sample of towns and the main conclusions were as follows:[24]

1   The cost of providing public health services was not affected much by differences in wage rates, rental levels, coal prices etc. Rather the supply of services exhibited massively diminishing returns to population increases, as noted earlier. Thus London's costs were especially high, not because wages were higher but because of the sheer problems of supplying services in the congested metropolis.

2   Expenditure on public health services, even after controlling for all other influences, was extremely sensitive to local income and wealth levels. The assessed value of property for purposes of raising local taxes ('rateable value') is our major source of information on local income/wealth levels. Thus a 10 per cent difference across towns in rateable value per head (or a 10 per cent increase over time in the same town) raised expenditure on services by a similar proportion even for towns with the same population and area.

3   The major provincial industrial towns (which attained the local governmental status of being called 'county boroughs') had a smaller problem than London in the cost of delivering services but this was more than offset by their lower average wealth levels. Expenditure per head was noticeably less but expenditure per £ of rateable value was actually higher. It was then the county boroughs which relied more on trading profits and estate income but which also finished up with higher rates per £ of rateable value.

How did this affect the pattern of spending on public health over time and its impact on the environment? Our answers to these questions can only be 'broad brush' in this chapter. There are two key indicators. First, the inputs to public health may be proxied by expenditures on staffing, fuel, capital works etc. Second, whilst mortality is affected by a wide range of variables, we shall use it, and especially infant mortality, as a rough indicator of the environmental impact of the public health effort.

What is striking about the public health effort is its timing. It is clear from Figure 4.2 that a major part of the spending occurred very late in the nineteenth century. In Figure 4.3 the capital expenditure data have been adjusted for price changes and for increases in the population. Even then the very large peak in the 1890s and early 1900s was such that expenditures expressed in real terms and per head of population, nearly trebled from the late 1880s to the early 1900s. This was especially noticeable for sewers and street expenditures, and applied to current as well as capital expenditure.[25]

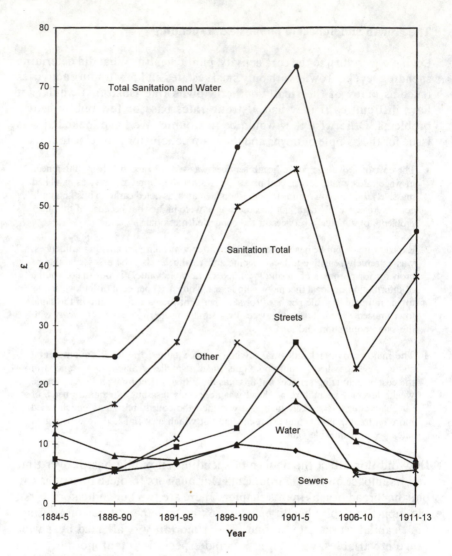

Figure 4.3 Sanitation and water supply: municipal capital expenditure per head at constant prices. (Sample of 36 towns in England and Wales, 1884–1913; annual average expenditure per 100 inhabitants in £)

Source: Local Taxation Returns England and Wales, 1884–1913 and Mitchell, 1988. Nominal expenditures are multiplied by 100/Rousseaux price index, further divided by the borough populations (census based) and then multiplied by 100.

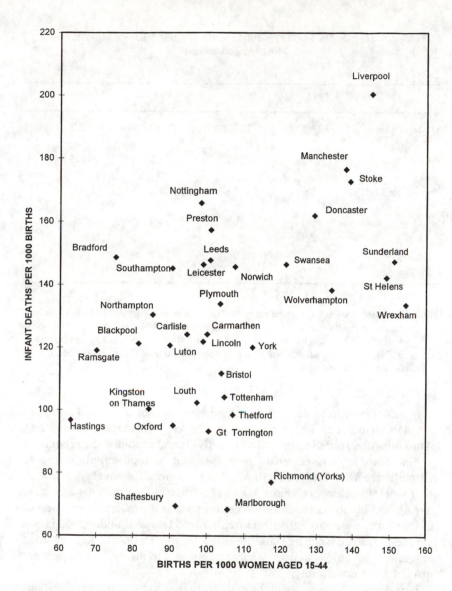

Figure 4.4 Fertility and infant mortality in 36 towns in England and Wales, 1906

Source: Annual decennial reports of the Registrar-General.

Table 4.5 Mortality by age, 1875–1905 (deaths per 1000; sample of 36 towns in England and Wales)

	1875	1885	1895	1905
Under 1 year	183.2	176.2	190.0	152.2
Child 1 to 4	31.2	27.3	24.2	18.2
Ages 5 to 34	6.6	5.6	4.8	4.0
Aged over 34	31.0	29.7	29.3	25.6
All ages	21.8	19.8	18.9	16.0

Note: The sources are the decennial reports of the Registrar-General, 1881–1911, which record, for each decade and age group, the mean populations and cumulative totals of deaths. The latter were divided by 10 and then by the mean population (in '000s) for that decade and the resultant age-specific death rate was centred on the middle of the decade.

Why was spending so delayed in the nineteenth century? The regulation and monitoring of the health environment in response to the new problems of urbanisation started in the 1830s and 1840s and included the regulation of new housing, inspection of premises and of food supplies (see in particular the 1848 Public Health Act,[26] the Nuisance Removals Act 1846,[27] the Town Improvement Clauses Act 1847). Some of the problems here were glaring and obvious though implementation was a problem. Provision of an appropriate sanitary infrastructure involved less well understood issues and the literature (such as Hamlin's work on the Thames)[28] has recorded how sewer technology and knowledge of optimal treatments of waste were areas of great uncertainty.

There were also governmental problems in that natural drainage systems often crossed local government boundaries. To develop a main sewer system consistent with the flow of water required co-operation across these boundaries and eventually a redrawing, as in Manchester which absorbed its outlying neighbours. Finally, the capital-intensive nature of public health expansion meant an increasing need for loan finance. Interest rates and repayment periods were ungenerous for the main central government loans, those of the Public Works Loan Commissioners. Prior to 1875 arrangements were *ad hoc* and often via Private Acts of Parliament. Not until the late nineteenth century do we see the Local Government Board playing a strong part in easing access to finance.

Conclusions: the implications for mortality

There are some rather specific implications for mortality and especially infant mortality. The latter is often regarded as a key indicator of the quality of the environment. Infant mortality was still very high in the early 1900s (Figure 4.4), reaching over 150 per 1000 births in many towns, many of which also still had relatively high fertility levels. This was at a time when the long-term decline of infant mortality had already set in. So, despite all the efforts from the 1830s onwards, Britain still had a hostile disease environment in the Edwardian era. The factors affecting infant mortality are very complex and include living standards, mothers' health and fertility, as well as the state of the domestic and community environments. A number of issues are, however, becoming clearer from our work on the sample of towns. First, mortality was declining for many age groups from about the 1870s if not earlier (Table 4.5). That fall cannot be explained by changes in the sanitary infrastructure since the major surge did not occur until the 1890s. An important contributory element was the housing stock. In all the different types of town (ports, rural settlements, textile towns, etc.) the number of houses was rising relative to population. In large industrial towns the increase over the period 1870–1914 was 40 per cent. All new houses were increasingly subject to regulations on spacing, drains, access to sewers, to light. It looks as though these qualitative improvements when added to smaller family size (and hence a smaller number of susceptibles) and the increase in the housing stock were an important aspect of the reduced exposure to disease.

Rising living standards, more generally, were also important. There is no dispute about the rise in this period and we should recognise what this meant. It was not simply a question of nutritional improvement. Indeed changes here may not always have been to the good in so far as rising real incomes generated extra spending on 'junk' foods like tea, sugar and condensed milk. More important perhaps was that rising real incomes allowed for household acquisition of health enhancing goods like toilets, sinks and soap, and a bigger tax base eased town council spending on sewers and cleaner water supplies.

Where the delayed improvement of the sanitary infrastructure may have had a key role was in infantile diarrhoea which showed no sign of secular decline until the early 1900s. We suspect that those high density towns which most delayed their public health programmes were the ones which were latest in seeing a fall in infant mortality. (Stoke seems to be a good example.) Even by 1906 we see from Figure 4.4 that infant mortality is still at horrendous levels – about 15 per cent of all infants. Since fertility levels were high, poor families still had to cope with constant infant problems in a hostile disease environment in which the most careful guard over health and hygiene was necessary. How that process worked out in different towns is part of our current research.

Notes

* Thanks are due to Frances Bell for research assistance and to the Leverhulme Trust for financial support.
1. J.R. Kellett, *The Impact of Railways on Victorian Cities* (London: Routledge and Keegan Paul, 1969).
2. P.J. Waller, *Town, City and Nation: England 1850–1914* (Oxford: Oxford University Press, 1983); *1847 Waterworks Clauses Act*, 10 Vict., c.17; J. Garrard, *Leadership and Power in Victorian Industrial Towns, 1830* (Manchester: Manchester University Press, 1983).
3. R. Millward, and S. Sheard, 'The Urban Fiscal Problem, 1870–1914: Government Expenditure and Finances in England and Wales', *Economic History Review*, 48 (1995), pp. 501–35; F. Bell and R. Millward, 'Public Health Expenditures and Mortality in England and Wales, 1870–1914', *Continuity and Change*, 13 (1998).
4. A.S. Wohl, *Endangered Lives: Public Health in Victorian Britain* (London: Methuen, 1983); S. Szreter and G. Mooney, 'Urbanisation, Mortality and the Standard of Living Debate: New Estimates of the Expectancy of Life at Birth in Nineteenth Century British Cities', *Economic History Review*, 51 (1998).
5. J.G. Williamson, *Coping with City Growth during the British Industrial Revolution* (Cambridge: Cambridge University Press, 1990), 1.
6. N.F.R. Crafts, *British Economic Growth in the Industrial Revolution* (Oxford: Oxford University Press, 1985), pp. 57–9.
7. Williamson, *Coping with City Growth*, ch. 10.
8. E.P. Hennock, 'Central-Local Government Relations in England: An Outline, 1850–1950', *Urban History Yearbook* (Leicester: Leicester University Press, 1982).
9. Millward and Sheard, 'Urban Fiscal Problem'.
10. Ibid.
11. B.R. Mitchell, *British Historical Statistics* (Cambridge: Cambridge University Press, 1988).
12. J.A. Hassan, 'The Growth and Impact of the British Water Industry in the 19th Century', *Economic History Review*, 38 (1985); J.A. Hassan, *A History of Water in Modern England and Wales* (Manchester: Manchester University Press, 1998); C. Hamlin, 'Muddling in Bumbledom: On the Enormity of Large Sanitary Improvements in Four British Towns, 1855–1885', *Victorian Studies*, 32 (1988), pp. 57–81.
13. M.J. Daunton, 'Urban Britain', in T.R. Gourvish and A.O. Day (eds), *Later Victorian Britain, 1867–1900* (London: Macmillan, 1988), pp. 37–67.
14. E.P. Hennock, 'Finance and Politics in Urban Local Government in England, 1835–1900', *Historical Journal*, 6 (1963), pp. 212–15.
15. Waller, *Town, City and Nation*, p. 304.
16. H.J. Gibbons, 'The Opposition to Municipal Socialism in England, *Journal of Political Economy*, 9 (1901), p. 254.
17. Millward and Sheard, 'Urban Fiscal Problem'.
18. R. Millward, 'The Emergence of Gas and Water Monopolies in Nineteenth Century Britain: Contested Markets and Public Control', in J. Foreman-Peck (ed.), *New Perspectives on the Late Victorian Economy* (Cambridge: Cambridge University Press, 1991).
19. H. Fraser, 'Municipal Socialism and Social Policy', in R.J. Morris and R. Rodger (eds), *The Victorian City: A Reader in British Urban History, 1820–1914* (London: Longman, 1993).

20. Ibid.
21. I. Maver, 'Glasgow and the Loch Katrine Water Supply', paper presented at the Conference on the Development of Water Resources in Britain (University of Aberystwyth, March 1998).
22. Ibid.
23. J.A. Hassan, 'Growth and Impact'; Hassan, *History of Water*; D. Knoop, *Principles and Methods of Municipal Trading* (London: Macmillan, 1912).
24. Millward and Sheard, 'Urban Fiscal Problem'.
25. Bell and Millward, 'Public Health Expenditure'.
26. *1848 Public Health Act* (11 and 12 Vict., c. 63).
27. *1848 Nuisance Removals Act* (9 and 10 Vict., c. 96).
28. C. Hamlin, 'William Dibdin and the Idea of Biological Sewage Treatment', *Technology and Culture*, 29 (1988), pp. 189–21.

CHAPTER FIVE

The role and influence of Glasgow's municipal managers, 1890s–1930s

Irene Maver

Introduction

How influential were municipal managers in British cities between the 1890s and 1930s, which represented a period of unprecedented expansion in the provision of services and utilities? This chapter focuses on the Glasgow experience, and the pivotal role that the civic bureaucracy came to play in implementing urban strategy during this time.[1] As a quantitative indicator of their importance, the number of full-time staff employed by Glasgow Corporation in the 1890s had more than tripled from approximately 10,000 to 34,000 by the 1930s. Yet Glasgow was distinctive because commitment to the public service was a phenomenon that went much further back than the 1890s. The traditional legal function of Scotland's royal burghs in the jurisdiction of urban areas had been consolidated at the start of the nineteenth century, in an attempt to come to grips with the problems of public order.[2] This laid the foundations of a formidable administrative machine, which was opened out substantially when a wide-ranging reorganisation of departmental structures occurred during the 1890s. By this time, the bureaucracy had become very conscious of its own self-image. While elected councillors were prone to shift and change according to the vagaries of political fortune, full-time officials represented a solid symbol of continuity. The public relations focus of Glasgow Corporation as a 'model municipality' prior to 1914 helped to enhance their status even further.[3] Leading officials came to be as well-known as local politicians, but with the added dimension of professional gravitas, intended to assure the public that the city was in trustworthy hands.

Yet for all their crucial importance in shaping the city's identity, the role and influence of municipal managers have not been a prime focus of Glasgow's civic history. Indeed, despite considerable interest in Scotland's early burgh history, there has been a dearth of general local government studies from the nineteenth century, and so comparisons are difficult to make. Even in the terrain of municipal studies for elsewhere in the United Kingdom, the presence of officials is often shadowy.[4] The most recent analyses of Glasgow Corporation have tended to concentrate on how the municipal ethos was consolidated in the years leading up to the First World War, with the role of elected representatives the subject of especial scrutiny.[5] A distinguishing feature of the pre-war civic leadership was its solid grounding in the business community, with men of substantial wealth consistently in key positions of power. The intensity of their commitment derived from a tradition of consensus in municipal affairs, identifiable from the mid-nineteenth century, and which vocally affirmed faith in an idealised notion of the public good. There was a strong religious underpinning to civic rhetoric, powerfully influenced by evangelical Presbyterianism and crucial for muting overt party political rivalries within the corporation.[6] The rationale was to promote the harmonious integration of urban society and give credibility to the more expensive municipal undertakings, with professionalism helping considerably in reinforcing such strategy. The image that evolved was one of beneficent paternalism and sound business sense, which meant that the advocacy of public ownership by the 1890s, even in contentious areas of new technology such as the electricity supply, was broadly accepted as in the best interests of the community.

However, as this chapter explains, Glasgow's carefully nurtured sense of civic cohesion became increasingly fragile as the new century progressed. There were two major contributory factors to this process. The first related to the sheer scale of the municipal function and fear that the rapid expansion of individual departments was causing control to fragment within the corporation, especially as far as the accountability of elected representatives was concerned. The intense discussion about the nature of governance in Glasgow was set firmly within a broader context, as urbanisation and its attendant social problems forced a reappraisal of civic responsibilities not just in the United Kingdom, but in Europe and North America. The creation of integrated administrative entities, such as London County Council in 1888 and the Corporation of the City of Glasgow in 1895, was an attempt to address the vexed question of controlling populous urban communities. That organisation constituted the key to effective local governance was emphasised by one Scottish student of political science in 1904:

> In the last century our predominant bias was in favour of liberty, the unrestrained action of the individual. In the coming century this attitude must be altered; we must learn to trust in corporate action; and as the Imperial Government is over-weighted, we must be prepared to see more and more functions delegated to the local bodies.[7]

However, corporate action at the local level inevitably necessitated funding, a controversial commodity which stimulated debate about finance and the need for administrative co-ordination to ensure economies of scale. Although held in check during the pre-war period, after 1918 cost-effectiveness in municipal management became a major concern of the city's influential ratepayer (i.e. taxpayer) pressure groups.

There was a second political factor relating to the integrity of the municipal function and perceptions of fragmentation. Despite expressions of neutrality at election time, competing interest groups were rife among the civic leadership, and their approach often reflected radically different priorities. Latterly, allegiances divided between Liberal and Unionist partisans. Bitter rivalries became apparent in the City Chambers, especially as the Unionists had defected from the Liberal Party in 1886 (precipitated by the crisis over Irish Home Rule), leaving a simmering undercurrent of betrayal. The Unionist split also undermined the long-standing Liberal hegemony on Glasgow Corporation which (whatever the reality) had been projected as a focus for community cohesion. To compound the sense of political flux, the intrusion of the Labour Party into the municipal domain from the 1890s created yet another serious political challenge. Labour activists directed their appeal towards working-class voters, with a programme favouring extensive municipalisation, notably in housing, perceived as the most intractable of the city's social problems. The forthright emphasis on civic collectivism helped them slowly then swiftly to strengthen their position, with the result that local politics polarised along stark socialist and anti-socialist lines. The politicisation of the electoral process contributed to the ongoing debate about the administration of the city, and leading officials came to be caught uncomfortably between growing Labour assertiveness and increasing calls for retrenchment. Over time, these contradictory pressures put the officials' previously unblemished reputation for professionalism severely to the test, and provoked unprecedented responses as the power struggle intensified.

The development of professionalism

While the role of the managers was consolidated towards the end of the nineteenth century, professionalism in Glasgow's municipal services had a long pedigree, stretching back at least to the 1800s.[8] The town clerks established a deeply entrenched position at this time, to ensure the smooth functioning of the civic apparatus, especially in the vital sphere of law enforcement. While electoral reform in 1833 fundamentally altered the exclusive, burgess-based system of representation in Scottish civic government, some key officials appointed under the former regime survived until as late as the 1870s, their position legally protected and therefore beyond the control of councillors.[9] In consequence, there were important continuities with pre-reform practices, even as the civic leadership embarked on ambitious new projects, such as the mid-century municipalisation of water and gas supplies. This helped to fuel the notion that officials represented tradition as well as progress, and that policies of expansionism were likely to proceed with caution because of the restraining influence of the professionals. The reality was more complex, with Angus Turner, the ageing principal Town Clerk, having to be bought off with a substantial pension in 1872 because his die-hard Toryism ran counter to the prevailing Liberal orthodoxy among councillors. His successor, James D. Marwick, who took office in 1873, was selected as much for his amenable brand of politics as his capabilities; civic leaders were anxious to avoid repetition of the embarrassing clashes with the irascible Turner. The Marwick example was important for demonstrating that the quest for civic efficiency depended on a comfortable working relationship between officials and elected representatives, and that in key administrative positions like the Town Clerk it was essential that there should be ideological compatibility.

However, Marwick proved to be no cipher for the civic leadership. After he was offered the then staggering annual salary of £2,500 to transfer from Edinburgh to Glasgow Corporation, he assertively continued the long-standing tradition of professionalism and single-mindedness in the bureaucracy.[10] Although aged 47 when he took office, Marwick remained in the Town Clerk's position for 30 years, overseeing the transition from the essentially burgh-based organisation of civic authority to the massive corporate structure of the 1900s. Marwick had made it his mission to see that the rigid confines of the old municipality were extended to include prestigious middle-class suburban communities, which had the benefit of adding lucrative rates revenue to the city coffers. A workaholic, with a hand-picked retinue of loyal assistants, Marwick overcame suburban scepticism by the active promotion of Glasgow's image, raising its national and international profile and demonstrating its mettle as a cosmopolitan and efficiently-run city. 'Greater Glasgow' was the chosen appellation for the extended city, reflecting the imperialist climate of the times as ambitions for 'Greater Britain' began to be articulated in the wider political arena. In his efforts to raise the public consciousness, Marwick cultivated a penchant for civic monumentalism, with the elaborate design of the City Chambers (Glasgow's new civic headquarters opened in 1888) visible testimony to the Town Clerk's ideas and influence at the height of his power. Marwick was knighted by Queen Victoria in 1888; an accolade not without controversy, as it was perceived as further bolstering his ego, and creating an undesirable 'social distinction' between the public servant and his less elevated masters.[11]

By the 1900s, Town Clerk Marwick had become a formidable role model for the burgeoning corps of municipal managers in Glasgow, although no one could hope to emulate the elevated status of the United Kingdom's highest-paid civic official. Nevertheless, the style was obviously apparent in men such as John Young, General Manager of the Tramways Department between 1894 and 1904, whose mode of working merited the epithet of 'masterly', to show how much he was able to hold together the various administrative strands in his municipal domain.[12] The metaphorical use of the reins of power was especially appropriate for Young, whose farming origins proved to be invaluable for running a department with (initially) a large establishment of horses. On the other hand, William Foulis, head of the Gas Department, had a wholly different public image; he was, according to one biographical appraisal in 1901: 'rather the professor of mathematics than the servant of a municipal Corporation. He brings to his duty the keen insight of a highly-trained intellect, the ready resource of a practical engineer, and a broad understanding of men'.[13] In the general running of Glasgow Corporation utilities, officials were described in the same publication as well ahead of the private sector in terms of their ambitions and commitment: 'They become possessed of the passion for success, which consists in making their department pay, show a good return, a big balance, a high record'.[14] These were soothing words to Glasgow's ratepayers, who were assured that the 'municipal machine' was being kept in prime efficiency by an array of experts, the best in their respective fields. There was also scope for professional commitment that was not tied in with money-making potential. In 1898 James Paton, Curator of Galleries and Museums, was described effusively as a nurturing force within the community, his priority the 'growth and education in culture and refinement' of the city's population.[15]

The focus on the individual attributes of managers was instructive, as the administrative changes during the late nineteenth century had set civic activists thinking about the best means of co-ordinating the diverse range of municipal functions to secure maximum efficiency and cost-effectiveness. Despite Marwick's efforts, it was recognised that local government was growing at too fast a pace for councillors to keep up with day-to-day administrative responsibilities, and that the larger departments were assuming the character of individual enterprises, with no overall control.[16] The notion of the general manager thus came to be vocally articulated in Glasgow as the solution to the hazy 'after Marwick' scenario. Importing influences both from Germany and the United States, the manager was perceived as an innovative and businesslike approach to civic organisation; a full-time administrative supremo who could oversee all municipal affairs, liaise with departments and ensure no unnecessary overlapping of functions.[17] However, efforts to alter the traditional function of the Town Clerk proved to be impossible, the essential Scots law qualifications limiting the choice of suitable candidates, despite optimistic hopes of importing an administrative heavyweight from south of the border.[18] In 1905 Marwick's successor was appointed after much toing and froing; he was Adam Whitson Myles, erstwhile County Clerk of Forfar, who could never quite shake off the stigma that he was an also-ran. Nor, to Myles's discomfiture, did the debate about the general manager diminish, but continued throughout the pre-war period as concern intensified about the seemingly relentless expansion of the multifaceted 'municipal machine'.

Political challenges

During the 1880s and 1890s influential civic leaders had made much about the benefits of 'Greater Glasgow', taking ideas from the copious dossier of evidence in favour of the extended city, beaverishly compiled by Town Clerk Marwick and his staff. To demonstrate their innovative approach towards the restructured city, a few even openly aligned themselves with the cause of 'municipal socialism', an ambiguous term, used generically in the United Kingdom to describe the growth of interventionism in local government. Above all, it came to be personally associated with Joseph Chamberlain, Mayor of Birmingham during the 1870s, before embarking on his high-profile parliamentary career.[19] The gleam cast by Chamberlain's fast-rising star had made a considerable impact in Glasgow, with several admirers (notably Town Clerk Marwick) following him into Unionism after the 1886 split within the Liberal Party. The Chamberlainite brand of 'municipal socialism' offered a daring populist edge to deliberations at election time, although precise definitions of such a radical-sounding option proved difficult to pin down. For instance, in 1889 one visiting American assured readers of the Scottish law journal, the *Juridical Review*, that municipal socialism was simply, 'a convenient term under which to discuss certain of the numerous and increasingly complex functions of the large modern town'.[20] In 1893 one commentator took the meaning further, suggesting that: 'Municipal socialism appears a valuable mediation between the still dominant individualism of England and the State as Universal Providence as in Germany'.[21] As for Glasgow, in 1896 the Unionist Lord Provost James Bell was adamant that the utilities of water, gas, electricity and tramways constituted 'natural monopolies', vital public services that could not be left to the vagaries of free market forces.[22] In this context, 'municipal socialism' proved to be a useful polemical device, but it was scarcely meaningful in the strictly political sense, as control of the corporation continued safe in business hands.

The breezy references to 'municipal socialism' had been made when the actual socialist presence within Scottish town councils was minimal. Thus, in Glasgow there had been a few 'working men' councillors from the 1880s, of doubtful socialist credentials, and whose success was sporadic thanks to uncoordinated electoral efforts. However, the position began to alter decisively from 1896, under the direction of Glasgow Trades' Council (a forum of local trade union organisation) and the steady consolidation of support for the newly formed Independent Labour Party (ILP).[23] Thereafter, the entry of a broad Labour alliance (the Workers' Municipal Elections Committee) had a crucial impact on Glasgow's civic elections. It was not so much the number of Labour or 'Stalwart' councillors who were elected that prompted anxiety among civic leaders, as these totalled only nine out of 77 in 1896. Rather, it was Labour's potential to disturb the carefully-nurtured tradition of non-partisanship within the Corporation, which was believed to have done so much to maintain the city's integrity in face of the challenges of precipitate urban growth. Of course, civic harmony was far less cohesive than the rhetoric implied, with competing Liberal and Unionist interest groups pursuing a much more subtle power struggle for control during the 1890s, especially in relation to social welfare strategies.[24] Nevertheless, hostilities were partly suspended when an organisation was formed in 1898 for the express purpose of eliminating the disreputable Stalwart presence from the corporation, and restoring the previous balance of representation. The Citizens' Union forthrightly declared its objective to be 'non-political and unsectarian', and initially attracted a range of eminent patrons.[25] One was Robert Crawford, a councillor of ardent Unionist convictions, who in the 1880s had been an outspoken champion of 'municipal socialism', but by 1898 was condemning socialism as 'the worst enemy of municipal progress'.[26]

By their incursion into Glasgow's civic affairs, the Stalwarts starkly redefined 'municipal socialism' as sinister and subversive, and created embarrassment for civic leaders as their own interventionist policies came to be equated with perceived Labour excesses. Most damaging for Glasgow's dignity was a series of articles which appeared in *The Times* during 1902, and singled out the city as an extreme example of civic collectivism.[27] Having constructed an impressive municipal empire, or 'city-state' as contemporaries liked to call it, the upstart Stalwarts were depicted as steadily building an alternative power base and biding their time in order to edge their way deftly into ultimate control. Negative views about the corporation's expansionist ambitions had been long articulated, but none in such a directly political or public way. Nor had there been an organisation like the Citizens' Union to argue quite so forcefully about the corrosive qualities of the monolithic 'municipal machine'. Together with fighting talk about the dangers of municipal socialism, its mission statement went on to emphasise the financial burden of expansionism, and the pressing need for 'economy in administration and the reduction of taxation'.[28] The phenomenon was by no means limited to Glasgow, as organisations like the London-based Industrial Freedom League were indefatigable publicists against the growth of the municipalities, especially as the acquisition of large-scale utilities such as the tramways and electricity supply were believed to be stifling competition.[29] In this respect, the Glasgow Stalwarts had helped to create hostages to fortune by tarnishing the corporation's hitherto exemplary record for business acumen and professionalism in civic dealings. It scarcely mattered that the strength of Stalwart representation initially depended on a fragile and unpredictable unity among assorted constituent organisations, or that electoral support had eroded drastically by 1908, with a solitary councillor surviving in office. Whatever the reality, the message was clear that Labour policies were committed to further extension of public ownership via the municipality.

Glasgow's changing civic image

Yet the Citizens' Union and a closely linked organisation, the Ratepayers' Federation Ltd, founded in 1903, could do little to dent the supreme self-confidence about Glasgow's municipal achievements during the pre-war period.[30] Civic expansionism continued to lie solidly at the heart of priorities, as was shown by the campaign throughout the 1900s to make Glasgow territorially even greater by drawing in the populous shipbuilding communities of Govan and Partick. Moreover, for all the practical considerations relating to additional rates' revenue and pooled administrative resources, there was still a burning desire to demonstrate the scale of Glasgow's magnitude, and give quantifiable substance to the lofty claim of being 'Second City of Empire'. In 1912 the boundaries were substantially extended and the city's population rose to over a million. The prospect of the redefined municipal entity meant that the preoccupation with efficiency intensified, the renewed debate about the general manager (notably in the press) indicating that tentative ideas were afloat to appoint such a supremo over the Town Clerk. Arthur Kay, businessman and driving force behind the Ratepayers' Federation, was in no doubt about the benefits for the city. He claimed that the candidate should be:

> an able businessman of great administrative ability, a paid general manager, as in Berlin – the best managed city in Europe; a judicial, judicious, masterful, broad-minded man, able to overcome friction amongst officials and discount that scheming which generally accompanies a too pronounced development of the departmental system; that evil form of development which turns what ought to be co-operation into rivalry.[31]

But others were less convinced, even those who shared the same Unionist politics as Kay. Councillor John C. King, for instance, was emphatic that the general manager proposal was a euphemism for 'uncontrolled autocracy', which would magnify the power of officials and undermine the democratic process in local government.[32]

Although the debate continued up to the war, nothing tangible was achieved, with the result that individual departments became even more self-contained under an array of municipal managers. In the interim, the Corporation workforce increased steadily, with over 15,000 on the payroll during the 1900s. The personnel factor was a point elaborated in 1906 by Frederic Clemson Howe, an American professor of civic administration and enthusiastic admirer of Glasgow Corporation and its representatives. He marvelled that one-tenth of city voters was employed by the municipality, yet manifestations of graft and corruption in the electoral process seemed to be non-existent. Glasgow, he was gratified to note, 'was a government of the taxpayers, by the taxpayers', the implication being that the restricted nature of the ratepayers' franchise was wholly positive for effective administration.[33] The pre-war right to vote was determined by residential or property qualifications, with a limited number of women householders enfranchised since 1881. However, all those in rates' arrears were excluded from the voters' roll, a proviso welcomed by Howe and others as it muted the unpredictable influence of the 'slum vote' and provided an incentive for the public-spirited citizen to keep up payments.[34] Yet the indefatigable Arthur Kay believed this to be too generous, arguing that those paying higher rates on their properties deserved proportionately more councillors.[35] Kay's rationale was that business interests were losing their grip on civic affairs, and that the electoral system needed a radical overhaul to redress the balance and restore credibility to the City Chambers. As Kay picturesquely put it, by this means socialism would 'find its wings – generally gilded with ratepayers' gold – clipped'.[36]

On the other hand, there were corporation enterprises that paid their way and helped reassure ratepayers that the 'municipal machine' could be cost-effective. The success of the Tramways Department was such that the profits came to form part of the 'Common Good', a general fund used for the social and cultural welfare of the city. The tramways was also the largest employer of all the corporation departments, with James Dalrymple, the General Manager, responsible for some 4,000 of the 15,000 corporation workers in 1905.[37] Trained as an accountant, he had spent all of his working life in the municipal service, thus exemplifying the Marwick brand of professional who maintained exacting standards and set great store by loyalty to the corporation.[38] Indeed, the Tramways Manager ran his all-male establishment with military precision, prospective employees recruited mainly from more salubrious districts well beyond the city limits and required to pass a rigorous test of physical fitness. The robust and manly image of the workforce in quasi-military attire became something of a trademark for the city which, together with state-of-the-art electric tramcars, established an enviable reputation for the department. The visible display of civic potency on the streets of Glasgow was a powerful advertisement for municipal enterprise, and between 1914 and 1918 became inextricably linked with the war effort, as Dalrymple turned his energies to military recruitment on the corporation's behalf. The Tramway's Battalion (or 15th Battalion of the Highland Light Infantry) was allegedly raised by him in 24 hours, and eventually well over 3,000 men from the department served in this capacity during the course of the war.[39]

The wartime emphasis on civic patriotism seemed to be the logical extension of the role and function of Glasgow's municipal managers from the 1890s, the city-state producing its own exemplary fighting force. This was undoubtedly how Dalrymple would have liked to be remembered, his efforts in both peace and war being seen to yield significant returns for the community. Yet ironically, as the politicisation of the electoral process intensified, the position of the full-time officials became less secure. By the 1914 municipal elections, the Labour Party had re-established a base within the City Chambers, helped by improved central organisation and added scope for representation due to the absorption of predominantly working-class outlying communities in 1912. Leading activists like John Wheatley and Patrick Dollan, who were astute publicists for the Labour cause, became well-known throughout the city for their rhetoric and leadership qualities.[40] Dollan was a journalist with a wry turn of phrase and a gift for political networking. Wheatley became inextricably associated with housing, an issue of prime concern to the local authority after the war, given the extensive government remit to embark on a major municipal house-building programme. Moreover, Clydeside, as one of the United Kingdom's key wartime centres of munitions production, had established a reputation for industrial militancy, which generally added to the fiery image that Labour was constructing.[41] After 1918 Labour represented a new way forward for a substantial body of electors, given that the war had discredited so much that was associated with the former regime. The Liberal Party, notably, had lost much of its allure because of irreconcilable leadership differences over the conduct of the war.

In 1914 there had been a record 19 Labour councillors out of 111 on the corporation. After the keenly contested 1920 elections this figure advanced to 44 representatives. To some extent the franchise reforms of 1918 had helped to bolster Labour's base, with the municipal electorate rising from

242,357 to 446,311.[42] On the other hand, the vote in local government elections remained more exclusive than the parliamentary equivalent. The former was based on the criterion of 'owner-occupancy', which tended to exclude single, working-class men and women from the voters' roll. Labour's post-war performance at the municipal polls must be set in this restricted context. Opponents recognised that it was not so much the weight of numbers, but Labour's assertive political stance that was winning support. In consequence, an anti-socialist alliance coalesced in 1920 under the designation of the Good Government Committee, its aim to challenge all Labour candidates in municipal elections.[43] Some of its leading lights (such as Chairman George William Black) had links with the Citizens' Union stretching back to 1898, so there was nothing novel about the committee's objectives. Indeed, true to its roots, it was argued that local government should be 'entirely a business proposition', with no room for overt political partisanship.[44]

By 1921 the committee had metamorphosed permanently into the Good Government League, with 'economy' as its prime watchword. There was also much emphasis on protecting the 'dignity' of the corporation from socialist extremism, with Black insinuating that the Labour Party was permeated with 'semi-alien' Irish influence.[45] Significantly, Dollan and Wheatley were the most prominent Labour leaders to come from an Irish immigrant background. The timing of all this was highly significant, as from that year Glasgow faced serious recession, due to declining global demand for shipping, the city's economic mainstay. The government's failure to maintain the momentum of post-war reconstruction and the association of Glasgow's industrial élites with economic decline had the effect of consolidating support for Labour, to the extent that ten out of the city's 15 Members of Parliament were returned for the party in the 1922 General Election, including Wheatley. This in turn prompted concerted efforts from the Good Government League to promote a 'Moderate' alternative to Labour and prevent the socialists from edging into overall municipal control. The Moderate rationale was 'non-party politics', and individual Unionists and Liberals rallied to the cause. Ironically, the effect was to divide the corporation openly into competing interest groups, of vocally declared ideological differences.

The crisis in municipal management

All this activity had a crucial impact on the position of the municipal managers, who came to be caught in the squeeze between Labour and the Moderates. As politics polarised, the nature of civic government became increasing cause for controversy, and probing questions began to be asked about alleged maladministration within the various municipal departments. The brief General Strike of May 1926 and prolonged coal strike thereafter proved to be a catalyst for exposing managerial deficiencies, with the hitherto omnipotent James Dalrymple the subject of especial public scrutiny. While the Tramways Department had consistently made financial surpluses prior to the war, profits had been plummeting during the early 1920s, so that by June 1926 a deficit was reported of over £100,000.[46] The pugnacious role of the tramways workers during the May strike seemed to confirm to municipal critics that the department was out of control and there began to be talk of wholesale changes, not least scrapping the tramways altogether and replacing the tramcars with that smart new symbol of automotive times, the omnibus.[47] This smacked of blasphemy to the beleaguered Tramways Manager, but he was already being depicted as a dinosaur in his loyalty to the old transport system, seemingly fossilised in the pre-war glory days.

The Ratepayers' Federation, together with the influential *Glasgow Herald* newspaper made vocal claims for the virtues of the 600 omnibuses plying the increasingly congested streets of Glasgow, particularly as these privately-run operations did not recognise trade unions, and were unlikely to be caught up in future strike activity. Characteristically, Dalrymple refused to reinstate the striking tramwaymen, a tactic intended to placate his Moderate critics. However, it found scant favour with a sizeable proportion of voters in the 1926 municipal elections. Labour's quota of councillors increased ominously to 50, and in early December Dalrymple cut his losses and abruptly resigned.[48] Sensationally for the time, he used the forum of a BBC radio broadcast from Glasgow to make the announcement, explaining to his listeners: 'Of course, a public official has to stand a lot and keep smiling, but there comes a time when even a Corporation servant must remember that he is a man. I have given up my post simply because the conditions have become intolerable'.[49]

Effectively, Dalrymple was declaring that attempts were being made from all sides to emasculate him. Indeed, one historian has subsequently suggested that there was Labour–Moderate collusion to precipitate Dalrymple's departure, because of his 'autocratic' demeanour and determined refusal to brook interference with his managerial style.[50] Whatever the personal circumstances behind the Dalrymple affair, the financial crisis in the Tramways Department was symbolic of a much deeper municipal malaise in Glasgow, at least according to the city's press. The individual departments, it was suggested, had too much autonomy, with councillors kept resolutely in the dark about the state of finances.[51] Complaints about non-accountability became tied in with appeals from a broad range of business interests, co-ordinated by the Chamber of Commerce and encouraged by the Ratepayers' Federation, for the burden of taxation to be reduced in order to stimulate the sluggish state of local industry. Immediately prior to the 1927 municipal elections an impressive list of 179 'employers and manufacturers' voiced concern via newspaper advertisements that there should be 'economy in administration and vigilant investigation' into corporation expenditure.[52] The utilities of tramways, electricity and gas generated the most debate, with lurid claims of 'squandermania' and internecine rivalries between the departments, bidding for municipal resources to boost their respective establishments. The climax was eventually reached in 1928, when a complex scandal unravelled about irregularities in the administration of the Electricity Department, which briefly thrust Glasgow Corporation into national notoriety.

The revelations related to overstaffing, uneconomic use of generating capacity, unauthorised expenditure (especially relating to land purchases), and most sensational of all, the provision of a generous range of welfare facilities for the workforce and their families.[53] In the context of growing unease among the business community over the city's unstable economy, such profligacy seemed to provide all too glaring evidence of drastically skewed civic priorities. Outside perceptions were summed up in the Edinburgh-based newspaper, *The Scotsman*: 'Glasgow's prestige as a centre of light and leading in municipal administration appears to be getting dimmed. Does the declension date from the advent of the strong Socialist element on the Corporation? Or is it that the 'second city' has outgrown its capacity to manage its affairs?'[54] Robert B. Mitchell, Chief Engineer and Manager of the Electricity Department since 1920, was compelled to resign in June 1928. Like Dalrymple he was a casualty of perceived mismanage-ment, his departure providing tangible evidence in both the city and beyond of action to redeem the corporation's tarnished reputation. Other managers fell under suspicion, and there were unsavoury accusations in the press, but no further resignations were forthcoming. Nevertheless, there was revived talk of appointing 'an expert to manage the city', based on the experience of a number of cities in the United States, where the post of City Manager formed part of a high-profile crusade against municipal corruption.[55] This was less of a practical option than useful-sounding rhetoric on the part of the Moderates, who prior to the 1928 municipal elections were able to make much of 'municipal socialism with its concomitant evils of departmental extravagance and lack of effective control'.[56]

The Moderates had been encouraged in their electoral endeavours by the city's business interests and the organisational skills of pressure groups like the Ratepayers' Federation, which were increasingly determined to winkle out evidence of municipal mismanagement. The fiercely anti-socialist editor of the *Glasgow Herald*, Sir Robert Bruce, also did much to promote the Moderate cause, believing firmly in a cross-party alliance to stem the tide of Labour. In some ways the campaign was successful, because the Labour Party did not gain overall control of the corporation until 1933. Yet the weakness of the Moderate stance was its inherent defensiveness, based on the negative concept of 'non-party politics' and the notion that the city had to be rescued from insidious corrosion. The debate about the corporation's fragmenting integrity reflected Glasgow's declining status as the recession began to bite hard, and fuelled fears by the end of the 1920s that Scotland was becoming an economic wasteland.[57] That the focus of industry seemed to be drifting southwards and emigration was reaching unprecedented proportions added disturbingly to the sense of deterioration. The post-war reversal of economic fortunes was attributed to a number of causes, with the 'socialist menace' one of the most readily identifiable. But Glasgow's municipal managers were also demonised, embodying apparent loss of direction in the city's government. Their claims to stand diplomatically aloof from controversy only fuelled the notion that the bureaucracy was out of touch with public feeling. For the Moderates, the journalistic element of scandal and corruption helped to heighten such perceptions, although their claim to serve as the legitimate custodians of the public good could not prevent the long-term hegemony of the Labour Party in the corporation after 1933.

Conclusion

As this chapter has explained, the status of the municipal managers had long reflected public confidence in Glasgow and the corporation, which had been relatively buoyant prior to the war but became increasingly depressed thereafter. From the nineteenth century, officials had worked in tandem with the civic leadership, and personal and political connections could be close. However, the growth of the Labour Party eroded this partnership. Corporation officials were consequently caught in the conundrum of growing Labour assertiveness, and the management approach that for decades they had carefully nurtured. By the 1920s, their personal influence and public status were seriously called into question as Labour made major inroads into Glasgow's electoral base. This led to a crisis in control of the civic administration, which reached a climax after the trauma of the 1926 General Strike. However, by 1929 the controversy was receding, partly because the anxiety of the business community about the rates and public expenditure issue was being addressed by central government. The provisions of the 1929 Local Government (Scotland) Act allowed for rates' relief to industry, in the hope that confidence could be restored to the economy.[58] The legislation also led to a drastic streamlining of Glasgow's 'municipal machine', with the rationalisation of the complex committee structure that lay at the heart of civic decision-making. Yet ironically, the Act also added substantially to the responsibilities of the corporation, with education (in terms of schooling) and public assistance coming under its remit for the first time. By 1933, when Labour took power, municipal provision had reached unprecedented proportions in Glasgow, with almost 34,000 permanent staff to serve the million-strong population.[59] Although their image had been forced to alter to make way for the new breed of local politician, the function of the municipal managers remained as vital as ever.

Notes

1. This is an amended and extended version of papers that appeared at Leeds and the Fourth International Urban History Conference at Venice, 3–5 September 1998. I am most grateful to Mhairi Dewar for access to her 'municipal scandals' file of the 1920s and the opportunity to discuss the role of the municipal managers.

2. Irene Maver, 'The Guardianship of the Community: Civic Authority Prior to 1833', in T.M. Devine and Gordon Jackson (eds), *Glasgow, Volume I: Beginnings to 1830* (Manchester: Manchester University Press, 1995), pp. 239–77.

3. See, for example, Sir James Bell and James Paton, *Glasgow, Its Municipal Organisation and Administration* (Glasgow: James McLehose, 1896); Glasgow Corporation, *Souvenir Handbook of Glasgow* (Glasgow: Glasgow Corporation, 1904); Glasgow Corporation, *Municipal Glasgow: Its Evolution and Enterprises*, (Glasgow: Glasgow Corporation, 1914). Glasgow's municipal status was approvingly described in Albert Shaw, 'Municipal Government in Great Britain', *Political Science Quarterly*, 4 (1889), pp. 197–229.

4. However, see P.J. Waller, *Town, City and Nation: England, 1850–1914* (Oxford: Oxford University Press, 1983), pp. 281–8.

5. Bernard Aspinwall, *Portable Utopia: Glasgow and the United States, 1820–1920* (Aberdeen: Aberdeen University Press, 1984), pp. 151–84; W. Hamish Fraser, 'From Civic Gospel to Municipal Socialism, in Derek Fraser (ed.), *Cities, Class and Commun-ications: Essays in Honour of Asa Briggs* (Hemel Hempstead: Harvester Wheatsheaf, 1990), pp. 58–80; W. Hamish Fraser, 'Municipal Socialism and Social Policy', in R.J. Morris and Richard Rodger (eds), *The Victorian City: A Reader in British Urban History, 1820–1914* (London: Longman, 1993), pp. 258–80; Irene Maver, 'Politics and Power in the Scottish City: Glasgow Town Council in the Nineteenth Century', in T.M. Devine (ed.), *Scottish Elites* (Edinburgh: John Donald, 1994), pp. 98–130; Irene Maver, 'Glasgow's Civic Government', in W. Hamish Fraser and Irene Maver (eds), *Glasgow, Volume II: 1830 to 1912* (Manchester: Manchester University Press, 1996), pp. 441–85; Tom Hart, 'Urban Growth and Municipal Government: Glasgow in a Comparative Context, 1846–1914', in Anthony Slaven and Derek H. Aldcroft (eds), *Business, Banking and Urban History* (Edinburgh: John Dodd, 1982), pp. 193–219.

6. Callum Brown, 'To Be Aglow with Civic Ardours: The 'Godly Commonwealth'

in Glasgow, 1843–1914', *Records of the Scottish Church History Society*, 26 (1996), pp. 169–95.

7. Mabel Atkinson, *Local Government in Scotland* (Edinburgh: William Blackwood, 1904), pp. 4–5.

8. Maver, 'Guardianship of the Community', pp. 254–5.

9. Maver, 'Glasgow's Civic Government', pp. 462–4.

10. Sir James D. Marwick, *A Retrospect* (Glasgow: privately published, 1905), pp. 136–8; John Gray McKendrick, *Memoir of Sir James D. Marwick, 1826 to 1908* (Glasgow: James McLehose, 1909), p. 136.

11. *The Bailie*, 10 February 1892.

12. William S. Murphy, *Captains of Industry* (Glasgow: Murphy, 1901), pp. 76–8.

13. Ibid., pp. 71–2.

14. Ibid., p. 71.

15. *The Bailie*, 2 March 1898.

16. Atkinson, *Local Government in Scotland*, pp. 51–9.

17. Ibid., pp. 57–8; *Glasgow Herald*, 6, 13, 16, 18, 19, 20 May 1908.

18. *Glasgow Herald*, 31 March 1905.

19. Linda J. Jones, 'Public Pursuit of Private Profit? Liberal Businessmen and Municipal Politics in Birmingham, 1865–1900', *Business History*, 25 (1985), pp. 241–4.

20. Albert Shaw, 'Municipal socialism in Scotland', *Juridical Review*, 1 (1889) p. 33.

21. Quoted in Fraser, 'From Civic Gospel to Municipal Socialism', p. 66. The statement originally appeared in the *Speaker*, 1 April 1893.

22. Bell and Paton, *Glasgow, Its Municipal Organisation*, pp. xxi–ii.

23. W. Hamish Fraser, 'Labour and the Changing City', in George Gordon (ed), *Perspectives of the Scottish City* (Aberdeen: Aberdeen University, 1985), pp. 168–9; James J. Smyth, 'The ILP in Glasgow, 1888–1906: The Struggle for Identity', in Alan McKinlay and R.J. Morris (eds), *The ILP on Clydeside, 1893–1932: From Foundation to Disintegration* (Manchester: Manchester University Press, 1991), pp. 35–42.

24. Maver, 'Glasgow Town Council in the Nineteenth Century', pp. 120–23. Housing was a particular bone of contention, with Glasgow's Liberals far more amenable to interventionism in this sphere. The temperance issue was also assertively pursued by Liberals.

25. For the original aims of the Citizens' Union, see its *Minute Book, 1898–1903*, Glasgow City Archives [GCA] TD 488/9.

26. *Glasgow Herald*, 25 October 1898.

27. *The Times*, 6 October 1902. See also Fraser, 'From Civic Gospel to Municipal Socialism', pp. 74–5.

28. GCA TD 488/9, *Citizens' Union, Secretary's Report, 1903*, p. 3.

29. Richard Roberts, 'Business, Politics and Municipal Socialism', in John Turner (ed), *Businessmen and Politics: Studies of Business Activity in British Politics, 1900–45* (London, Heinemann, 1984), pp. 22–4.

30. For the Ratepayers' Federation, see Maver, 'Glasgow's Civic Government', pp. 475–6.

31. Quoted in the *Glasgow Herald*, 18 May 1908.

32. Quoted in ibid., 19 May 1908.

33. F.C. Howe, 'Glasgow', in Simon Berry and Hamish Whyte (eds), *Glasgow Observed* (Glasgow: John Donald, 1987), p. 183. The article originally appeared in *Scribner's Magazine* in 1906.

34. Atkinson, *Local Government in Scotland*, pp. 35–6.
35. *Glasgow Herald*, 13 November 1907.
36. Ibid.
37. Howe, 'Glasgow', pp. 183–4; see also Bernard Aspinwall, 'Glasgow trams and American politics, 1894–1914', in the *Scottish Historical Review*, 56 (1977), pp. 64–84.
38. Irene Maver, 'Glasgow's Municipal Workers and Industrial Strife', in William Kenefick and Arthur McIvor (eds), *Roots of Red Clydeside, 1910–1914? Labour Unrest and Industrial Relations in West Scotland* (Edinburgh: John Donald, 1996), pp. 224–5.
39. Charles A. Oakley, *The Last Tram* (Glasgow: Glasgow Corporation, 1962), pp. 63–8.
40. William Knox (ed), *Scottish Labour Leaders, 1918–1939* (Edinburgh: Mainstream, 1984), pp. 92–9, 274–84.
41. Iain McLean, *The Legend of Red Clydeside* (Edinburgh: 1983), especially part 1; Joseph Melling, 'Work, Culture and Politics on "Red Clydeside": The ILP during the First World War', in McKinlay and Morris (eds), *The ILP on Clydeside*, pp. 83–122.
42. Figures taken from Glasgow Corporation Diaries, 1918–21, in Glasgow City Archives. A significant majority of the new voters were women, who constituted just under 50 per cent of the eligible electorate.
43. *Glasgow Herald*, 28 October 1920; McLean, *Legend of Red Clydeside*, p. 161.
44. *Glasgow Herald*, 28 October 1920.
45. Ibid., 22 October 1921.
46. Ibid., 1 June 1926.
47. Paul Carter, 'The West of Scotland', in Jeffrey Skelley (ed.), *The General Strike* (London: Lawrence and Wishart, 1976), pp. 132–4; Ian McDougall, 'Some Aspects of the 1926 General Strike in Scotland', in I. McDougall (ed.), *Essays in Scottish Labour History* (Edinburgh: John Donald, 1978), pp. 170–206; *Glasgow Herald*, 26 and 28 June 1926.
48. Oakley, *The Last Tram*, pp. 77–80.
49. *Glasgow Herald*, 2 December 1926.
50. McLean, *Legend of Red Clydeside*, p. 219.
51. See GCA TD 488/2, Glasgow Ratepayers' Federation Newscuttings, for newspaper comment between 1927 and 1929.
52. *Glasgow Herald*, 24 and 31 October 1927.
53. Ibid., 28 January 1928.
54. *Scotsman*, 2 February 1928.
55. Indeed, the calls predated the Electricity Department revelations. See the *Glasgow Herald*, 9 January 1928. For the United States, see also Leonard D. White, *The City Manager* (Chicago: Chicago University Press, 1927), especially pp. 232–69.
56. *Glasgow Herald*, 1 November 1928.
57. For a discussion of perceptions of Scotland in decline, see Richard J. Finlay, 'National Identity in Crisis: Politicians, Intellectuals and the End of Scotland', 1920–1939', *History*, 79 (1994), pp. 242–59.
58. Robert Burns, 'Local Government: Past and Present', in *Proceedings of the Philosophical Society of Glasgow*, 60 (1931–32), pp. 113–28.
59. David Stenhouse, *Glasgow, Its Municipal Undertakings and Enterprises* (Glasgow: Glasgow Corporation, 1933), p. 17.

CHAPTER SIX

Urban governance in Montreal and Toronto in a period of transition*

Michèle Dagenais, translated by Susan Dalton

Municipal Government has ceased to be a matter of construction and maintenance ... The chief problems we have to deal with are not the construction of
sewers and sidewalks and that kind of thing. These things ... a few years ago ...
constituted the whole sphere of municipal government. But we have got a long
way past that and the problems we have to deal with now are problems affecting
human welfare, problems of prevention, the problems looking to the betterment
of the people of cities ... It is work that looks to the serving of those human
instincts which when properly provided for make a health, moral, and intelli-
gent community.[1]

It was in these terms that the Mayor of Toronto, Horatio C. Hocken, spoke
before a group of businessmen in 1914, in a speech entitled, 'The New
Spirit in Municipal Government'. His words reflect a new way of conceiving
of the role, the spheres of activity and the style of governing Canadian
municipalities which arose at the beginning of the twentieth century and
which I would like to examine in this chapter. The change which Mayor
Hocken refers to arrived in a crucial period of transition – that in which
what Eric H. Monkkonen has called 'the active city'[2] was born. In place of
the *ad hoc* measures previously favoured by cities, the operation of this
new type of urban government was driven by the principle of direct
provision. As historian Jon C. Teaford has shown, it was also the period in
which municipalities, despite being the object of negative press, succeeded
in responding to the challenges of diversity wrought by significant changes
in the population and rapid urban growth, and of financing of services,
with remarkable success.[3]

At their origins, municipal governments were perceived as and acted as
regulatory bodies, charged with assuring the existence of services which
encouraged the development of real property. During the period of transition
described above, they became more directly involved in governing the city
as a whole. At the same time, a new concept of municipal management
developed, which became manifest through the local government's direct
appropriation of an entire series of services and by a broadening spectrum of
municipal activity. The notion of public service was at the heart of this change
in urban government; it is the key idea which translates the meaning of
changes taking place in the governance of Canadian cities.

To show the development of this transition, I have chosen to compare two of the largest Canadian cities: Toronto and Montreal. Instead of adopting a more institutional approach, analysing only the changes which took place inside municipal governments, I have also taken account of the dynamics of the local political scene to shed light on the more specific phenomenon of urban governance. This line of questioning is inspired by Patrick Le Galès's work on urban governance which, in his terms, 'points to the interactions between the state and society and to coordination strategies that make public action possible'.[4] The question of governance encourages one, as he explains, 'to take into account the strategic capacity of the actors, the diversity of the process of legitimation and the negotiation dynamic present between the actors'.[5]

This chapter is divided into two parts. First, I will give an overview of the situation in Montreal and Toronto in the second half of the nineteenth century, a time when municipal government was characterised by the practice of regulation. Second, I will present the principal causes which led the two municipalities to conceive of their role and their place in the city differently, and which led to the adoption of interventionist policies. In order to grasp the conditions which limited public action in the nineteenth century, as well as those which favoured its development at the turn of the twentieth, I will consider changes in the local political scene and those which arose within municipal governments. Two sets of variables are at work here: on the one hand, the composition of the élite, the electoral regime and political practices, and on the other, the structure of municipal institutions, the organisation of services and, to a lesser extent, the composition of the workforce.

Urban governance in nineteenth-century Canada

The characteristics of urban governance in Canada were intimately linked to the conditions in which the municipal system was born in the middle of the nineteenth century. With the exception of the few towns that were granted municipal charters at the end of the eighteenth century, the mid-nineteenth-century Canadian municipal system was created in one stroke at the same time as the rise of the liberal state.[6] In the 1830s and 1840s, the establishment of municipal 'corporations', including Montreal and Toronto,[7] represented an important step in this process. What was at stake, then, was not the idea of local autonomy, but increased efficiency and economic growth in the management of state affairs. Therefore, although local institutions in Britain and the United States served as models in many ways, Canadian municipalities were not established in response to a local demand. This is not to deny, however, that they disposed of a variety of powers which gave them a certain amount of political autonomy. The breadth of these powers varied according to the size of the city: the largest cities were granted charters, whereas smaller towns were submitted to the conditions of the general laws.

The Canadian municipal system was thus developed in aid of property management, and the voluntary obligations and responsibilities which they subsequently assumed continued to be determined by this initial conception. For example, for a long time the municipalities' financial resources all derived essentially from property taxes. The fact that, in the beginning, only property owners had the right to vote and run for office was justified with reference to municipalities' primary function and to their sources of revenue.[8]

In this context, political life remained the privilege of a small group, an elite; consequently, between the years 1840 and 1890, few people were politically active. The eligibility rating constituted the first sizeable obstacle.[9] In Montreal, an aspiring mayor had to own property worth a minimum of $4,000, the equivalent of ten years' salary for a skilled worker. Also, only owners of property of a certain value could vote. And even though in the course of the second half of the nineteenth century rate-paying tenants obtained the franchise, several conditions continued to limit its exercise. First, tenants had to live in lodgings of a certain value, which excluded the most destitute citizens from political life. Moreover, only those who paid their taxes before the first of January of each year could exercise their right.[10] At the other extreme, more well-to-do citizens were decisively favoured. Not only could they vote in the neighbourhood of their residence, but also in all others in which they possessed property. Those who owned a business of a certain value could also obtain the right to vote.

Over the course of this period, elected officials were mostly drawn from the world of business: mainly bankers but also affluent merchants and manufacturers. As wealth constituted the best entryway into politics, candidates came from the highest social classes and were small in number. In this context, it is not surprising that the municipal council resembled a very select club open mainly to the financial élite. As Monkkonen astutely observed, 'the city corporation truly represented an élite club whose commercial interests were identical with those of the city'.[11]

At this time, Montreal's and Toronto's city halls[12] were run by elected officials, with the mayor and councillors representing different municipal districts. After every election, the councillors chose from among themselves the members of the committees charged with the administration of municipal affairs. The number of committees varied over the course of the years according to the extent of the services assumed by the municipality. Each was directed by a president who, in concert with members of council, managed the budget of his committee. The Finance Committee[13] held the pre-eminent place in this system, as it was responsible for forecasting the annual budget. Furthermore, it had the right to review all expenditures and contracts not included in the budget and had to approve them before they were submitted to the municipal council for a vote.

The aldermen's committees, which represented an early form of executive power, literally held the fate of the city in their hands, but as they were constituted solely of elected officials, their composition could change from one election to the next. This situation compromised the continuity of local government. In addition, no formal body was charged with assuring the co-ordination of committee operations, resulting in numerous overlaps between the various jurisdictions. In the nineteenth century, the first committees included those governing the police, fires, lighting, markets and water. However, it did not mean that they themselves managed corresponding services. The formation of commissions indicated, rather, the establishment of a process of regulations meant to assure the existence of various services, either by their direct management or by the granting of contracts to private companies.

From the 1860s on, a distinction between political, technical and administrative functions was introduced with the creation of the first municipal services, which subsequently were accorded a budget for operations and for regular employees.[14] Services gradually became structured over the course of the second half of the nineteenth century, often appearing in moments of crisis then disappearing when no longer needed or at election time. As few formal arrangements existed (aside from specific obligations such as public security), municipalities had a lot of latitude to define their actions according to how they understood the role of municipal affairs.[15]

The developing road to public services

Police services were among the first to be established in Montreal and Toronto. In Toronto, however, the most pressing concern was not so much the creation of a permanent police force as the manner in which it was recruited.[16] Given that police officers were directly chosen by members of the municipal council, for many years their appointment and their dismissal were determined by their political allegiances rather than their competence. As conservative sympathisers dominated the municipal political scene in the middle of the nineteenth century, it was the liberal-reformists who denounced the situation. Under these circumstances, the population was hesitant to submit to police authority, which it judged to be excessively partisan.

Nevertheless, in order to sustain Toronto's growth, it proved to be increasingly necessary from the middle of the nineteenth century on to put forward an image of the city as a prosperous commercial metropolis. This is why questions of efficiency and order won out over partisan considerations. Even elites from opposing political camps rallied to the idea of hiring a permanent police force and handing over the recruitment of officers to an independent commission charged with hiring future personnel according to professional competence as opposed to political considerations. From this point on, evidence of partisan behaviour on the part of police became cause for immediate dismissal. This also meant that local elected officials could no longer intervene in the recruitment of police and had to allot the service's director the necessary powers to manage the force and evaluate its labour and budget needs.

The water supply represented another important factor favouring economic and industrial growth, not to mention its critical role in preventing and fighting fires especially in large cities such as Montreal and Toronto which, in 1850, had populations of 57,715 and 30,775 respectively.[17] None the less, the municipalisation of the water supply was not seen as the solution to all of these problems at first. Thus, while the Montreal municipal government decided, in the middle of the nineteenth century, to acquire a private company which provided a large proportion of the water to Montreal,[18] Toronto instead chose to continue to rely on the services of a private firm. Faced with the inability of the company to expand its system to respond to the growing demands of the city, however, Toronto finally acquired the existing system in 1872.

In this case, although both cities faced the same problem, the solutions they adopted were originally different. Nevertheless, because the technology required to ensure the development of the provision of water (like the provision of gas and means of communication, such as telephone and public transportation) rested on collective solutions, they would strongly contribute to the formation of the notion of a public interest which transcended individual, particular interests. This is why, even though these utilities were originally developed to respond to élite interests and economic development, debates surrounding their operation included many segments of the population, obliging either the companies supplying these services or the municipalities to take the demands of the public into account as well. In this way, these debates not only favoured the emergence of a public conception of the water question, but gave rise to consideration of the public dimension of the supply of gas and electricity in cities.

The issue of health would also become a public concern over the course of the second half of the nineteenth century.[19] In Montreal, the anticipation of epidemics led to the establishment of health boards by municipal authorities on several occasions. In every instance, however, health officers, appointed temporarily, only had the power to make recommendations to the health committees, which in turn held the sole authority to make decisions affecting this one area. Most often the resulting measures consisted of the adoption of by-laws to control the quality of products offered on the market, the circulation of animals, the organisation of (most notably) *ad hoc* vaccine campaigns and attempts to establish garbage collection systems. The attitude of the municipal authorities can be explained as much, if not more, by the refusal of elected officials to share the power whose exercise they jealously guarded as by the difficulty that doctors had in garnering recognition for and legitimising their expertise.

It was only from 1870 on that health officers were admitted to the meetings of the health committees. At the same time, the few employees of the health board, who until that point had been lodged in the central police station, were provided with their own office. These modest advances were followed, shortly after the 1879 elections, by a retreat when the new municipal council decided to abolish the health board and restrict access to the health committee only to elected officials; the council decided that the police force would be able to sufficiently control changes of the population and ensure the enforcement of certain minimal hygiene standards. All measures aimed at improving public health in the city were not suspended as such, but were subsequently under the supervision of the Road Committee. In the end, advances in medical knowledge (notably in the development of bacteriology), the growth of the urban population, the provincial government's strict control over the municipalities and especially the terrible smallpox epidemic of 1885–86 overcame the resistance of elected officials. In 1886, the health board was re-established permanently under the direction of Dr Louis Laberge and, from this point on, the value of medical expertise and the public character of the health question became evident.

In the nineteenth century, Canadian urban élites generally sought to establish their legitimacy foremost by affirming the private character of the municipal 'corporation', which, according to this formulation was put to the service of property owners and not the urban populace.[20] As a result, city governments sought to limit their projects and preached the adoption of economical budgetary practices. Besides, many of Toronto's ratepayers agreed with the adage that 'the government which governs least governs best',[21] and although the establishment of certain services favoured the development of the idea of public service, this notion still remained vaguely associated with the municipal élite's idea of the role of urban government.

The changing landscape of city politics

Several factors came together at the turn of the century to bring a series of changes to the urban governance of Montreal and Toronto. The origin of these changes is generally attributed to reform movements.[22] There is no doubt that movements such as the Reform Party of Montreal and the Toronto Guild of Civic Art played an important role in this process by exerting pressure on elected officials, by presenting their own candidates in elections and by sensitising the public to urban issues and to the necessity of more sustained intervention on the part of municipal authorities. However, their influence should not be overestimated: reformers only held power for short periods of time and most reforms actually occurred during the reign of populist leaders. Therefore, it is necessary to take a variety of other factors into account in order to explain the changes to urban governance. In short, the advent of reformers occurred in the larger reorganisation of forces on the political scene.

The 1880s were, above all, the prelude to the renewal of elected officials. In both Toronto and Montreal, new candidates were drawn increasingly from the middle class, including members of the liberal professions such as lawyers and doctors, groups of local merchants and small entrepreneurs, especially those in the field of construction.[23] Although the motivations behind the renewal are not entirely clear, it seems as though the movement corresponded in part to the traditional élites' flight from urban politics as their economic activities began to take place on a national scale. Thus, with the advent of monopoly capitalism, the fortunes of businessmen and bankers no longer depended as strictly on that of the city, and this is why they did not need to control local affairs to the same extent.[24] But the phenomenon of renewal can also be attributed to the rise of new urban élites whose activities, often more modest in size, continued to be directly dependent on the city. In the case of Montreal, the process of political renewal was doubly acute because of the increasing presence of francophones on the local scene, growing out of the rise of the movement to annex several suburbs surrounding Montreal.[25] The renewal of local elites was also accompanied by a change in political practices, the most important of which the prolongation of the careers of local elected officials. This resulted in a certain professionalisation of the group. In this context, wealth no longer constituted candidates' most important resource, as their popularity became much more decisive in winning elections.

At the same time, political life began to become more democratic. The adoption of a series of new procedures, including the secret ballot, facilitated the holding of elections and allowed voters to express themselves more freely. Trade unions turned their attention to organised political action. In

1899, militants founded the Parti Ouvrier in Montreal. A few years later, they successfully fought for the elimination of property qualifications for elected officials, which permitted tenants to run for office. In Montreal as well as Toronto several workers' candidates were elected, including Jos Ainey, a Montreal carpenter and Jimmy Simpson, a Toronto printer. Both won seats on the boards of control of their respective cities in the 1910s.

Moreover, in the context of the rapid growth of Canadian cities at the end of the nineteenth century, urban governments were called on to play a larger role. Municipal management also became a critical political question. In fact, many of the reform groups created in this period made this their top priority. These groups sprung mainly from three sources: the local business élite, the growing body of professionals and experts (such as engineers, doctors and social workers), and women's benevolent associations.[26] Although pursuing specific goals, these groups would lead to the adoption of reforms in the way municipal institutions functioned. The most important concerned the division of powers. The goal was to reinforce the executive such that, as historians Armstrong and Nelles explained, 'individual aldermen did not play such a large role in making policy and spending money'.[27] First in Toronto, then in Montreal, reformers were successful in obtaining the creation of boards of control charged with executive authority.[28] These new institutions were composed of four members elected by the entire electorate in each city, as opposed to by the citizens of each district, in order to curb the negative influence which ward-voting was thought to have on the integrity of councillors. Subsequently, executive and administrative functions were conferred on the new institution, while the council retained its role in the legislative domain. The Board of Commissioners thus inherited all the administrative powers previously held by the aldermen's committees.[29]

Whether they were treasurers, accountants, city clerks, lawyers, engineers, doctors, assessors, police officers, firefighters or white-collar workers, all these bureaucrats constituted another group of actors emerging in this period of transition. Present only in small numbers during the major part of the nineteenth century, their ranks continued to grow over time. It is in large part due to their work to solve numerous urban problems of the period that municipal governments consolidated their hold on the city. The expertise that they possessed, both through their training and their experience in municipal management, made them an incontrovertible part of municipal government and their influence was sometimes considerable. Even more than elected officials, they were responsible for maintaining continuity in municipal governments. Motivated both by their desire to solve the problems which confronted rapidly growing cities and by their desire to extend their sphere of activity and obtain recognition of their expertise, bureaucrats would play a fundamental role in the development of the field of municipal action.

Renewal of élites, democratisation of political life, municipal institutional reform, professionalisation of the civil service – all these factors converged to favour the growth in the role of city governments in the management of local problems. In turn, the increased activity of municipal institutions helped to give substance to the notion of public interest, and, subsequently, public service. Thus, it was increasingly in the public interest that politicians promised the electorate that they would furnish quality services and see to the needs born of urban growth. It was also in the public interest that, on their side, reformers militated for a rationalisation of municipal management. And it was to better serve the public that department managers and local government employees demanded more power and the growing deployment of their skills. Thus, through their reliance on this concept, both groups succeeded in becoming increasingly important forces on the municipal scene over the course of the years. In doing so, they strongly contributed to the transformation whereby the concept of 'public' gradually became the principle according to which urban government changed and the guiding principle of municipal government from that point on.

Certainly, as this increased worry over the public often made its way into electoral rhetoric, municipal leaders followed their own interests more keenly, reformers fought for changes in order to shield municipal management from political influences, and department managers sought to obtain more power. But the contradiction between word and action is not as stark as it appears. The sharply underlined objective of working in the public interest was the manner in which all actors sought to legitimise their positions and their actions. Consequently, from the beginning of the twentieth century, the municipal government appeared less like a private corporation and more like a public administration, like a bureaucracy propelled by a logic of its own.[30] It was again in response to the demands of elites that urban governments became involved in new areas.[31] But they were no longer the only ones to do so, and the battles which arose concerning the growth in municipal prerogatives or the direct provision of new services were also fought by segments of the *petite bourgeoisie* and by militant workers.

A new spirit in municipal government

The movement for public ownership of utilities which was born at the beginning of the twentieth century in Toronto is of this ilk.[32] But here, as historians C. Armstrong and H. V. Nelles explain, the fight in favour of the municipalisation of public services was not inspired by any type of municipal socialism, as was the case in certain British cities. In fact, motives of economics and efficiency, rather than democratic ideals, were at the origin of the mobilisation. At the heart of the movement were found a large proportion of the economic élite, 'the solid bourgeois ratepayers' and union leaders, all of whom united for different reasons to demand functional, efficient and inexpensive public services. Not all utilities were municipalised – far from it. In fact, problems were more often solved by the establishment of increasingly strict regulation of private enterprises. Only in 1921 would public transport become municipalised. In their study, the authors show that it was only after being worn down, when faced with the private company's refusal to enlarge its street railway system to service the cities annexed by Toronto at the time, that the citizens envisioned municipalisation as the only solution to their problems.

This conflict, among others, reveals the existence of a second fight, just as important: local élites (including local politicians and businessmen) were seeking to hold their own in their battle with the big businesses and trusts which controlled public utilities in Canadian cities at the time, leading Armstrong and Nelles to class their actions under the heading of 'civic populism'.[33] Therefore, the fight for the municipalisation of public transport offered local élites the possibility of increasing their hold on the municipal scene. It also favoured the development of a conception of what should be controlled by public authorities and, in doing so, rendered legitimate the idea of the involvement of municipal powers in the management of public utilities, previously considered to be proper to the private sphere. Thus, the notion of public interest was forged in the process of debate in this instance also.[34]

The increasingly systematic involvement of the Montreal municipal government in public assistance also attested to the transformations taking place in urban governance. At the beginning of the twentieth century, the rapid rise in urban squalor resulting primarily from the massive arrival of immigrants in the ports of Canadian cities, was in large part responsible for this involvement.[35] In 1907, the Montreal government created a permanent department charged with caring for the most destitute: The Bureau of Municipal Assistance under the direction of the experienced municipal employee Albert Chevalier. In the beginning, the new service gave grants to institutions ministering to the needs of the homeless, just as the municipal council had done previously. Then, starting in 1913, the city itself ran a shelter. In addition, it consented to accord sizeable tax breaks to charitable institutions.

The extent of the resources mobilised towards assistance none the less caused financial problems, as money was drawn from the city's general pool of funds. Therefore, in 1915, the municipal government adopted the principle of an amusement tax, already in place in other cities, particularly those in Europe. One penny from every ticket to shows, concerts, etc., went towards taxation. The result was that within ten years, Montreal had a policy of systematic public assistance with specific financing. Contrary to what was happening in the nineteenth century, the municipality's direct provision of this service was no longer seen 'only as a contingent necessity, but also as a social duty – a duty of intervention which would give way to permanent and systematic, as well as financial and bureaucratic, action'.[36]

It was actions like these, undertaken in the area of welfare, that led the mayor of Toronto to say, in 1914, in his speech to a group of Canadian businessmen, that the well-being of the population was an integral part of the municipal government's mandate. Although the numerical data available on the development of municipal spending in the areas associated with it have not yet been tabulated in a systematic way, certain indications point to a tangible growth in the responsibility of city governments in the first decades of the twentieth century. This tendency was part of a larger movement of growth in public spending in all sectors. While in 1900 Toronto spent $5.00 per capita in the areas of parks and leisure, education and libraries and health and welfare, this amount rose to $35.00 in 1930.[37] Spending in all these areas accounted for 28 cents of each dollar derived from property tax in 1900, compared with 45 cents in 1930. Certainly, this increase in spending linked to services benefiting people, as opposed to property, did not mean that the municipality would leave aside its first priorities. Rather, it meant that it could not solely concern itself with municipal problems; it would also have to address urban problems. Furthermore, the enlargement of the city's mandate was also accompanied by a different strategy for managing problems – that of the direct provision, and indeed the creation, of new municipal services.

Conclusion

In Canada, at least in Toronto and Montreal, the transition in urban governance was similar to the process of 'municipal reform' as Derek Fraser[38] defined it a few years ago, but took place later than it did in Britain. This can be explained by a number of factors, the most important of which were the dependence of Canadian cities on capital,[39] the absence of a tradition of civic responsibility which existed in Scottish cities[40] and also the weakness of a working class which only sporadically engaged in political action. Despite the delay, and although we cannot link the changes that happened in Canada to municipal socialism, Montreal and Toronto were also moving increasingly towards direct provision. In Canada, this change was the result of the renewal of local élites, the democratisation of political life and the formation of a municipal bureaucracy. Together, these factors contributed to the reformulation of the role of urban governments.

Notes

* This research was funded by a grant from the Social Sciences and Humanities Research Council of Canada and the Fonds pour la formation et l'aide à la recherche (FCAR). My thanks for Susan Dalton for translating this chapter.

1. Horatio C. Hocken, 'The New Spirit in Municipal Government', Canadian Club, *Addresses*, 85 (1914–15), from Roger E. Riendeau, 'Servicing the Modern City, 1900–30', in Victor L. Russell, (ed.) *Forging a Consensus: Historical Essays on Toronto* (Toronto: University of Toronto Press, 1984), p. 167.

2. E.H. Monkkonen, *America Becomes Urban: The Development of U.S. Cities and Towns, 1750–1980* (Berkeley: University of California Press, 1988).

3. J.C. Teaford, *The Unheralded Triumph: City Government in America, 1870–1900* (Baltimore and London: The Johns Hopkins University Press, 1984).

4. Our translation. Patrick le Galès, 'Du gouvernement des villes à la gouvernance urbaine', *Revue française de science politique*, 45 (1995), p. 95.

5. Our translation. Ibid., 60.

6. For an overview of the question, see Jean-Pierre Collin and Michèle Dagenais, 'Evolution des enjeux politiques locaux et des pratiques municipales dans l'île de Montréal, 1840–1950', in Denis Menjot and Jean-Luc Pinol (eds), *Enjeux et expressions de la politique municipale (XIIe–XXe siècles)* (Paris: l'Hamattan, 1997), pp. 191–5; and Katherine A. Graham et al. (eds) *Urban Governance in Canada: Representation, Resources and Restructuring* (Toronto: Harcourt Brace, Canada, 1998).

7. Montreal was granted its initial charter in 1832 for a period of four years. Because of the political instability wrought by the rebellions between 1836 and 1838, Montreal's charter was not renewed. It received its permanent charter in 1840. For its part, Toronto's charter, which was never suspended, was granted in 1834: Engin F. Isin, *Cities Without Citizens: The Modernity of the City as a Corporation* (Montreal: Black Rose Books, 1992), pp.143–9.

8. Warren Magnusson, 'The Development of Canadian Urban Government', in Warren Magnusson and Andrew Sancton (eds), *City Politics in Canada* (Toronto: University of Toronto Press, 1983), pp. 7–8.

9. On the regulations pertaining to elections, see Michèle Dagenais, *La démocratie à Montréal, de 1830 à nos jours* (Montreal: City of Montreal, 1992).

10. Added to this is the obligation of paying the statute labour, a tax imposed on those who only paid water taxes, in this case, the renters. (Michèle Dagenais, *La démocratie à Montréal*, p. 16).

11. E. Monkkonen, *America Becomes Urban*, p. 112.

12. On Montreal, see Paul-André Linteau, *Histoire de Montréal depuis la*

Confédération (Montreal: Boréal, 1992), chs 5 and 10; J. Cléophas Lamonthe, *Histoire de la Corporation de la Cité, de Montréal depuis son origine jusqu'à nos jours*, Laviolette and Massé (eds), (Montreal: Montreal Printing and Publishing Co., 1903), pp. 65–197. On Toronto, see J.M.S. Careless, *Toronto to 1918: An Illustrated History* (Toronto: James Lorimer, 1985); S. Morley Wickett, 'The Municipal Government of Toronto', in S. Morley Wickett (ed.), *Municipal Government in Canada* (Toronto: University of Toronto Studies, History and Economics, 2, 1907).

13. In Toronto, an executive committee fulfilled basically the same functions as the Finance Commission in Montreal. Patricia Petersen, 'The Evolution of the Board of Control', in Victor L. Russell (ed.), *Forging a Consensus*, (see note 1), p. 182.

14. Dany Fougères, 'Le public et le privé dans la gestion de l'eau potable à Montréal depuis le XIXe siècle', in Louise Pothier (ed.), *L'eau, l'hygiène publique et les infrastructures* (Montreal: Groupe PGV – Discussion de l'archéologie, 1995) p. 51.

15. As John Taylor skilfully explains in speaking of the charter of municipalities, 'There was an abundance of "may" clauses and very few "must" ones': 'Urban Autonomy in Canada: Its Evolution and Decline', in G.A. Stelter and A.F.J. Artibise (eds), *The Canadian City: Essays in Urban and Social History* (Ottawa: Carleton University Press, 1984), p. 479.

16. Nicholas Rogers, 'Serving Toronto the Good: The Development of the City Police Force, 1834–1884', in Victor L. Russell (ed.), *Forging a Consensus* (see note 1), pp. 116–40.

17. Careless, *Toronto to 1918* (see note 1), p. 200.

18. Dany Fougères, 'Le public et le privé dans la gestion de l'eau', in Christopher Armstrong and H.V. Nelles, *Monopoly's Moment: The Organization and Regulation of Canadian Utilities* (Philadelphia: Temple University Press, 1986), pp. 11–33.

19. See Heather MacDougall's *Activists and Advocates: Toronto's Health Department, 1883–1983* (Toronto: Dundurn Press, 1990); see also M. Farley, O. Keel and C. Limoge's 'Les commencements de l'administration montréalaise de la santé publique', *HSTC Bulletin, Journal of History of Canadian Science, Technology and Medecine/Revue d'histoire des sciences, des techniques et de la médecine au Canada*, 20–21 (1982) pp. 24–46, 85–109.

20. This situation was similar to the one that existed in nineteenth-century American cities. See for instance Sam Bass Warner's *The Private City: Philadelphia in Three Periods of its Growth* (Philadelphia: University of Pennsylvania Press, 1968); and Robin Einhorn's, *Property Rules: Political Economy in Chicago* (Chicago, Chicago University Press, 1991).

21. With regards to this, see the debates surrounding the development of public health in Toronto in Heather A. MacDougall's article, 'The Genesis of Public Health Reform in Toronto, 1869–90', *Revue d'histoire urbaine/ Urban History Review*, 10 (1982), p. 3. See also Catherine Brace's 'Public Works in the Canadian City; the Provision of Sewers in Toronto, 1870–1913', *Revue d'histoire urbaine/Urban History Review*, 23 (1995), p. 36.

22. Paul Rutherford, 'Tomorrow's Metropolis: The Urban Reform Movement in Canada, 1880–1920', in Gilbert A. Stelter and Alan F.J. Artibise (eds), *The Canadian City* (see note 15), pp. 435–55; John C. Weaver. 'The Modern City Realized: Toronto Civic Affairs, 1880–1915' in Alan F.J. Artibise and Gilbert A. Stelter (eds), *The Usable Urban Past: Planning and Politics in*

the Modern Canadian City (Toronto: MacMillan of Canada, 1979), pp. 39–72.

23. For Montreal, see Paul-André Linteau, 'Le personnel politique de Montréal, 1880–1914: Evolution d'une élite municipale', Revue d'histoire de l'Amérique française, 52 (1998), pp. 189–215; Guy Bourassa, 'Les élites politiques de Montréal: de l'aristocratie à la démocratie', in R. Desrosiers (ed.), Le personnel politique québécois (Montreal: Boréal Express, 1972), pp. 117–42. For Toronto, see Careless, Toronto to 1918; Keith Walden, Becoming Modern in Toronto: The Industrial Exhibition and the Shaping of a Late Victorian Culture (Toronto: University of Toronto Press, 1997), pp. 16–19.

24. John H. Taylor, 'Urban Autonomy in Canada', pp. 493–4. Eric Monkkonen noticed the same phenomenon in the case of the United States, America Becomes Urban, pp. 122–3.

25. Paul-André Linteau, 'Rapport de pouvoir et émergence d'une nouvelle élite canadienne-française à Montréal, 1880–1914', Études canadiennes: Revue interdisciplinaire des études canadienne en France, 21 (1986), pp. 163–72.

26. Paul-André Linteau, Histoire de Montréal, pp. 211–13.

27. C. Armstrong and H. V. Nelles. 'The Rise of Civic Populism in Toronto, 1870–1920', in Victor L. Russell (ed.), Forging a Consensus, p. 210. See also, P. Petersen, 'The Evolution of the Board of Control', in V.L. Russell (ed.), Forging a Consensus, (see note 1), pp. 181–91.

28. Petersen, 'The Evolution'; Michèle Dagenais, 'Une bureaucratie en voie de formation: L'administration municipale de Montréal dans la première moitié du XXe siècle', Revue d'histoire de l'Amérique française, 46 (1992), pp. 177–205.

29. They were also given the important task of preparing and managing the budget, after its approval by council. In addition, the new Board of Commissioners was responsible for the nomination and dismissal of the majority of its employees, Dagenais, 'Une bureacratie', p. 185.

30. On this point, see Michèle Dagenais, Des pouvoirs et des hommes: L'administration municipale de Montréal, 1900–1950 (Montreal and Kingston: McGill-Queens University Press, 2000).

31. As Jon Teaford writes in speaking of American cities, the upper middle class continues to exert a strong influence on the formulation of municipal politics: 'municipalities proved especially effective in providing services for that class, with its devotion to flush toilets, public libraries, and suburban parks', The Unheralded Triumph, p. 10.

32. Armstrong and Nelles, 'The Rise of Civic Populism in Toronto', pp. 192–237.

33. By employing this term, they make reference to the movement opposing large capital and monopolies which developed in the same period in the United States in the rural milieu. See Armstrong and Nelles, 'The Rise of Civic Population in Toronto', p. 208.

34. Armstrong and Nelles, Monopoly's Moment, p. 36.

35. Jean-Marie Fecteau, 'Un cas de force majeure: le développement des mesures d'assistance publique à Montréal au tournant du siècle', Lien social et Politiques – RIAC, 33 (1995), pp. 106–7.

36. Our translation, p. 109.

37. Roger R. Riendeau, 'Servicing the Modern City', p. 167.

38. Derek Fraser, 'Introduction: Municipal Reform in Historical Perspective',

in D. Frazer (ed.), *Municipal Reform and the Industrial City*, (Leicester: Leicester University Press, 1982), pp. 2–14.

39. Robert J. Morris, 'The Reproduction of Labour and Capital: British and Canadian Cities During Industrialization', *Urban History Review/Revue d'histoire urbaine*, 18 (1989), pp. 48–62.

40. Richard Rodger, 'L'interventionnisme municipal en Ecosse, civisme local, préoccupations sociales et intérêtes de possédants', *Genèses*, 10 (1993), pp. 6–30.

CHAPTER SEVEN

A spirit of improvement: improvement commissioners, boards of health and central–local relations in Portsea

Ann Day

During the first half of the nineteenth century the interplay of central–local administrative relations was a crucial element in the appropriation of space in the industrialising urban centres of Britain. The transition to a 'modern' state system, which was mediated through a number of practices at this time, necessitated a reorganisation of existing power structures. Within this process local community representation was essential for the construction of a framework of power based on consensus. A number of historians have focused on the political decisions of the 1830s as instrumental in providing a channel for the establishment of consensual political practices, as well as the basis for discussion of central–local patterns of authority. For example Derek Fraser concurs with Brian Keith-Lucas's view that, whilst the 1835 Municipal Reform Act did not of itself revolutionise local government, 'the profound transformation of town government during the nineteenth century derived from ... 1835'.[1] Indeed, Fraser sees the nineteenth-century 'revolution' as a continuous process stretching from the reform of corporations in 1835 to the 'municipal socialism' of the 1890s. But there is a much longer precedent for the transformatory processes, dating back several decades before the reform movements of the 1830s. The specific ways in which positions of power were constructed within the local sphere during the second half of the eighteenth century were to have an important impact on the processes of change that took place during the mid-nineteenth century. Yet this is an area of study that has often not received its due significance in historical writings on urban governance.[2]

The implementation of urban reform schemes stemming from the mid-eighteenth century resulted mostly from the concerns and interests of very localised bodies of authority, such as the boards of improvement commissioners which were established during this period.[3] When analysing such schemes it becomes apparent that the definition of what was seen as a new 'social order' was predicated on the notion that those who had the means to avoid the worst aspects of urbanisation and industrialisation could alleviate the effects of these forces on those who did not have such means. This process, Patrick Joyce argues, was a link between the management of self and the management of the city.[4] Also, it was through the establishment of localised administrative bodies, such as boards of Improvement Commissioners that some individual inhabitants were able to construct an identity for themselves based on their activities within a particular type of collective action. The foundation of group action was therefore not only the sharing of common interests and objectives but perceptions of individual group members by each other, as well as by those outside the group, as 'fit and able' to carry out certain functions which affected the social whole.[5] As many of the individuals concerned were local tradesmen and businessmen, their legitimisation for such activities arose from the imbrication of family and business, through which they were able to construct for themselves an appearance of respectability and moral authority.

Using the 1830s as a starting-point for debate has led some writers to emphasise a transition from local autonomy to greater government intervention and, therefore, a move from local to central forms of authority. However, to talk of a shift from these *ad hoc* forms of local urban governance to a more formalised central–local relationship of control tends to overlook the more subtle complexities of local and state interaction, obscuring what both John Garrard and E.P. Hennock have identified as the legitimation of local autonomy through a process of negotiation with central government.[6] As Garrard points out, although local governing bodies in the eighteenth and early nineteenth centuries were less dominated by legislative and political institutions outside their boundaries than in later periods, their positions of power were to some extent shaped by an ability to obtain legal recognition for their sphere of activities. Such was the case with the boards of Improvement Commissioners, who were able to construct their power base fairly autonomously at a local level but required an Act of Parliament in order to legitimate their role as 'improvers' of urban space. The Improvement Commissioners played a pivotal role in establishing strategies to 'police' the local urban community through the regulation of patterns of individual behaviour which impinged on the convenience of other inhabitants, and it was the initiation of these infrastructural systems that highlighted the continuing need for reform measures to alleviate the more adverse aspects of urban life. A close study of the reasons underlying the gradual decline of such statutory authorities as the Improvement Commissioners, and the emergence of bureaucratic styles of authority found in municipal government from the second quarter of the nineteenth century, throws into relief the tensions engendered by the renegotiation of the ways in which power and authority were expressed.

In this respect, as Miles Ogborn argues, it should not be assumed that the measures for sanitary reform initiated during the mid-nineteenth-century period clearly reflect a binary opposition between centralised administrative authorities and local bodies embedded in forms of resistance and hostility.[7] Whilst antagonism existed between the need for effective systems of administration (based on a move towards a national uniformity) and the concerns of the local, it could be argued that the shift towards the centralisation of authority was aimed not at eradicating local power but at reconfiguring the ways in which it functioned. This reformulation of central–local relations was a continuous process of negotiation involving a collectivity of interest and action at a local level, and a degree of flexibility by government bodies in the enforcement of central policies. Without the accepted legitimisation of central policy decisions by local authorities, their effective implementation was almost impossible. The collection of statistical data during the eighteenth century and neighbourhood surveys initiated in the 1830s at a nation-wide level were crucial to this process as a national concern. This information facilitated the establishment of a normative evaluation of health issues and the provision of an effective sanitary infrastructure as part of the urban landscape constructed through an increasingly formalised regulatory system. However, it was often in the local arena that opposition to changes in the authoritative structures were most keenly felt and that the necessity for conciliation was most pronounced. By using the example of the Portsea Improvement Commissioners, established in 1764 and disbanded in 1864, it will be possible to look more closely at the ways in which the interests of different social groups at a local level either collided, intersected or conflated during the transitional period from the mid-eighteenth century to the establishment of the 'modern' state from the 1830s onwards.

The Portsea Improvement Commissioners

The emergence of boards of improvement commissioners exemplifies the changes that were being made during the mid-eighteenth century in response to the perceived ineffectiveness of the old corporations and to the oligarchical style of local administration. A number of the large towns, particularly those which had been incorporated under charters, were dominated by an oligarchy of merchants and local gentry, notably in Leeds[8] and in Liverpool.[9] The appearance of statutory bodies to deal with matters pertaining specifically to local concerns in developing urban areas was a fairly *ad hoc* process. A very early example was the Court of Sewers, the first of which has been traced back to the thirteenth century.[10] However, it was not until the mid-eighteenth century that the increasing process of urbanisation led to the establishment of the boards of improvement commissioners as statutory authorities for special purposes. The boards owed their initial existence to the efforts of individual members of the populace, who collected together to propose an Act of Parliament that would empower them to exercise certain responsibilities outside the domain of existing corporations. Whilst the creation of local boards of improvement commissioners did not in itself negate the power of the local elite, as the commissioners needed representatives from the landowning class (usually local Members of Parliament) to represent them in Parliament, the boards' members did go some way to construct an alternative sphere of authority. The commissioners justified their leadership through social status acquired by means of ownership of local property and through moral and economic investment in the local community.

Although Portsea Island was far from unique in its establishment of a board of improvement commissioners, the particular way in which it emerged was linked to the island's military and naval domination. Richard I granted the first charter to Portsmouth (the only urban settlement on Portsea at this time) in 1194 in recognition of its function as a port for the embarkation of troops to serve abroad.[11] Three centuries later, Henry VII, anxious to develop his naval strength, recognised Portsmouth's advantages as a naval port. Situated in the centre of the south coast, it offered an ideal location for a royal dockyard and the first graving (or dry) dock was constructed in 1495, effectively bringing Portsmouth into being as a dockyard town.[12] The dominance of the Admiralty and the military forces on Portsea Island was to have a profound effect on its geographical and economic development over the following centuries. With the growth of the dockyard and its body of labour, the consequent need for more housing forced expansion outside the medieval town of Portsmouth, spilling its surplus population on to what was then known as Portsmouth Common.[13] These separate townships established their own boards of improvement commissioners and remained largely unconnected in terms of statutory control up until the mid-nineteenth century. The expansion of the dockyard and consequent increases in the number of inhabitants meant that by the eighteenth century Portsmouth Common had outrun Portsmouth in size and population levels; under a second Act of Parliament in 1792, although remaining a Liberty of Portsmouth,[14] the common renamed itself Portsea, undoubtedly in a bid to emphasise its identity as separate from that of the old town of Portsmouth.

The Borough of Portsmouth had been ruled since 1627 under the terms of a charter granted by Charles 1. The oligarchical-style corporation consisted of a mayor, a recorder, 12 alderman and an unlimited number of burgesses, or freemen, who generally totalled around 110 up to 1835.[15] In the latter part of the eighteenth century the borough was dominated by the Carters, a brewing family,[16] who had succeeded in wresting power away from the previous Admiralty-nominated incumbents (in the earlier part of the century Portsmouth had been an Admiralty borough[17]). But rapid urban growth on Portsmouth Common, with accompanying demographic changes, and the seeming ineffectiveness of the borough in dealing with the problems raised by this situation, resulted in the initiation of a petition by 75 local inhabitants of the common to request an Act of Parliament. After the passing of the Act the new Commissioners resolved to send their thanks to the Duke of Richmond and Sir William Heathcote, Baronet 'for their patronage and assistance in the business of passing the Act of Parliament'.[18] Their inaugural meeting was held at the Royal Oak public house in June 1764 and was attended by 31 of the Commissioners. These included a large percentage of local tradesmen such as bakers, grocers, linen drapers and stationers.[19] Senior dockyard officials were elected as *ex officio* members but rarely attended meetings; their inclusion may well have been in recognition of the Admiralty's grip on land development in the area. The occupational composition of the first Commissioners would suggest that their main concerns would have been the haphazard system of street layout and the impassability of the thoroughfares because of mud and sewage build-up, neither of which was conducive to good trading access. Indeed, the main activities of the Commissioners during the first years of their existence were the paving and repair of the streets and the provision of effective drainage, not as a health measure but to enhance accessibility. Funding for this work was based on rates levied at 3d. in the pound of the annual value of property and payable by individuals whose premises faced on to the area of paving to be constructed or repaired.[20] This practice continued up until 1843 when the principle of a general rate was first mooted.

A key aspect of the Portsea Improvement Commissioners was the way in which the board's reflection of the social structure of the area established a pattern of representation that spread across a number of local initiatives during the period. Arguably the stranglehold of the state, through its military and naval presence on the Island, precluding as it did any significant commercial development in the area, impacted strongly on the constitution of the power blocs in Portsea. Without a distinctive and permanent urban middle class with the level of wealth and status identified elsewhere by such writers as Dror Wahrman, Rick Trainor and Bill Rubinstein,[21] positions of authority in Portsea were appropriated by what Crossick and Haupt describe as *petit bourgeois* groups, that is, small shopkeepers, artisans and minor professionals.[22] It was these men who considered that their responsibilities as arbiters of reform should be conducted in 'a well regulated spirit of improvement founded on just and reasonable principles'.[23] Yet an analysis of the board's composition indicates a shift by the early nineteenth century towards the more substantial tradesmen and more established professional men of the town, together with members of the local urban gentry. During the 1850–60 period, the percentage of solicitors and gentlemen elected each year was approximately 25 per cent of the total number re-elected or newly elected (a third of the commissioners had to be replaced annually and at this time the figure for replacement was 21).[24] The work of the improvement commissioners by this time increasingly necessitated the services of local professional men, particularly solicitors, and it was their roles as recorders, clerks and treasurers which helped to enhance their professional status within the local community.[25] This work, part of the process of professionalisation to which Mary Poovey refers in her study of the medical profession, lay at the heart of wrangles between the Portsea Improvement Commissioners and the General Board of Health in 1850.

Throughout their 100-year history, the Portsea Improvement Commissioners were largely unchallenged in achieving a balance of control over local inhabitants. Their self-elective continuity reflected the constitution of the town council prior to 1835 whereby the Alderman of Portsmouth appointed the magistrates and also elected new burgesses.[26] The concept of election, although introduced in principle by the rules of the Portsea Improvement Commissioners whereby a certain number of members had to be re-elected, was in practice often ignored in favour of a system of membership renewal based on carefully chosen candidates or through re-election amongst existing Commissioners. This was not a practice peculiar to Portsea; the Webbs found that in the vast majority of instances, the Improvement Commissioners were in effect 'a self-elected and self-renewing little clique of "principal inhabitants"'.[27] Criticisms of the system for election began to appear in the local newspaper. A report in the *Hampshire Telegraph* on a meeting of the Commissioners held in 1850 refers to the 'smug' way in which the elections were staged, going on to say that 'it seemed to have become the vogue in Portsea for retiring members or those who wished to be re-elected to have a quiet meeting amongst themselves and to enter into an engagement to support and vote for each other'.[28] This tight hold on office and this sense of insularity undermined the role of the improvement commissioners in urban governance by the mid-nineteenth century, when the drive for representative local self-government became irresistible and the sanitary reform movement demanded increasing professionalisation of sanitation and health matters. The Commissioners were isolated from popular politics and aloof from the growing enthusiasm for public health reform, which – in the form of the 1848 Public Health Act – threatened to invest bodies such as town councils with specialised powers and experts operating under central government scrutiny.[29]

The first Portsea Improvement Commissioners widened their powers of administration through further Acts in 1792 and 1826, but it was the fourth Act in 1843 that identified a clear cleft in the objectives and ideals of the Commissioners and revealed a playing out of growing political and personal tensions. The main issue was the proposal to raise the level of rates by imposing the principle of a general rate; this seemingly radical departure from previous practices greatly antagonised one section of the board members, who believed that it undermined the prevailing concept of individual responsibility. But this issue of widening the rating system had a deeper resonance in the ensuing factionalism of the Commissioners. By the 1840s many members had also been elected to the Portsmouth town council, thus straddling both spheres of local power. Opposition to the terms of the 1843 Act was a starting-point in the overarching resistance to a lessening of the power and authority of the boards of improvement commissioners; the successors of the 'old guard' of the late eighteenth century were resisting the 'young Turks' of the mid-nineteenth century.

The anti-Act faction of the Portsea Improvement Commissioners continued in their hostility, even after the 1843 Act was adopted, resisting any proposal to bring the board's responsibilities under what they viewed as a central administrative system drawing together the separate townships of Portsmouth and Portsea. The Portsmouth town council first suggested such an idea in 1846, at which time it drew fierce opposition from members of the Portsea Improvement Commissioners.[30] The introduction of the Public Health Act in 1848 was also viewed warily by this firmly entrenched hostile group; in January of that year they set up a parliamentary committee in a bid to preserve their rights as they saw them. A sanitary committee had already been appointed in 1845, to investigate aspects of sanitation and health in response to the serious outbreaks of cholera in the town during the early 1840s. However, the Commissioners considered their own power under the local Act of 1843 sufficient to cover the issues raised by the Public Health Act and decided not to adopt the latter.[31] Of course, it has to be borne in mind that, in Portsmouth as elsewhere, the functions of the Improvement Commissioners, as they were first established, envisaged town improvements not to enhance the health of the populace but to regularise the physical development of the town for the sake of the greater convenience of its inhabitants.[32] Issues of health and sanitation were not prominent in general perceptions until outbreaks of epidemic disease from the early 1830s resulted in rising concern. Whilst by the 1840s the Portsea Improvement Commissioners were beginning to recognise the need for more efficient drainage methods and sewage removal, many of them undoubtedly viewed the adverse report of the Board of Health's Inspectorate, and the ultimate imposition of the Public Health Act, as a slight on their abilities and a 'muscling in' on their area of authority.

The proceedings of the Portsea Improvement Commission reveal an unprecedented number of meetings between 1843 and 1852 – the decision-making period about implementing a new Act. The flurry of attendance by the main protagonists shows that this was indeed a struggle for power within the board and not just a battle about extending the powers of the Commissioners generally. Yet from the 1850s there seems to have been an abatement in the level of antagonism to the board's seemingly inevitable subsumption to the town council. Declining attendance may indicate that the power play in local politics by this time was taking place elsewhere. Individuals on the board of the Portsea Improvement Commissioners, many of whom were firmly established local councillors by that time, evidently no longer needed board membership as a springboard for their personal ambitions. Their eventual capitulation in the 1860s, in contrast to the level of resistance during the 1840s and early 1850s, was somewhat of a damp squib. The last entry in the proceedings states that 'the Powers and Authorities hitherto exercised by the Commissioners, have ceased, and the same are now vested in the Town Council of the Borough of Portsmouth, as the Local Board of Health'.[33]

The Rawlinson Report

Yet before this final surrender the Commissioners vigorously resisted an assault on their powers and competence by an alliance of central government and local sanitary reformers. Under the Public Health Acts, a centralised General Board of Health was established with powers to create a local board of health in areas where the death rate exceeded 23 per thousand. The General Board could also act on the basis of a petition from 10 per cent of the ratepayers, a more usual practice. An inspector was sent from the General Board of Health to each locality to report on its sanitary conditions and make recommendations on the adoption of the Act; in the case of Portsea Island the inspector was Robert Rawlinson. Outbreaks of cholera, spreading from Bengal to Britain in the early nineteenth century,[34] more than any other disease of the period focused fears about the supposed degeneration of urban society and, together with policies on poor relief, helped to crystallise ideas about reforming administrative structures. The Portsea Improvement Commissioners reacted to the first outbreak of cholera in 1831 by appointing superintendents to police specified areas of the town in a bid to ensure that the removal of rubbish and sewage was carried out efficiently. This emphasis on cholera epidemics is more easily understood when set within the national context, as when seen in relation to other endemic diseases in Portsmouth and Portsea it would appear irrational that cholera should cause the most anxiety.

Portsmouth had the third worst smallpox rates in the country in the mid-century period; its inhabitants also suffered severely from typhus epidemics. Deaths from smallpox on Portsea Island between 1848 and 1854 were nearly three times higher than in Liverpool and over twice as high as in Bristol at that time (both seaport towns).[35] But it was a 'moral panic' which focused attention on cholera, as R.J. Morris maintains: '[C]holera was a deep test of the values of British society, of the care which society felt it "ought" to provide for those threatened, and the resources which it "was" in fact prepared to provide'.[36] On Portsea Island, as elsewhere in the country, it was the responses to cholera and proposed remedies for its eradication, as initiated by central government, which underlay much of the local hostility to Robert Rawlinson's report in 1850.

Numerous debates abounded at the time as to the causes of cholera. It was often the urban poor who were seen as the agents for outbreaks of cholera because of its supposed connection to profligate behaviour. One of the overriding concerns of middle-class reformers was the fact 'that the disease [could] spread from the dissolute to the sober and industrious'.[37] In fact, the local newspaper on Portsea Island exhorted the poor of the area to '[S]pend less money on beer and other drinks and spend more on flannel and coals' in order to achieve cleanliness and avoid disease.[38] Whatever the origins of the disease, the debates clearly illustrate a growing concern with the health of urban areas and the inadequacies of existing systems to deal with the problems of increasing urbanisation.

The Rawlinson Report had been set in motion by a petition forwarded to the General Board of Health from the ratepayers of three wards, none of which were either covered by a local Act or represented by a board of Improvement Commissioners.[39] The petition had stemmed from a meeting which was attended by a number of local representatives, including members of the Portsea Improvement Commissioners. Rawlinson had been sent to Portsea Island to set up a preliminary enquiry into the problems of sewage disposal, drainage and efficient supply of water. It was noted in the resultant report that in 1832 there had been 192 attacks of cholera identified as such and 88 deaths. The first case of cholera in the 1848 outbreak occurred in July of that year and the epidemic continued until September 1849, during which time there were 335 deaths from the disease on the island. In the return of Dr Henry Carter for the town of Portsea, the locations of cholera cases were seen to cluster around the numerous small courts and narrow alleys of the town, where 110 cases of cholera and 38 deaths had occurred. The report noted the close proximity of houses, the absence of good drainage, the scarcity of privies and the bad quality of the water supply in the town.[40]

One of the returns to the Rawlinson inquiry came from the Portsea Improvement Commissioners, in which they outlined the wide range of their responsibilities under the various Acts of Parliament and indicated that,

> [W]hile the commissioners fully admit the necessity of some sanitary regulations as regards the out districts [referring to the petitioning wards], they earnestly hope that it will not be considered necessary to extend the 'Act for promoting the Public Health' to the town, or in any way to interfere with the present system of local government and management under which they are now acting, being persuaded that to do so would be to entail a heavy amount of annual expenditure which the town is very unable to bear, as well as a heavy debt.[41]

There are two very clear agendas here. The first is a hostility to central government intervention, articulated as 'interference' in 'long-existing arrangements', which through the 'strenuous exertions' of the Commissioners and the 'expenditure of very large sums' are now working well. The second concern is a reluctance either to raise the level of rates or to incur a debt through a large capital outlay for what they deemed an 'inapplicable, unproductive, and most expensive system'.[42]

Thus the stage was set for a contest between the advocates of sanitary reforms – led by Dr Henry Slight, a local surgeon – and those ratepayers unwilling to adopt the proposal for a single authority with borough-wide responsibilities in place of the individual board of Improvement Commissioners. This dispute became the crucible for local power struggles. The anti-Act lobbyists were referred to as the 'Muckabites'[43] and their antagonistic stance was related not only to the increased costs of the proposed sanitary reform but also to the abolition of traditional local methods of dealing with environmental issues. The Act, if adopted, would also have introduced a new exemption for government property on Portsea Island, currently contributing 16 per cent of the total borough rate income, and it was this issue that again fragmented the local authorities in 1852. The opposition group, dominated by Portsea Commissioners and councillors, used this element of the Act to mount a successful campaign early that year, mobilising the local ratepayers and winning by a small majority vote. The pro-Act contingent based their support on the premise that the improved health of the local population, engendered through the implementation of the Act, would reduce the call on poor rates and also enhance property values. The exemption of properties with low rateable values from poor rates became another area of contention. Under the new Act such properties would be subject to rates; in Portsea Parish there were over 4,000 non-rateable properties,[44] many of which were owned by members of the Portsea Improvement Commission.[45] Dr Slight took up this point when he referred to the 'wretched property' owned by some of the opponents of the Act, referring particularly to the 'Hebrew opposition'[46] whom he perceived as the ringleaders of the anti-Act lobby.[47] Such accusations reveal the degree of animosity aroused during the debates around the implementation of the Act. They indicate not only the sharp rivalries for positions of power but also that the platform for urban governance was shifting towards a more centrally focused and formalised municipal council.

The Portsea Improvement Commissioners continued to state their case, claiming that their measures were efficacious in complying with the terms of their responsibilities under the previous Acts of Parliament, but there was much contrary evidence. In the conclusions to his report, Rawlinson (concurring with Dr Carter's findings) states that, 'the borough is not so healthy as it may be, on account of ill-paved and undrained streets, imperfect privy accommodation, crowded courts and houses, with large exposed middens and cesspools ... no adequate powers for effective local government at present exist'.[48] This last statement was a damning indictment of the Portsea Improvement Commissioners, and it is not surprising that they largely rejected the proposals of the report at that time. Although the Act was adopted later in the 1850s, it was not until 1865 that a comprehensive plan was drawn up for a new drainage and sewage system, and not until 1879 that it was finally completed.[49]

Robert Rawlinson's inquiry into the sanitary conditions on Portsea Island served to highlight the inadequacy of local boards of Improvement Commissioners in eradicating dirt and disease in many of the poorer areas. Reactions to Rawlinson's proposals emphasised the parochial and insular nature of local government at this time, whilst also revealing widespread resentment of governmental dominance on Portsea Island as manifested in the exemption of the Admiralty and the Board of Ordnance from paying rates. The overwhelming presence of the state on Portsea Island through its military and naval bases had a quite obvious effect on attitudes towards what was perceived as increased government intervention in issues of health and sanitation. Vigorous hostility to the Public Health Act of 1848 was often couched in a rhetoric of resistance to what was seen as enforcement from the centre, but whilst this may have been the dominant perception, such concerns also acted as a forum for the voicing of individual interests and antagonisms. The whole debate around the need for sanitary improvements exemplifies Geoffrey Crossick's argument that the concerns of the *petite bourgeoisie* were irreducibly local and that '[T]he parochial character of its culture must have severely impaired the ability of the British petits bourgeois to cope with change, and must have been responsible for much of the rigidity of values that only hardened as the period progressed'.[50] For the anti-Act lobbyists, the 'rigidity of values' appeared to rest mainly on maintaining acceptable levels of rates and thus on protecting their own legitimation for authority.

Conclusions

The example of the Portsea Improvement Commissioners demonstrates the complex ways in which the local government system of the mid-nineteenth century emerged over the course of the previous hundred years. This period acted therefore as a conduit, where the customs and practices founded in the *ad hoc* tendencies of the eighteenth century were gradually transmuted, through a universal style of social reform, into a systematised and bureaucratised approach to urban governance that was to become the basis for the modern state. However, the resistance shown by the anti-Act lobby in Portsea reveals that the transition was not a seamless move from one structure of authority to another. Instead, throughout the course of the nineteenth century a series of innovatory social reforms were introduced through a continuous system of negotiation and the reconciliation of different interests at both a national and a local level.

The interplay of group relations in establishing central–local administrative structures, and the accompanying renegotiation of the power nexus at a local level, was inevitable in the process of modernising the social order of urban space. Such progression can be viewed as the move towards a municipal consciousness: debates about the health of the city were shifting way from an authority founded on the moral worth of small-scale producers and tradesmen to what Robbie Gray refers to as one of 'rational knowledge'.[51] Such knowledge was disseminated through burgeoning forms of bureaucracy and a concomitant increase in the power and status of the professional man and the qualified expert, as outlined by Irene Maver in her work on Glasgow in this volume.

Thus the issue of health and sanitation should not be accepted as an automatically perceived 'problem' of urbanisation and, therefore, as an inevitable aspect of local administrative control. This is particularly so before the early part of the nineteenth century, bearing in mind that authoritative bodies like the first boards of improvement commissioners were established with a somewhat different agenda. The whole problematic of health was only defined as such as the progress of urbanisation necessitated a redefining of the social order, and consequently a widening of the parameters of urban governance. As pointed out in the introductory section of this volume, what is of importance to the historian is not merely to define that a 'problem' occurs at any given time, but how contemporary perceptions serve to construct the problem and the impact of this construction both on decisions made to alleviate or ameliorate such problems and on structures of authority and power.

Notes

1. D. Fraser, *Municipal Reform and the Industrial City* (Leicester: Leicester University Press, 1982). See also B. Keith-Lucas, *The Unreformed Local Government System* (London: Croom Helm, 1980).
2. For example, Mary Poovey sees the acceleration of urbanisation that took place during the last three decades of the eighteenth century as the prelude to a wider recognition of urban poverty and its effect on the health of the population; these concerns acted as a fulcrum in the reform process. She argues that as such problems became more visible, they were judged as more problematic, culminating in the social reform movement of the mid-nineteenth century. M. Poovey, *Making a Social Body: British Cultural Formation 1830–1864* (London and Chicago: University of Chicago Press, 1995).
3. S. Webb and B. Webb, *Statutory Authorities for Special Purposes* (London: Frank Cass, 1963; first published 1922).
4. P. Joyce, *Democratic Subjects: The Self and Social Control in Nineteenth Century England* (Cambridge: Cambridge University Press, 1994).
5. E.P. Hennock, *Fit and Proper Persons* (London: Edward Arnold, 1973).
6. Hennock, 'Central/Local Government Relations in England: An Outline 1800–1950', *Urban History Yearbook* (Leicester: Leicester University Press, 1982); J. Garrard, *Leadership and Power in Victorian Industrial Towns 1830–1880* (Manchester: Manchester University Press, 1983).
7. M. Ogborn, 'Local Power and State Regulations in Nineteenth Century Britain', *Transactions of the Institute of British Geographers*, ns 17 (1992).
8. Hennock, *Fit and Proper Persons*, p. 179.
9. D. Fraser, *Power and Authority in the Victorian City* (Oxford: Blackwell, 1979).
10. Webb and Webb, *Statutory Authorities*.
11. J. Chapman, 'The Geographical Evolution of Portsmouth', in J.B. Bradbeer (ed), *Portsmouth Geographical Essays*, vol. 1 (Portsmouth: Portsmouth Polytechnic, 1974).
12. R.S. Horn, *Her Majesty's Dockyard at Portsmouth* (Portsmouth: Portsmouth Dockyard, 1966).
13. J. Chapman, 'The Common Lands of Portsea Island', *Portsmouth Paper*, 29 (Portsmouth: Portsmouth City Council, 1978).
14. J. Cramer, 'The Origins and Growth of the Town of Portsea to 1816', unpublished PhD thesis, Portsmouth Polytechnic, 1985.
15. S. Peacock, 'Borough Government in Portsmouth, 1835–1974', *Portsmouth Paper*, 23 (Portsmouth: Portsmouth City Council, 1975).
16. P. Eley, 'Portsmouth Breweries 1492–1847', *Portsmouth Paper*, 51 (Portsmouth: Portsmouth City Council, 1988).
17. A. Temple Patterson, *Portsmouth: A History* (Bradford-on-Avon: Moonraker Press, 1976).
18. Portsmouth City Records Office (PCRO), G/ICP/1/1, Proceedings of the Improvement Commission, June 1764–January 1775.
19. J. Noon, 'The Improvement Commissioners of Portsmouth and Portsea to c.1800', *Moody Essay* (Portsmouth, 1979) (PCRO).
20. Noon, 'The Improvement Commissioners', p. 9.
21. D. Wahrman, *Imagining the Middle Class, the Political Representation of Class in Britain, c.1780–1840* (Cambridge: Cambridge University Press, 1995); R. Trainor, *Black Country Elites: The Exercise of Authority in an Industrialised Area, 1830–1900* (Oxford: Clarendon Press, 1993); W.D. Rubinstein, *Men of Property* (London: Croom Helm, 1981). For an analysis of the Portsmouth middle class see J. Field, 'Wealth, Style of Life and Social Tone amongst Portsmouth's Middle Class, 1800–

75', in R.J. Morris (ed.), *Class, Power and Social Structure in British Nineteenth-Century Towns* (Leicester: Leicester University Press, 1986), pp. 68–106.

22. G. Crossick and H.G. Haupt, *Shopkeepers and Master Artisans in Nineteenth Century Europe* (London: Methuen, 1984).

23. PCRO, G/ICP/1/7, Proceedings of the Portsea Improvement Commissioners meeting, 22 March 1842.

24. PCRO, G/ICP/1/9, Proceedings of the Portsea Improvement Commissioners, October 1852–October 1863.

25. Keith-Lucas, *The Unreformed Local Government System*, p. 152.

26. J. Field, 'Bourgeois Portsmouth: Social Relations in a Victorian Dockyard Town, 1815–1875', unpublished PhD thesis, University of Warwick, 1979.

27. Webb and Webb, *Statutory Authorities*, p. 245.

28. *Hampshire Telegraph (HT)*, 19 November 1850.

29. Mary Poovey (*Making a Social Body*, 4) locates this shift to greater bureaucracy and professionalisation within the strategies for general social reform and argues that 'the sanitary idea constituted one of the crucial links between the regulation of the individual body and the consolidation of those apparatuses we associate with the modern state'.

30. R. Otter, 'Aspects of Environmental Public Health in Portsmouth 1764–1864', unpublished PhD thesis, University of Portsmouth, 1994.

31. PCRO, G/ICP/1/8, Proceedings of the Portsea Improvement Commissioners, June 1843–October 1852.

32. Webb and Webb, *Statutory Authorities*, p. 252.

33. PCRO, G/ICP/1/10, Proceedings of the Portsea Improvement Commissioners, November 1863–July 1864.

34. R.J. Morris, *Cholera 1832* (London: Croom Helm, 1976).

35. Field, 'Bourgeois Portsmouth', p. 435.

36. Morris, *Cholera 1832*, p. 21.

37. F. Mort, *Dangerous Sexualities* (London: Routledge and Kegan Paul, 1987).

38. PCRO, 16A/143, Newspaper cutting from the papers of Captain James Anderson RN.

39. PCRO, Robert Rawlinson (Rawlinson Report), *Report to the General Board of Health on the Sewage, Drainage and Water Supply of Portsmouth, 1850*. The three wards, All Saints, St Mary and St Paul, lay outside the townships of Portsmouth and Portsea.

40. Rawlinson Report, p. 28.

41. Rawlinson Report, pp. 34–5.

42. Rawlinson Report, p. 35.

43. R. Otter, 'Aspects of Environmental Public Health', Appendix 3.

44. Ibid., Appendix A1.2.

45. PCRO, Poor Rates Books for Portsea Parish, 1815–1885.

46. A. Weinberg, 'Portsmouth Jewry', *Portsmouth Paper* 41 (Portsmouth: Portsmouth City Council, 1985). Two of the main opponents of the Public Health Act were Emanuel and Ezekiel Emanuel, local silversmiths who both served as Commissioners. Emanuel Emanuel went on to become the first Jewish Mayor of Portsmouth.

47. Otter, 'Aspects of Environmental Public Health', Appendix 3.

48. Rawlinson Report, p. 86.

49. Otter, 'Aspects of Environmental Public Health', Appendix 3.

50. G. Crossick, 'The Petite Bourgeoisie in Nineteenth-Century Britain: the Urban and Liberal Case', in Crossick and Haupt, *Shopkeepers and Master Artisans* (see note 22).

51. R. Gray, 'Bourgeois Hegemony', in J. Bloomfield (ed.), *Class, Hegemony and Party* (London: Lawrence and Wishart, 1977).

CHAPTER EIGHT

Expediency, authority and duplicity: reforming Sheffield's police, 1832–40

Chris Williams

Before 1964, Britain's cities policed themselves. Given that the state is the body with a monopoly on the legitimate use of force, then the control of the police – the institution charged with using this force – is an important function of any central or local government. This chapter examines how control over police and criminal justice occupied a central place in the debates over the best form of government for the town of Sheffield in the second quarter of the nineteenth century. It falls into four main sections. The first explains why the topic of urban police reform ought to occupy a central place in any study of the nineteenth-century city and advances some explanations as to why this has hitherto not been the case. The second offers an interpretation of the ways in which the idea of governance will be treated. The third explains the course of events in the 1830s whereby Sheffield got its new police and its charter, stressing the extent to which these outcomes were under-determined by social and political trends, owing much to contingency. The fourth offers some general conclusions demonstrated by this process, and their bearing on the contexts and structures within which it occurred.

The significance of policing

The history of policing is central to the study of the history of the city. Even so, in the past it has often been overlooked as a key theme by historians exploring the politics of the city in the modern era. This has been the case owing to the initial orientation of the history of local government.

The Webbs started a tradition that saw democratic municipal government as fundamentally benign and generally consensual. Utilitarian analysis had battled with unaccountable Old Corruption and won, allowing it to restructure local government and services on a logical basis.[1] Sanitary reform was the obvious change to concentrate on as an exemplar of this process. Local attitudes to education and health were also seen as unequivocally reformist and progressive.[2] So a whole body of work on the government of Victorian cities exists which does not mention the local police force, or does so only in passing.[3] Significantly, one exception to this trend – Foster's work on Oldham – is a work that concentrates whole-heartedly on the city as a site for class antagonism.[4] But the prevailing trend is doubly odd given that control – or lack of it – over their own police force, is one of the key ways in which British cities of today differ from those of the past. It is worth noting that more recently there have been exceptions to this tendency, notably Trainor's work on the Black Country, and Etheridge's study of police in Northampton, where she states that the creation and development of Northampton's new police has to be understood in the context of corporation reform.[5]

There are several reasons why the history of policing needs to occupy a central position in any study of nineteenth-century urban governance. First, policing is an expensive task, and in the period under consideration, especially before municipalities began to spend large amounts of money on capital and improvement projects from the 1870s onwards, it often consumed the lion's share of local government expenditure. In the period under study here, 'watching' accounted for about 40 per cent of the Sheffield Improvement Commission's expenditure: this does not cover the expenses of the petty sessions jurisdiction, the parochial constable system, the private subscription police forces set up in this period or the measures some Sheffield townships took under the 1833 Lighting and Watching Act.[6] In the 1850s policing accounted for more than four-fifths of the borough's expenditure, although this figure decreased as it took over the non-police functions of the Improvement Commission, and began to invest in capital projects.[7]

Second, control over the police force is the chance to apply coercive power locally: often this has great commercial significance, given that the police authorities are regulating property as well as people. In looking at nineteenth-century police forces, the older, wider, meaning of the word police – those activities required to keep a place functioning – is more useful than the current meaning which pertains more to anti-crime activities.[8] Sheffield's police authority had the power to regulate all manner of activities ranging from obstructions on the footpath, through overly smoky chimneys, to unsafe walls, cellars and middens.[9] It had a great deal of control over disputed transactions through the right of the police to determine what was and what was not a crime. Such cases were normally determined by the police themselves, but the chief policeman had been appointed from the ranks of the Improvement Commission, and its monthly meetings saw a number of appeals from individuals, debates over priorities, and contested interpretations of its statutory powers: in short, it exercised a degree of executive control over and above its prerogative of hiring, firing, disciplining and promoting police officers.[10] Winstanley has noted a similar set of preoccupations in the case of the Oldham police.[11]

Third, the police had a symbolic function as an indicator of local independence and power, which was sometimes displayed on a ceremonial level. In 1836, when Sheffield's Collegiate School was opened, the newly created day police force marched in company with all the assembled dignitaries of the town to celebrate.[12] Other towns saw their police forces as signs of local idiosyncrasy, as actors in civic ceremonial, or as a last sign of the independence of a borough fallen on hard times.[13] The police were a symbol of cherished autonomy and difference, one of the things separating Sheffield from humble places.[14]

Fourth, policing could have a major direct impact on the history of a town: it was the reason that Sheffield incorporated as a borough. It was not alone in this – Oldham's incorporation, for instance, was also a result of police considerations.[15]

A consideration of governance

The term governance is seen here as something that was both exercised by, and applied to, a point reasonably close to the top of the town's social hierarchy. The Improvement Commission and its successor the borough Watch Committee were at the centre of power in Sheffield.[16] These men were very conscious of their position among the governors – in 1860 one chair of the Watch Committee offered to resign because he had not received his customary *ex officio* invitation to the Cutlers Feast, the symbolic centre of Sheffield's social year.[17]

The men who controlled the police in Sheffield, however, were also among the governed, and they realised this. All that they did rested on statutory authority conferred by local or general legislation, or by traditional forms of organisation such as the township vestry or the town trust, which could be subject to challenge in the courts, or to redefinition by statute.[18] Common law and tradition were no proof against statute: they could be swept away. The right of the Court Leet to name local constables was ended by the 1842 Superintending Constables Act, which granted a right of veto to the local magistrates.[19] The men who laid down the law locally were at the mercy of the opinion of the Secretary of State, and although they could stay in anxious daily touch with their Members of Parliament (MPs) while bills went through Parliament, they could not make their lobbying magically effective.[20] The central state made its decisions on the basis of a number of factors, and the interest shown in their own affairs by the large towns, no matter how insistent, was never allowed to dominate proceedings.

State power as a theoretical abstract also featured in the desire for social and governmental change. Weber has persuasively defined the state as that body with a monopoly of violence, and Klockars has pointed out that it is police forces that exercise that right internally but, as Elias has shown, monopolies of violence have been historically linked with monopolies of taxation.[21] This power is crucial because it overcomes the limits to social intervention that are felt by voluntary bodies, no matter how highly motivated. Voluntary collective institutions could not create the institutions they needed in order to have a significant impact without the power to tax – in the local context, to levy a rate. Such a power always needed a basis in statutory authority. Even so, the governance of Sheffield, and the definition of its ruling groups, did make use of voluntary association, mainly on a symbolic level. Networks of intellectual societies served to knit together an emerging urban middle class.[22] Public subscriptions for worthy causes allowed prominent individuals to broadcast their commitment to the town, while social functions such as the annual Cutlers Feast identified the town's worthies: however, Sheffield as an unincorporated town, was under-governed in this way compared to older towns such as Leeds.

Governance therefore, refers here both to governance of the populace by the burghers, and of the burghers by the state. It has instrumental components such as the ability to coerce and the right to collect taxes. Yet it also has symbolic components: the right to autonomy for its own sake and the need to preserve the symbols of power as well as the substance.

Municipal reform in Sheffield, 1832–40

In 1831, Sheffield's population was 91,000: an increase of 26,000 over the 1821 figure. By 1841, it reached 111,000. Most of this increase was driven by expansion in the old-established grinding trades and in the newer heavy steel sector.[23] As Smith has shown, Sheffield's working class was characterised by strong neighbourhood and occupational solidarities, and the attempt on the part of the middle classes to deal with these was part of a general process whereby impersonal and universalistic institutions increasingly took over the tasks of local government.[24] The process whereby Sheffield was incorporated has already been examined in general terms: here it will be studied in terms of the precise and significant impact that was made by the issue of control over criminal justice.[25]

In 1818 an Improvement Act was passed for Sheffield, creating the Improvement Commission, with 120 Commissioners. A maximum value on the rate it could levy was set. Its jurisdiction only covered an area within three-quarters of a mile from the town centre. This encompassed about

90 per cent of the boroughs population but only around 10 per cent of its area. As the population increased, the proportion covered by the police force steadily sank. Commissioners were mainly elected on a ratepayer franchise, serving for life or until they failed to attend once a year.[26] It met monthly, but by 1830 it had set up a number of committees, including a Watch Committee that met more often. By 1830 it was responsible for cleansing, lighting and watching and employed around 60 night watchmen. As well as the Commission, Sheffield was governed by: the six township vestries, which controlled poor relief (until 1834) and rate collection and nominated constables; the township boards of highways; the Courts Leet which annually appointed constables and many other local officers such as inspectors of weights and measures; the Cutlers Company, whose master carried out many functions of a mayor; and the Town Trust, which administered property held for the benefit of the town.

The judicial functions of local government were exercised by the Petty Sessions Magistrates. These were local clergy and gentry, members of the West Riding county bench. None lived in the town. They sat in petty session in the Town Hall twice a week. The local acting constables served under them: there were between two and four of these, plus assistants. Hugh Parker, JP, was the most active member of this bench: he sat at over half of the sessions in the 1830s. He was a Whig in his politics, and as will be seen, his recommendations were listened to with great respect by all but a tiny minority of the élite. The local bench was only a subset of that of the whole Riding and all the West Ridings JPs had the right to sit in Sheffield, although few of the rest ever exercised it. The county government was responsible for quarter sessions, for maintaining prisons, for refunding prosecution expenditure, and for reimbursing constables. Lord Wharncliffe chaired the West Riding Quarter Sessions in the late 1830s. A prominent Tory, he was in favour of reforming the police arrangements of the county.

Politically, the improvement commission was divided between Liberal reformers and their opponents. Some of these were doctrinaire Tories, some were apolitical, and the last mentioned contained the majority of men who had formed the core of the Commission's various committees (watch, rate, light, cleansing) which performed more of its tasks between monthly meetings. The man who generally held the initiative in the arguments that led up to incorporation was Luke Palfreyman: a lawyer, Improvement Commissioner and prominent member of the Reform Association in the 1830s. Some of his opponents implied that his zeal for daily justice might have been linked with the amount of cases he took on at Petty Sessions.[27]

An election riot occurred in 1832: five people were killed when troops fired into a crowd protesting at the defeat of a local radical reformer.

Significantly the event was always seen in terms of the non-local magistrate who had ordered non-local troops to fire into the crowd. The deaths were seen not as justification for a change in structure but as an occasion for personal praise and blame. The inquest jury, though, was packed with reliable men to ensure that this potentially troublesome institution did not deliver an uncomfortable verdict at a politically dangerous time.[28] But subsequent moves to incorporate did not attempt to use the deaths as a reason for incorporation: a link Cobden tried to make with Peterloo in Manchester.[29] The 1830s in Sheffield continued to be disorderly: January 1835 saw the Medical School systematically and carefully burnt to the ground by an angry crowd who suspected its proprietors of body-snatching.[30] This was a reminder of the power of the autonomous crowd and of the otherness of many popular attitudes compared to those of the town's ruling élites, the majority of whom supported the medical establishment. There were some calls to remedy the lack of a police presence during the day – the immediate cause of the destruction – but they quickly lapsed.

Also in 1835, the Municipal Corporations Act was passed. This created a ready-made option for the town if it wished to reform its government. The issue was highly politicised and the local Liberal paper, the *Sheffield Independent*, was as consistently for incorporation as the local Tory paper, the *Sheffield Mercury*, was against it. As the town grew beyond the three-quarter mile radius more people – especially the wealthier inhabitants of the Western suburbs – began to live in the unpoliced area. Some of these raised voluntary subscriptions for their own watchmen.[31] In addition, in 1837 and 1839 two of the constituent townships adopted the provisions of the 1833 Lighting and Watching Act. These steps tended to be taken as an immediate reaction to a perceived crime wave, and to lapse into disuse after the wave ended: they were unable to establish themselves as institutions.

In the spring of 1836 the Improvement Commission requested that the Justices sit daily. Both Hugh Parker and the Commission as a whole were worried by the cumulative effects of the increasing population on the ability of the justices at Petty Sessions to deal with the everyday problems of the town. Parker replied to the Commission, and offered them three choices: they could incorporate under the 1835 Act; appoint a stipendiary magistrate via a new local Act; or augment the local bench by appointing men from the town itself to it. A deputation from the Improvement Commission, with strong representation from pro-incorporation Reformers, decided on the third option – more local justices. As well as this, the Commission voted to establish a day police force, increasing its complement from two to 16. The day police were recognised as the only way to secure the peace of the streets. After they had been introduced, the *Mercury* welcomed them in the following terms: 'such a force has long been wanted in Sheffield, the disorderly state of the streets, especially in the evenings, having been such as would not be tolerated in any other large town'.[32]

The proposal to add to the bench did not succeed. The normal process of addition to the bench moved slowly and involved the extension and replication of existing gentry-based social networks. This proposal would have given a significant degree of stature and power within the West Riding bench as a whole (the members of which numbered around 200) to 12 members of the urban bourgeoisie. It is therefore unsurprising that it happened very slowly: by 1837 only one of the 12 suggested had qualified. In view of this, in 1837 the Commission proposed a new Improvement Act with a stipendiary magistrate. Consideration of this draft bill, though, fell off the bottom of the agenda.[33] The Commissioners, meeting monthly to deal with the business of running the town, were unwilling to give it time, and no other local institutions were actively supporting or debating it enough to take the proposal from draft form to one that could pass a town meeting.

On its failure, the Reform Association put forward a formal proposal to incorporate in 1838. This was defeated by 4,589 votes at an average value of £16 to 1,970 at £27. There was a three-way split politically. In the middle, in favour, were the Whig reformers and richer ratepayers. On one wing, against, were the Tories because they knew Sheffield would automatically become a Whig stronghold. On the other wing, against, were the radicals speaking for the poorer ratepayers, since they were convinced that they would be more heavily taxed by a corporation that they too could not control.[34]

Between 1838 and 1840, the Improvement Commission became polarised and contested between a reformist, liberal wing who began to stand slates for the annual elections, and their Tory and localist opponents who were anti-incorporation. When advocating incorporation, Palfreyman had accused the Commission of being an 'irresponsible life-elected body', yet he felt able to chair the meetings in June, September, November and December 1838.[35] At the general meeting of ratepayers to elect new members to the Commission in August, there was a challenge to the vote for the chair, normally a formality.[36] The incorporators won. The Liberals won the elections, too: the nine new members included two of the incorporators, Corden Thompson and George Roebuck, near the top of the poll. The names of those not elected included several prominent Tories. Those apolitical Commissioners who served on its subcommittees tended to be more likely to be against incorporation. This exacerbated existing tension between the committees and the Commission as a whole. The tension had not been resolved by the appointment of a Watch Committee member – Thomas Raynor – to head the police force: after Raynor's appointment the

Commission vetoed the Committee's recommendations for his four subordinates, and appointed their own choices.[37]

In 1839, then, the town was deadlocked on the issue of reform, but this situation was about to change, prodded by an external stimulus. This was the move by central government to offer a means whereby counties could set up their own police forces, controlled, as were all other local government functions at county level, by the bench of magistrates. In order to take effect, this measure needed two-thirds of the magistrates to support it. While Parliament considered it, the Commission attempted to get one of its members, John Parker, MP, to amend the bill so that it would not apply to unincorporated towns that already provided for their own police.[38] To no avail: when it was passed in 1839, the County Constabulary Act only exempted incorporated boroughs from its provisions, in counties that chose to adopt it.[39] The genesis of the Act was found in concern for the problems of the vagrant poor, but when it was passed (and amended in 1840) the immediate problem of Chartism was one of the main spurs to its creation.[40] In 1839, the West Riding bench began to consider the County Constabulary Act. This move was sparked off by Chartism, and then spurred on by Samuel Holberry's attempted revolt in Sheffield, which was stopped by Sheffield's own police in January 1840. There was a notable lack of panic among the majority of the Improvement Commission: despite the fact that an attempted revolution had taken place on their doorstep, nobody called for the police to be reformed. Lord Wharncliffe, however, used the event to underline what he had been personally calling for since the previous year: the application of the County Police Act to the industrial districts of the riding.[41]

This would mean a police force controlled by the riding bench, which would pay for it out of a rate levied on the policed areas. Sheffield would have no control over the actions of the force, or over its level of expenditure. All the Commissioners joined to lobby against the proposal via petitions and their justices. During the bench's debates on the Acts, the magistrates active in Sheffield vigorously supported the town's position, and gave glowing testimonies to the competence of its police force. Even though they were non-resident, they appear to have seen their role as representing Sheffield to the West Riding, rather than vice versa.[42] Indeed, during the various meetings, JPs generally acted in the interest of their home districts, rather than attempting or claiming to speak for the riding as a whole.

In March 1840, Parker intervened locally for the second time, and proposed a local police bill based on the Birmingham and Manchester Acts.[43] This was a major gaffe, not rescued by attempts at backtracking. These Acts involved a government-appointed commissioner who was also a stipendiary magistrate. They were passed in response to a perception that the cities involved were deadlocked by intra-corporate feuds, or were dominated by unreliable elements.[44] It was anathema to the burghers of Sheffield that they should so abnegate their own responsibility, and the Commission decisively voted to reject the proposal. Eventually, a consensus was built around a conservative new Improvement Act that would give Sheffield a stipendiary magistrate and a police board.

It was at this stage that the duplicity began to occur. Palfreyman and his pro-incorporation allies took the initiative and scuppered the proposal for a new Improvement Act, claiming that the *status quo* was entirely acceptable.[45] Once this was done, they talked up the possibility of the County Constabulary Acts being applied to Sheffield. The only infallible way to avoid this, they claimed, was to incorporate. They made use of the genuine localist feeling in the town, its opposition to taxation without representation, and the fact that Wharncliffe was a Tory.[46] In addition they were not above calling attention to the serious disorder associated with the implementation of the County Police Acts in Lancashire. Eventually they won opinion round. Ironically, over the summer and autumn of 1840, the West Riding bench began to run out of steam. Wharncliffe could not find the required two-thirds majority to agree on the exact areas that were to be policed and taxed. These signs were ignored by Palfreyman and his faction, and by their mouthpiece, the *Independent*.

Eventually they got what they wanted: in October 1840, Parker decided that the only way for Sheffield to avoid the County Constabulary Acts was to incorporate as a borough. This played right into the reformers' hands, and created a situation where they could be sure of getting the proposal through a public meeting. Once more the ratepayers voted, and this time, in 1841, the petition to incorporate passed. In 1843, Sheffield received its Charter of Incorporation.

Conclusions

There are three main conclusions to be noted here. The first is that in order to understand what happened, we have to avoid hindsight. While to us the situation may appear as a high road to incorporation, to those involved this was merely one of many possible outcomes. The merits of incorporation were always tested against the *status quo*, against a stipendiary magistrate or against a new local improvement Act. The most obvious feature of these debates was that Sheffielders seemed to want as much self-respect and autonomy as they possibly could, provided it did not increase the rates. In 1838, during the first attempt to incorporate, finance was more important. By 1840, the supposed external threat of the County Constabulary Acts outweighed worries over possible extra expenditure: under the Acts, Sheffield would be taxed by an unaccountable County bench. The control of urban policing was not altered by concern over crime or riot: it was altered by reaction to an external factor, the ambitions of the West Riding.

The second conclusion concerns the role of the state. The legal framework had changed in 1835, and changed again in 1839. The Improvement Commission may have been masters in their own house, but they were helpless in the face of statute law. The urban polity knew it was actively dependent on the sanction of the central state in order to exercise its power. Even the simplest plans to levy a subscription to deal with public order problems needed a statute to be effective. Voluntary association was too ephemeral to achieve institutional permanence, and too susceptible to the free rider problem.[47] In order to extend usefully the policed area and thus make sure that the town was able to comply with the minimum nationally acceptable standards of civility, it was necessary to obtain parliamentary backing to levy a rate.

Third, a sense of legitimacy was necessary: some form of local accountability in the form of a public meeting was needed to get reform through. Property qualifications were always present, and the right of the ratepayers to control an institution that policed the bodies and property of all their fellow townsfolk was not generally questioned. However, the example of Colne and other parts of Lancashire – where the imposition of the new police had led to sustained and violent working-class opposition – was noted in Sheffield: there was a sense of the real balance of power on the streets, which had probably been reinforced by the Medical School riot of 1835.[48] Reform could not afford to be overly unpopular. Aside from this consideration, the critical path of events was located within the middle classes.

The choices that were made had wider significance. Incorporation meant that the body controlling the police, the borough, was now the major organ of local government, whereas the Improvement Commission had only been one of several. The stage was set for the borough to arrogate an increasing number of governmental and service functions to itself. The mayor would now serve both as a magistrate in petty sessions and as a member of the Watch Committee, responsible for controlling the police force. In Sheffield, as in other towns and cities, the police force was under the direct control of the borough council, which rendered this institution pre-eminent as the local government.

Notes

1. See for instance S. Webb and B. Webb, 'English Local Government from the Revolution to the Municipal Corporations Act', Vol. 3: *The Manor and the*

Borough (London: Longmans, 1908), p. 405.

2. Even so, recent criticism has tended to show that the field of public health in general is a politicised and ideologically contested terrain. This view is summed up in M. Niemi, '"Making the Unknown Known": Town and Townspeople in Public Health Discourse in Birmingham and Gothenburg 1890–1920', in H. Power and S. Sheard (eds), *Body and City: A Cultural History of Urban Public Health* (Aldershot: Scolar, 1999).

3. Examples of failure to consider boroughs' policing responsibilities include: E.P. Hennock, 'Compositions of Borough Councils', in H.J. Dyas (ed.), *The Study of Urban History* (London: Edward Arnold, 1968), pp. 317–18; D. Fraser, *Urban Politics in Victorian England: The Structure of Politics in Victorian Cities* (London: Macmillan, 1979); and A. Elliott, 'The Incorporation of Bradford', *Northern History*, 15 (1979), pp. 156–75, p. 160. Other historians who have mentioned policing once and then go on to explain urban government primarily in the context of other needs include R.J. Morris, 'The Middle Class and British Towns and Cities of the Industrial Revolution, 1780–1870', in D. Fraser and A. Sutcliffe (eds), *The Pursuit of Urban History* (London: Edward Arnold, 1983), pp. 286–305, p. 303; and Trainor, who characterises civic preoccupations before 1870 as consisting of sewers and water, R. Trainor, 'Urban Elites in Victorian Britain', *Urban History Yearbook* (Leicester: Leicester University Press, 1985), p. 9 (although see note 5 below).

4. J. Foster, *Class Struggle and the Industrial Revolution: Early Industrial Capitalism in Three English Towns* (London: Weidenfeld and Nicolson, 1974), p. 58.

5. See R.H. Trainor, *Black Country Elites: The Exercise of Authority in an Industrialized Area, 1830–1900* (Oxford: Clarendon Press, 1993) pp. 167–73 and R. Etheridge, 'Nineteenth-Century Northampton: The Nature of the New Police, Crime and Disorder', *Northamptonshire Past and Present*, 2 (1995–96), pp. 172–84, 183.

6. Improvement Commission Accounts, printed annually in the *Sheffield Independent*, 1818–44.

7. In 1860, the Town Council spent £14,400: £12,017 of this was spent on the police force: *General and Commercial Directory and Topography of the Borough of Sheffield, etc.* (London: Francis White and Co., 1862). It is worth noting that until the 1880s, the borough's chief source of cash for capital investment was the police force pension fund.

8. When Adam Smith lectured on the theory of state regulation in the 1760s, he defined police as the inferior parts of government, namely, cleanliness, security and cheapness or plenty: A. Smith, *Lectures on Justice, Police, Revenue and Arms* (New York: Kelley and Millman, 1956), p. 154.

9. Sheffield Improvement Act (58 George II c. liv), s. xl, xlii, xlv.

10. *Sheffield Iris*, 7 July 1818; *Sheffield Independent*, 9 June 1833; 5 April and 10 May 1834; 10 June 1837 and 6 June 1840.

11. M. Winstanley, 'Preventive policing in Oldham, c.1826–56', in *Transactions of the Lancashire and Cheshire Antiquarian Society*, 96 (1990), pp. 17–35, 20.

12. *Sheffield Independent*, 8 Oct. 1836.

13. Luton police wore hats made of straw in the summer, in acknowledgement of one of the town's staple industries: T.J. Madigan, *The Men Who Wore Straw Helmets: Policing Luton 1840–1974* (Dunstable: The Book Castle, 1993); in Hereford the police carried the corporation's banner and mace in parades up to the 1930s: G. Forrest and T. Hadley, *Policing Hereford and Leominster: An Illustrated History of the City of Hereford Police 1835 to 1947 and Leominster Borough Police 1836 to 1889* (Studley: Brewin, 1989), pp. 29, 47, 54; while

tiny boroughs like Malton paid higher rates in order to preserve their own police forces for as long as possible: J. Woodgate, *The Essex Police* (Lavenham: Terence Dalton, 1985), pp. 172–3.

14. *Sheffield Independent* 12 Dec, 1840.

15. Oldham Corporation, *Oldham Centenary: A History of Local Government* (Manchester: Grove, 1949), p. 81.

16. C. Steedman, *Policing the Victorian Community: The Formation of English Provincial Police Forces, 1856–80* (London: Routledge, 1984), p. 67.

17. Sheffield Borough Watch Committee Minutes, 6 Sept. 1860, Sheffield City Archives A295/3.

18. In the period before the passage of the 1818 Improvement Act, the status of the Town Trust was subject to a challenge in Chancery over whether the franchise belonged to the freemen or the householders (J.D. Leader, *Records of the Burgery of Sheffield, Commonly Called the Town Trust* [London: Stock, 1897], p. 1). Parish and township vestries across England had their electoral franchise altered by the Sturges Bournes Act of 1818 (58 George III c. 69).

19. An Act for the Appointment and Payment of Parish Constables (5 and 6 Vict, c.109); *Sheffield Independent*, 8 Apr. 1843.

20. *Sheffield Independent*, 7 Sept. 1839, Letter from John Parker MP to John Staniforth, Improvement Commission Law Clerk.

21. M. Weber, *The Theory of Social and Economic Organisation* (New York: Free Press, 1947), p. 156; K.B. Klockars, *The Idea of Police* (Beverley Hills, CA: Sage, 1985), p. 12; N. Elias, *The Civilising Process: The History of Manners and State Formation and Civilisation* [trans. E. Jephcott] (Oxford: Blackwell, 1994) (fp. 1939), pp. 345–6.

22. I. Inkster, 'Social Class and Popularised Culture in Sheffield during the 1840s', *Transactions of the Hunter Archaeological Society*, 12 (1983), pp. 82–7, esp. p. 83.

23. S. Pollard, *A History of Labour in Sheffield* (Liverpool: Liverpool University Press, 1959), pp. 125–6.

24. D. Smith, *Conflict and Compromise: Class Formation in English Society, 1830–1914, A Comparative Study of Birmingham and Sheffield* (London: Routledge, 1982), pp. 7, 45.

25. See M. Walton, *Sheffield: Its Story and Achievements* (Sheffield: Sheffield Telegraph, 1952), pp. 176–7; and B. Barber, 'Sheffield Borough Council, 1843–1893' in C. Binfield and D. Martin, et al. (eds), *The History of the City of Sheffield 1843–1993, Vol. 1: Politics* (Sheffield: Sheffield Academic Press, 1993), pp. 25–52, esp. pp. 27–8.

26. The exception were the 16 members of the Town Trust, and officers of the Cutlers Company, who sat on it *ex officio*.

27. *Sheffield Independent*, 6 Jan. 1838.

28. See E.P. Thompson, 'The State of the Nation' *Writing by Candlelight* (London: Merlin, 1980), p. 207.

29. Morris, 'The Middle Class', p. 299.

30. See F.K. Donnelly, 'The Destruction of the Sheffield School of Anatomy in 1835: A Popular Response to Class Legislation', *Transactions of the Hunter Archaeological Society*, 10 (1979), pp. 167–71.

31. For details see C.A. Williams, 'Police and Crime in Sheffield, 1818–1874', unpublished PhD thesis, University of Sheffield, 1998, p. 69.

32. *Sheffield Mercury*, 10 Sept. 1836.

33. *Sheffield Independent*, 8 Jul., 5 Aug. and 9 Sept. 1837; *Sheffield Mercury*, 12 Aug. 1837.

34. Barber, 'Sheffield Borough Council' p. 27.
35. *Sheffield Independent*, 9 June, 8 Sept., 10 Nov. and 10 Dec. 1838.
36. *Sheffield Independent*, 11 Aug. 1838.
37. *Sheffield Local Register*, 15 May 1833, p. 254; *Sheffield Independent*, 5 Apr. and 10 May 1834.
38. John Parker was the son of Hugh Parker, the JP (*Sheffield Independent*, 7 Sept. 1839).
39. An Act for the Establishment of County and District Constables by the Authority of Justices of the Peace (3 + 4 Vict. c. 93).
40. See S.H. Palmer, *Police and Protest in England and Ireland, 1780–1850* (Cambridge: Cambridge University Press, 1988), pp. 423–27, 438–45, on its creation: notwithstanding the arguments advanced by David Taylor, who opposes Palmer's Chartist-driven interpretation, and considers the 1839 Act best considered as an addition to the range of policing options that had developed in the previous ten years or so: D. Taylor, *The New Police in Nineteenth Century England: Crime, Conflict and Control* (Manchester: Manchester University Press, 1997), pp. 28–9. John Parker's own words gainsay this: 'The necessity of establishing the foundation of a police force, before Parliament separates, in the present state of the country, is the only justification for taking up so large and difficult a subject at this period of the Session': Letter of Parker to John Staniforth of the Improvement Commission, 10 Aug., in *Sheffield Independent*, 7 Sept. 1839.
41. *Sheffield Independent*, 26 Sept. 1840.
42. *Sheffield Independent*, 11 Apr. and 26 Sept. 1840.
43. *Sheffield Independent*, 15 Feb. 1840: report of Improvement Commission meeting.
44. An Act for improving the Police in Manchester ... (2 + 3 Vict. c. 87); An Act for improving the Police in Birmingham ... (2 + 3 Vict, c. 88). In Parliament, these measures prompted heated characterisations of them as French-style centralising innovations (C. Emsley, *The English Police: A Political and Social History* [Harlow: Longmans, 1991], p. 42).
45. *Sheffield Mercury*, 4 Apr. 1840.
46. See, *inter alia*, the editorials in the *Sheffield Independent* for 3 Oct., 10 Oct., and 24 Oct. 1840.
47. Between 1818 and 1848, many voluntary associations with a concern with public order were extant in Sheffield, among them the Association for the Prosecution of Felons, the Association for the Protection of Trade, and the Sabbath Observance Society. All these were unable significantly to intervene in the arena they had chosen for themselves, or to establish an institutional existence. This is consistent with the patterns analysed by R.J. Morris, 'Voluntary Societies and British Urban Elites, 1780–1850 – an analysis', *Historical Journal*, 26 (1983), pp. 95–118.
48. The editorial of *The Independent* described how the activities of the new Lancashire police in Bury 'a gratuitous and officious meddling with the harmless amusements of the people ... produced retaliation, and the policemen had their heads broken. Such is the natural effect of the system': *Sheffield Independent*, 10 Oct. 1840. The level of popular antipathy to the New Police has been described by R.D. Storch, 'The Plague of the Blue Locusts: Police Reform and Popular Resistance in Northern England, 1840–1857', *International Review of Social History*, 20 (1975), pp. 61–89.

CHAPTER NINE

Politics, ideology and the governance of health care in Sheffield before the NHS*

Tim Willis

Introduction

The recent increased use of the term 'governance', is related to late twentieth century political developments such as decentralisation, devolution, and privatisation which have seen an increase in the use of agencies and a boom in the complex nexus of bodies forming the networks and partnerships that shape and implement policy. Governance has been related to the emergence of the minimal state, where local authorities were part of a network involving government and other agencies.[1] For Rhodes 'governance stands for a change in the meaning of government, referring to a *new* process of governing; or a *changed* condition of ordered rule; or a *new* method by which society is governed'. He uses the term to 'refer to *self-organising, inter-organisational networks*'.[2]

The key novelty of governance has been to blur the distinction between the state and civil society.[3] The concept can also help with the description of the increased differentiation in the formation and delivery of policy from 1979, and the allied decrease in the government's role in public service provision. Such novelty can be questioned if we examine the nature of local government in the interwar years. This is demonstrated here through a discussion of the medical and health services in Sheffield in the 1920s and 1930s.

The governance of health care before the NHS featured a network of separate agencies with local authorities as a key political element. A recent study of maternity care in Sheffield in the late nineteenth and early twentieth centuries, concluded that 'both the Council and voluntary groups, pursued policies that were based on pragmatism and consensus … the tone of all groups was pragmatic rather than ideological'.[4] However an examination of specialist health care journals, political party records, voluntary group records and Medical Officer of Health (MOH) reports, showed that health policy before the NHS was more than a technical matter of service delivery.[5] The governance of health was an arena determined by ideology as much as pragmatism, and where conflict was as common as consensus.

The governance of nineteenth-century Sheffield set the context for the social and political processes of the 1920s notably the anti-socialism espoused by the Liberal and Conservative Citizens Alliance, in office from 1919 to 1926. In office since 1926, the Labour Party in Sheffield brought a variety of approaches to the pre-NHS health service. Municipal socialism was especially important.[6] The example of the medical crisis of an epidemic of smallpox in late 1926 and early 1927 brought ideological concerns to the fore. The chapter argues that politics and ideological debate were very relevant to the formulation and implementation of health policy in Sheffield, in the decades prior to the NHS.

Sheffield and its governance

For most of the nineteenth century the administration of Sheffield had been conducted along the lines of a minimal local state. Bodies such as the Town Trustees, the Cutlers Company, and the Church Burgesses had a variety of seignorial, industrial and religious origins and performed functions which were largely uncoordinated. Even after its late incorporation in 1843, Sheffield was slow to develop a municipal mentality.[7] Civic pride, in terms of nineteenth-century 'gas and water' municipal socialism, was a late and brief episode in Sheffield's history which occurred in the closing years of the nineteenth-century. The water supply was purchased for the borough in 1888, largely as a reaction to the loss of 240 lives in the Sheffield Flood of 1864, when the privately owned Dale Dyke Reservoir burst its banks.[8] The gas supply remained in private hands until nationalisation in 1948. The Conservative administration in the last decade of the nineteenth century purchased the markets from the Duke of Norfolk in 1899, as well as purchasing the tramways and the electricity supply. The ultimate symbol of civic pride, the Town Hall, was opened in Sheffield in 1897, much later than other northern towns, and some 50 years after Leeds Town Hall.[9] In the late nineteenth-century cities, such as Birmingham, with a record of strong civic and municipal vision had a well-developed middle-class associational life with strong urban institutions. By way of contrast, Sheffield, with its peculiar class structure and overwhelming reliance on metal trades, had strong integration at the working-class neighbourhood level through networks of workshop, chapel, pub, and home, but a weak integration at a city-wide level.[10] Middle-class attempts at instigating an associational culture such as the athenaeum movement were spectacularly unsuccessful in nineteenth-century Sheffield.[11] Labour organisations, on the other hand, thrived.[12]

Urbanisation

Urbanisation and its parallel process industrialisation, forged the basis of the social and political character of Sheffield. For one of England's largest cities Sheffield is unusual in being neither a port, nor an administrative centre nor a communications centre. In his *Sheffield: A Civic Survey*, in 1924, Abercrombie stated that 'Sheffield is perhaps the largest purely manufacturing town in the country.'[13] Sheffield exists because of its industry.[14] In 1920, 70,000 worked in the steel industry and large numbers were also engaged in allied trades such as cutlery, edge tool manufacture and engineering.[15] Manufacturing industry remained the largest sector of employment in Sheffield until well into the 1960s.[16] The population of the six townships that made up the parish of Sheffield in 1801 was 45,755. By the time of the first census after borough incorporation (1843), the population had trebled to 135,310. The city's population trebled again, so that by the early twentieth century there were half a million people living in the city.[17] Such a 'contagion of numbers' invited a response from those in authority to deal with the social stresses and strains.[18] Politicians and administrators in the twentieth-century city, were required to deal with the effects of nineteenth-century urbanisation. The 1920s was a crucial decade in the formation of effective working-class urban social movements.[19] In Sheffield, working-class political and cultural leaders made claims to represent the city which, as a generic spatial unit, has generally been regarded by historians as a middle-class locale.[20] British cities were adjusting to wider democracy with the increased franchise, and seeking to accommodate the radicalism inspired by the First World War. Efforts to elect a distinct working-class political party were deeply involved in the debates and controversies over health care in British cities and, in the case of Sheffield, in the formation of a working-class city.

Sheffield, 1919–26: the Citizens Alliance

There was a sense in the 1920s that Sheffield was developing a more 'civic' character, and that its township mentality, as a place divided by neighbourhood and topography, was in decline.[21] The prospect of Labour taking control of the council resulted in Liberal and Conservative forces uniting in a single political entity, the Citizens Alliance, which was in office from 1919 to 1926. Labour were developing a popular municipal vision, while the cheeseparing Citizens Alliance made a series of political blunders. The Citizens Alliance *raison d'être* was an entirely negative one of anti-socialism. In 1926, its right-wing Liberal leader, Sir William Clegg, declared 'the Socialist party policy [of municipalisation] is largely impractical and impossible to carry out'.[22] The 1920s saw consolidation in party politics, electoral politics and in the administration of the borough. Labour fought every municipal seat in the city for the first time in 1919, winning 45 per cent of the vote and 12 seats in a chamber of 64.[23] The Labour Party steadily increased its presence on the council until the victory of 1926.[24] In 1920 the Sheffield Federated Trades Council, a Lib-Lab body mainly concerned with workers in the 'light trades' of cutlery and tool manufacture, merged with (or was taken over by) its rival, the Sheffield Trades and Labour Council, a more left-wing organisation concerned with workers in the 'heavy trades' of steel manufacture and engineering.[25] Through consolidation at the urban scale the Labour movement in Sheffield enabled a civic mentality for a working-class city.

At local elections the Labour Party campaigned on such issues as the municipalisation of the milk supply, which under Liberal and Labour pressure was introduced by the Citizens Alliance in 1919, only to be abolished in 1922.[26] Where Labour developed a zeal for municipalisation, stating that, 'what the Citizens [Alliance] did with water, we want to do with coal, milk and other things', the anti-socialist group failed to deliver a coherent vision for the city.[27] Its main philosophy was one of 'economy' rather than investment. In 1921 the mouthpiece of the Right in the city, The *Sheffield Telegraph* supported the Citizens Alliance minimal state approach and boasted that spending per child on the school medical service was lower in Sheffield than in places like London, Manchester, Liverpool and Birmingham.[28] The Alliance's record in office was unlikely to make it electorally appealing to voters in a city with a large working class. It ended the policy of compounding where rates were collected as part of the weekly rent, and introduced a twice yearly lump sum. This reform favoured the landlord, but made life much more difficult for the tenant and resulted in high rent arrears and the imprisonment of 289 people in 1927 for non-payment of rates.[29] In 1923 the Citizens Alliance was involved in a scandal over housing when it was revealed that 147 notices had been sent by the Medical Officer of Health to members of the Health Committee including its Chairman, Councillor Kaye, regarding the poor state of properties which they owned.[30] The scandal resulted in Kaye, who had been tipped as a future council Leader, losing his seat and typified the Citizen's Alliance ambivalent attitude towards improving the fabric of the city.[31]

Health services

Aspects of health and medicine in Sheffield had long been based on a network of relationships involving local government and other agencies in partnership, which blurred the boundary between public and private sectors. In 1904, Sheffield was the first city to introduce a tuberculosis notification scheme.[32] This required the Medical Officer of Health to develop a good working relationship with general practitioners (GPs).[33] The university medical school established links with local industry and the local authority. Medical Officers of Health were made honorary professors of Public Health, and the university carried out the laboratory testing for the Public Health Department, until the authority opened its own laboratories in 1947.[34]

Since the mid-nineteenth century, health care in Sheffield had developed without any formal co-ordination, through the proliferation of a variety of separate agencies such as the Poor Law, public health, education, health insurance, local and central government initiatives as well as voluntary bodies. Hospital provision was split between charitable or voluntary hospitals, each with their separate governing boards, and hospitals provided by the state through the Poor Law. The interwar years were a time when the role of the local state in health service provision expanded, but the voluntary sector faced mounting problems of rising costs and falling charitable donations. In Sheffield the four voluntary hospitals responded by moving into the area of inter-hospital and inter-service partnerships. Some degree of co-ordination and co-operation between the state sector, the voluntary sector and private practice was legislated at the national level with the introduction of National Health Insurance in 1911, where GPs worked as Panel Doctors, and with the Local Government Act of 1929 which required local authorities to consult with voluntary hospitals before embarking on any expansion of local authority hospital facilities. The only area of state monopoly was preventive medicine. Initially this had been concerned solely with environmental improvement strategies. From the turn of the century preventive medicine or public health care, became increasingly involved in the delivery of personal health services and concerned with the health of the individual.

The local state acquired powers and local authority health care expanded within a wider patchwork of provision. Some 20 pieces of legislation were passed between the wars extending the role of local authority health care, into maternity and child welfare provision, tuberculosis, cancer schemes, the school medical service and venereal disease measures. After the Local Government Act of 1929, Sheffield City Council appropriated two former Poor Law hospitals to be run as general hospitals under the Health Committee, rather than the Public Assistance Committee. Limiting the operation of the Poor Law in the city was an important element of Labour ideology.[35]

The state provision of hospitals created potential tension between Medical Officers of Health and local authority Health Committees, and the GPs and voluntary groups involved in these networks of self-organising agencies. Although these agencies had totally separate administrative functions, there were significant points of contact. The personnel of committees and bodies involved in health care in Sheffield frequently overlapped in a city with a small middle class. Members of the Labour movement were therefore deeply involved in the voluntary bodies that provided health care.[36] As Labour formed the ruling group on the City Council from 1926, the boundary between the local state and local civil society was constantly blurred.

Although the Ministry of Health was established in 1919, it was in the localities on hospital boards and in the council chamber, that decisions were made over the direction of hospital policy. In Sheffield, the post 1918 hospital funding crisis facing the four voluntary hospitals prompted them to come together in the Joint Hospitals Council, chaired by the Lord Mayor and including representatives from the hospitals, the Chamber of Commerce, the Cutlers Company, the City Council, The Trades Council, the Insurance Committee, the Boards of Guardians, the British Hospitals Association, the press and the university. The council's aims were to secure the finances of the voluntary hospitals and make the people of Sheffield 'hospital conscious'.[37] The chosen means was a workers contributory health scheme, 'The Penny in the Pound Scheme' launched in 1921, built on strong traditions of working-class self-help and depended on the co-operation of voluntary hospitals, municipal hospitals, business, the Labour movement and the local authority. The Joint Hospitals Council introduced an element of grassroots democracy to its scheme through the creation of the Sheffield and District Association of Hospital Contributors, whose committee included representatives from the voluntary hospitals, the local authority, the Trades Council and the Poor Law Guardians. The scheme collected pro rata contributions in the workplace from wages, and entitled contributors and their dependants to free treatment at any of the Sheffield hospitals. The branches of the two retail co-operative societies in Sheffield were amongst the collecting points.[38] The Sheffield firms involved in the scheme paid their contribution which was one-third of the amount collected by employees.[39]

The Joint Hospitals Council scheme reduced the waiting lists of the voluntary hospitals by making use of the municipal hospitals; contributors were also covered by a reciprocal arrangement with other schemes if they needed to use hospital facilities when they were away from Sheffield.[40] Although the Labour movement was involved in the 'Penny in the Pound Scheme', and heavily represented on the boards of other voluntary groups concerned with health,[41] this was not a simple acceptance of the principle of voluntarism or deference to the existing arrangement of services. The Sheffield Trades Council initially condemned the principle of workers contributory schemes, and feared that the offer by the voluntary sector of workers representation in hospital control, was likely to be tokenism.[42] Though Sheffield appears to have been a city where co-ordination between the voluntary and municipal hospital service worked well, the official Labour policy throughout the period was for a complete public medical service administered by local authorities.[43] The Labour Party felt that voluntary hospitals would gradually be absorbed into a state-run health service as the public finance of health care increased.

The style of local governance of hospitals developed in Sheffield was due to a mix of pragmatism and ideology on both sides of the hospital divide. The voluntary hospital boards and consultant staff wished to maintain their control in the face of mounting financial problems. Labour wished to see a state-run health care system administered through local government.[44] Before 1948 there was no nationally defined hospital system. In most of Britain individual hospitals existed in isolation. The general lack of collaboration at city level and on a regional or national basis was a constant point of contention for critics of pre-1948 hospital arrangements.[45] Sheffield's nascent foundation of a system of local hospital governance was unusual and was ended by the central government decision to nationalise rather than 'municipalise' the health service in 1948. The decision to remove any semblance of local democratic control in British health care split the Cabinet, and 'pluralism fundamentally lost out when Aneurin Bevan defeated Herbert Morrison's wise argument for the new health service to be run by local government'.[46] When Labour came to power in Sheffield as early as 1926 notions of municipal socialism informed the health policy of the city.

Sheffield from 1926: municipal socialism

The Sheffield Labour Party manifesto in the municipal elections of 1926 proclaimed that the party was 'pledged to unfettered extension and development in every phase of municipal activity'.[47] From 1926, urban governance in Sheffield became synonymous with municipal socialism. The Labour Party in Sheffield appropriated the term 'municipal socialism' from critics as a positive expression of their civic vision. In the party's published assessment of its first six years in office under the heading *Municipal Socialism* Labour claimed that its programme 'has been wherever possible to use the great municipal machine for the improvement of the city and bring the greatest health, educational and cultural benefits to the people'.[48] The Labour Party's vision for the city included slum clearance, house-building, the provision of public wash-houses, maternity and child welfare facilities, and an extended tuberculosis service.[49] The first reforms instigated by Labour, after coming to power in 1926 showed a zeal for municipal government. Labour established a Direct Works Department to build schools and houses, introduced superannuation for council employees, replaced the old shambles with a new market centre, created a municipal printing works, banned the Officer Training Corps from city schools, and set about streamlining the administrative efficiency of local government in Sheffield.[50]

Health care was in the foreground in this programme of reform. The reorganisation of the council committee system resulted in the Health Committee being increased from 15 to 21 members; it also took on parks and burial grounds, weights and measures and the care of the mentally defective for the first time. The Citizens Association objected to this rationalisation on the grounds that care of the mentally defective should not be part of the health committee and that the new rationalised committee would be unwieldy. Labour were not afraid to combine public health measures with a direct intervention in the market economy, and in 1929 the Labour Council closed down the city's 166 private slaughterhouses and replaced them with a single municipal abattoir.[51]

The ideological meaning of this restructuring of urban government was openly expressed. The Leader of the council stated that, 'In Sheffield we are hoping to make our local contribution to bringing about a real socialist commonwealth'.[52] National Labour leaders, such as Arthur Greenwood, agreed that 'the best and easiest path to socialism in this country is through local government'.[53] Recognising the influence of this ideological mindset on the formulation of social policy is a useful way to examine key concerns such as democracy, power, and the public interest. In the 1920s, the Labour Party in Sheffield began a process of adjusting to democracy. After 1926 there were tensions in the Labour movement over where the Labour movement ended, and where the City Council began.[54] To all intents and purposes, in terms of candidate selection, deciding which wards to contest and in drafting election manifestos, the Trades Council was the borough Labour Party. Once Labour had been elected to office, Communist and ILP elements of the Trades Council complained that policy was being made by the City Council Labour Group without recourse to its parent body, the Trades Council. In 1927, a motion to have the Executive Committee of the Trades Council attend the meetings and vote on all decisions of the City Council Labour Group was defeated, among calls that the Trades Council was being used, 'as a jumping off ground for second rate politicians'.[55]

Like several other British cities Sheffield has a reputation as a Labour citadel. However historians need to be careful of painting an essentialist picture of places; for instance, Liverpool did not see a Labour majority on the City Council until 1955. Even though Sheffield has been under Labour control since 1926, its reputation as a Labour citadel and as a centre for municipal socialism was made through a process of struggle and re-invention.[56] The identity of a place is therefore best seen as a dynamic phenomenon, as a process, something which is made and remade, and is therefore a protean form. In Massey's terms, 'it may be useful to think of places, not as areas on maps, but as constantly shifting sets of social relations'.[57] The history of Sheffield as told by the Labour movement, for example in 1966 at the height of Wilsonian corporatism, painted the city as a national leader and exemplar, as both a Labour citadel and a progressive centre for social policy:

> The Sheffield Labour Party can be said to have anticipated the welfare state as we know it today by taking advantage of all the permissive legislation available, some of which only became mandatory later.[58]

This portrayal of the Left in Sheffield, as being constantly in the vanguard of health reform, is wrong. It ignores the role of conflict in the shaping of policy, such as ideological differences between voluntary and Poor Law hospitals before the NHS, and between the Medical Officer of Health and the Chairman of the Health Committee. The teleologically progressive narrative of Sheffield as a Labour city keen to develop municipal services, also ignores contrary cultural traits, such as a strong commitment to working-class self-help and independence such as that seen in the popularity of the Penny in The Pound Scheme. The scheme raised £5 million during 1922–48; it had 3,800 contributing firms, with a total of 360,000 individual contributors by 1948.[59] It still exists today as the non-profit-making Westfield Contributory Health Scheme.[60] The Labour movement's review of its own history also ignores the individualistic views of key protagonists involved in health care, and how these views were manifested in policy terms. Sheffield City Council from 1926 to 1948, showed a desire to provide a range of health services from maternity care through to cremation. However, over the issue of vaccination policy the attitude of key elements of the Labour movement in Sheffield such as the Trades Council, the left-wing press and the Chairman of the Health Committee, were in direct conflict with the attitude of the city's Medical Officer of Health.

Historians of British local government and social policy have praised the local authority health service in Sheffield before 1939.[61] Against this assessment, Mike Savage, in his analysis of working-class politics in the late nineteenth and early twentieth centuries, has stated how the health policy of Sheffield City Council could be cited as an example of statist patriarchy. This was most apparent in the fact that the council was keen to promote care for tuberculosis sufferers (which in a metal town like Sheffield was a predominantly male disease), with hospital provision, rent rebates and rehousing schemes, while its record in the provision of maternity care was poor by comparison with other Labour areas such as the London Borough of Poplar or the Lancashire town of Nelson.[62]

In fact by the 1930s the lack of maternity and child welfare clinics on the new working-class suburban estates was regarded as scandalous by the Labour Council's critics on the left. The Communist Party noted how demand far outstripped supply for maternity and child welfare clinics, and argued that in a city with nearly half a million inhabitants there ought to be more than one clinic.[63] Sheffield's second maternity and child welfare clinic was not opened until 1938.[64] The Sheffield Women's Welfare Clinic, which was the local branch of the Family Planning Association, repeatedly contacted its London headquarters recommending that further branches be set up in Rotherham and other surrounding towns, as the Sheffield clinic was unable to cope with demand, and was swamped with requests for appointments from women in Sheffield and its region.[65] Rather than see the council as simply prioritising tuberculosis treatment over maternity care, in an expression of 'patriarchal statism', the limitations of the scope for local agency under the aegis of national legislation have to be taken into account. Under the system of *ultra vires*, the role of the local state was limited to the implementation of reforms sanctioned by central government in permissive and mandatory legislation. Whereas the 1921 Public Health (Tuberculosis) Act increased the responsibility of local authorities to treat tuberculosis sufferers, it was not until the late 1930s that legislation was introduced officially to regulate maternity care and introduce a professional midwifery service. Rather than criticise the council for failing to provide adequate maternity care perhaps it was more just to criticise all the agencies of maternity care in Sheffield.

Health policy for Labour in Sheffield was not simply a case of providing direct medical services but was part of the indirect municipal socialist policy of house-building. Health, housing and local government were intrinsically linked by statute, being the responsibility of the Ministry of Health. Housing was a contentious issue in Sheffield well before Labour came to power, and saw a cleavage along party lines between the Conservatives who favoured inner city tenement blocks and the Liberals and early Labour Party who promoted the idea of greenfield suburban developments.[66] Once in power from 1926, Labour took full advantage of national government subsidies and instigated a house-building programme that used direct labour and a substantial contribution from the rates. Three thousand houses were built by the council every year throughout the 1930s. The national figure for public sector compared to private sector building in the inter war years was 27.6 per cent, whereas in Sheffield the council was responsible for building 53.8 per cent of houses between the wars.[67] The targets for slum clearance and house-building were raised in the 1930s, and the new estates were significantly built along 'garden city' lines rather than inner city tenements. Private owner-occupied building was predominant in the west of the city, and council house-building in the east, which added to Sheffield's characteristic east–west polarisation.[68]

It is possible to see the Labour council's housing policy as showing signs of a statist and patriarchal approach, in the sense that Labour councillors from a tradition of temperance and Methodist non-conformism, argued that the new housing estates should be 'dry', or devoid of public houses.[69] However, it is also possible to appreciate housing policy, as part of an holistic health policy, and one that was ideologically driven. The Labour Council in the interwar years saw its first priority as the provision of decent accommodation. The first Labour Chairman of the Health Committee wrote, in his preface to the MOH Report of 1928, that it was no good removing tuberculosis sufferers to sanatoria, only to put them back into conditions where the disease thrived.[70] He also expressed how, through direct labour and council employment policies, the authority aimed to improve the economic position of the 'great mass of our fellow citizens' in order that they could afford good food and clothing to strengthen their resistance to disease.[71] Council housing and council employment became an important aspect of the city's identity.[72] In the 1930s the provision of health facilities including hospitals was also a major tenet of Labour's governance of the city, and an important aspect of municipal socialism in Sheffield.

Ideology and reactions to smallpox

In late 1926 and early 1927 there was an epidemic of smallpox in Sheffield, with 700 notified cases and one death. Smallpox epidemics had occurred in Britain in the nineteenth century and had led to compulsory infant vaccination; however, its application tended to be lax and in 1898, conscientious objectors were allowed to refuse to have their children vaccinated.[73] This crisis tested the health services of the city, and inadvertently revealed much about the ideology and pragmatism inherent in the governance of health care in Sheffield.

Lodge Moor isolation hospital had been built rapidly in 1888 to deal with a major smallpox epidemic.[74] From 1893 to 1922 Sheffield was free of smallpox, and Lodge Moor became an isolation hospital for other infectious diseases. However, from the early 1920s Sheffield and its surrounding counties noted an increase in the number of infections.[75] Conflicting notions over the management of the disease, and especially over vaccination, led to heated exchanges between the MOH and the new Labour Chairman of the Health Committee. Debates over vaccination were rife in Sheffield in the 1920s at a time when they had been largely settled in other towns. In late nineteenth-century Leicester, these debates had centred around opposition to state compulsion, and around the safety of the procedure. They had led to the development of an alternative strategy to deal with smallpox, relying on isolation rather than vaccination.[76] Unlike Leicester, the anti-vaccinators in Sheffield were offering no such alternative strategy. In Sheffield the Labour movement, in terms of the Trades Council and the Chairman of the Health Committee, were adamantly against smallpox vaccination in the 1920s, but on somewhat differing political and ideological grounds. The Trades Council felt that vaccination was a commercially driven treatment, designed to profit the drug companies. On the other hand William Asbury, the Chairman of the Health Committee argued that in order to prevent infectious disease like smallpox, it was the duty of the local authority to provide decent living conditions, rather than waste time and money on vaccination programmes. These views were aggressively expressed at the annual conference of The Royal Sanitary Institute in 1927. Compulsory vaccination not only infringed citizens' rights in Asbury's view but diverted attention from the fact that

> Smallpox is a filth disease and like all zymotics is amenable to sanitation. Our job is to work for a decent standard of life for the working class, place them in clean and healthy surroundings, and make them fully acquainted with the laws of personal hygiene.[77]

He noted that in 1926–1927 all but one of the 700 Sheffield cases reported were found in Attercliffe, a densely populated area of largely unregulated back-to-back housing and industry in the east end of the city.[78] In December 1926, the Trades Council newspaper expressed its brand of anti-vaccinationism: 'not until Socialism is achieved will we be free of the horrors of commercialised medicine, with its vaccines and vivisection and all the loathsome practices, some of which are unprintable here in which this pseudo-scientific spirit practices on the bodies of men'.[79]

On the other side of the debate was MOH, Fred Wynne, university trained, a career professional, appointed to Sheffield after serving as MOH in Wigan and Leigh. He was a strong and unusual character, an author, playwright and columnist for the *Manchester Guardian*.[80] Typical was his proposal in 1928 to ensure the safety of the milk supply in Sheffield, not by pasteurisation but through the even more drastic measure of having the entire milk supply of the city converted to powdered milk. Wynne argued that it would eradicate tuberculosis, and make milk easier to transport.[81] His background and training contributed to Wynne's science-based attitude to vaccination.[82] He noted how the public had rushed to be vaccinated in the outbreak of 1926–27 so that 100,000 people or one-fifth of the population of the city had been vaccinated against smallpox after 1925.

The police supervised queues outside many surgeries.[83] Wynne dismissed the anti-vaccinators' arguments that vaccination led to adverse reaction by saying that 'a certain class of patient attributes every ailment to vaccination.' He recognised that universal vaccination was impossible under modern democracy, but he still complained about the decision to allow people a choice of whether to be vaccinated and stated that this had given rise to 'the Conscientious objector who has never been asked to produce any evidence of being in possession of a conscience'.[84]

The two men interpreted the fact that the epidemic had been limited to the industrial area of Attercliffe in different ways.[85] For Asbury this was proof that overcrowding and unsanitary conditions made the inhabitants of the heavy industrial quarter of the city prone to disease. For Wynne this was proof of the success of the medical intervention of the Public Health Department in co-operation with the city's medical practitioners. Through a commitment to vaccination and medical intervention the MOH defended his role. As the smallpox hospital was used for tuberculosis patients, arrangements were made with a neighbouring local authority so that notified cases could be removed to a West Riding county council hospital (Hallwood Hall, Grenoside), but there were only 20 beds. The contacts of those infected had their keys confiscated and were accommodated at isolation cottages in the centre of Sheffield, where they were vaccinated and while their house was cleaned and fumigated with disinfectant by the Public Health Department. Those rehoused complained about the accommodation, and about having sheets, curtains, and linen ruined.[86] As the numbers of infected cases increased from October 1926 to February 1927, the city's accommodation for infectious disease cases was quickly filled and arrangements were made to isolate carriers and contacts in a 'campment' at Redmires, and eventually to isolate patients in their own homes. Asbury's argument that smallpox vaccination was an infringement of liberty could also stem from the practice of the MOH of publishing the initials and the full address of notified smallpox cases in his annual report.[87]

Wynne believed wholeheartedly in vaccination and said that in nearly 1,000 cases of smallpox from 1925 to 1927, the disease had not appeared in those that had been vaccinated within the last ten years.[88] With one-fifth of the population vaccinated against smallpox, by the end of the epidemic Sheffield was referred to as a 'vaccinated town'. Although there are many reasons affecting the incidence and spread of infectious disease, smallpox notifications in Sheffield showed a sharp drop after 1929, very different from Leicester which suffered over 1,000 cases a year in the early 1930s.[89]

Although public support seemed to go with the professional authority of the MOH validated by universities and career success, rather than the radical Labourist views of Asbury, both men were part of the policy network of governance and both drew on 'science' in their own way. Asbury was a key member of the council, Deputy Leader, Chair of the Health Committee, a Poor Law guardian, a JP, Chairman of the Public Assistance Committee from 1930, and Chairman of the Regional Smoke Abatement Committee. He was a signatory of the Minority Report of the Royal Commission on Unemployment in 1932. After serving on the City Council for 22 years he went on to be Deputy Regional Commissioner for Civil Defence Southern Region from 1942 to 1945, Land Commissioner for North-Rhine-Westphalia from 1946 to 1948, and Land Commissioner for Schleswig-Holstein from 1948 to 1950. He was made Deputy Chairman of the National Assistance Board in 1954.[90] Asbury and Wynne both argued their case on smallpox vaccination through the evidence of scientific experts. Asbury referred to papers in *The Lancet* linking vaccination and encephalitis. He noted that that other diseases such as measles and whooping cough were far bigger killers, but that the government and the medical profession appeared to be obsessed with smallpox. Wynne wanted more severe government control and believed that 'infected areas' should be declared and 'the government should have powers to prescribe any measures in that area' which they believed necessary after consultation with their expert advisers'.[91]

As well as viewing smallpox vaccination as scientifically unsound, irrelevant and expensive, Asbury saw vaccination as an ideological issue, as an infringement of liberty. The practice of vaccination in the 1920s was no mere injection with a modern hypodermic syringe. Vaccinators applied calf lymph to three or four fairly large lesions made on the patient's arm or leg. Vaccination in the early twentieth century was a serious assault on the body, and employers in Sheffield reported heavy absenteeism during the height of the epidemic, following the rush to vaccination.[92]

The episode illustrates how the ideology of the Left questioned the right of the central state, backed by the medical profession to frame the city's approach to health care. From Asbury's sanitarian perspective, vaccination as public health was nothing more than a palliative and a distraction from the main problem of providing decent living conditions for the inhabitants of the city. For Asbury the governance of local authority health care in Sheffield, was primarily concerned with improving the environment through better housing. Despite implementing the policy of vaccination under its legal obligation as the local authority, elements of the Labour movement in Sheffield showed a vehement reluctance to defer to the expert public health knowledge of the MOH. Answering questions over the epidemic in the council chamber, Asbury attempted publicly to undermine the work of the MOH, by stating that a patient had to have her arm amputated after an adverse reaction to vaccination. His evidence was based on the testimony of a fellow councillor. After investigation by the MOH the story turned out to be a fabrication, although it had achieved its purpose of publicity for anti-vaccinationism.[93]

In the 1920s, Labour in Sheffield saw public health as a matter of improving the environment. By the 1930s many medical aspects of health policy were embraced by a council which was increasingly keen to consolidate its local powers and to develop its role as a provider of general hospitals. Following the 1929 Local Government Act a former Poor Law hospital, Firvale Infirmary, became the City General, with a resident staff, and a full-time radiologist and pathologist who worked with the university medical school in a similar manner to the voluntary hospitals. The City General also saw the building of a maternity block, operating theatres, a casualty and out-patient department. Ideological and class concerns were behind the development of the City General, as it was located in the industrial east end of the city, whereas the other former Poor Law hospital appropriated, was at Nether Edge, in the more affluent west side of Sheffield and, although improvements were made, Nether Edge Hospital was not developed to the same extent as the City General. As well as hospital development in the 1930s, the council introduced a domiciliary midwife service, a child guidance clinic and a radiography service; in 1937 the council attempted to take over control of South Yorkshire Mental Hospital from the West Riding County Council.[94] In showing a progressive attitude towards the development of an increasingly comprehensive health service, Labour in Sheffield fully expected to play a significant part in the National Health Service (NHS) of 1948.

Although Labour in the localities became very much a part of the formation of health services before the NHS, notions of Labour's 'progressive' attitude towards health policy require careful reading over issues such as vaccination. The episode illustrates that conflict and ideology were an important element of the governance of health care before the NHS.

Conclusion

Use of the term 'governance' can be seen as a mere linguistic development; on its own it does not constitute an advance, or indeed shed any new light on the history of policy-making. The complex of interorganisational networks of service providing agencies, that have been a feature of the last two decades of the twentieth century are not necessarily a new development. Notions of governance refocus attention away from mono-causal and linear accounts of health care. An analysis of the variety of ideological strands that shaped aspects of the pre-NHS health policy, produces a more pluralistic picture of the form and style of urban government in the early twentieth century when questions about 'who governed?', and 'where did power lie?' are asked. The decisions that were made by elected politicians and appointed officials, as well as the use of the specialist knowledge of experts, were not entirely based on pragmatism. The influence of ideology in the development of health and welfare policy in twentieth-century British cities shaped many choices. There is scope for fruitful work in the archives of town halls, local political parties and the not-for-profit organisations that existed before 1948, exploring the blurring of the boundary between the state and civil society and dissecting the power relations between appointed officials and elected politicians. Adopting an analytical approach which embraces the governance of health care rather than tracing the development of the government of health care, it is useful to identify a more politicised definition of governance. Conflict and ideological debate are an essential aspect of healthy civil society, just as differing notions over the legitimate exercise of power, are essential to politics. The tendency to see governance as the consensual management of partnerships and networks, tends to leave out a role for politics and ideology. Health policy in Britain before the NHS is one example where ideology can be seen to have informed local governance. Policy is not made in an ideological vacuum, and a broad definition of ideology helps us to appreciate the ways in which politics has an influence on networks of policy-makers in all epochs. Jones has stated in relation to the 1990s and the twenty-first century: 'Whether it is local government or local governance someone somewhere will be taking key decisions affecting the welfare of citizens and their local communities'.[95] Whether we recognise this pattern of decision-making, as 'governance', 'pluralism' or as the 'mixed economy of welfare', we can be certain that ideology has been in the past, and will continue to be an important contributory factor in shaping decisions.

Notes

* I would like to thank Mick Worboys, the editors and participants at the Urban History Group meeting at Leeds 1998 for their helpful comments on earlier versions of this chapter. All mistakes remain my own.
1. G. Stoker, *Local Governance in Britain*, University of Strathclyde, Department of Government Papers (Glasgow: 1994).
2. R.A.W. Rhodes, 'Diplomacy in Governance', *Politics Review*, 7 (1998), p. 24 (emphasis in original).
3. R.A.W. Rhodes, *Understanding Governance: Policy Networks, Governance, Reflexivity and Accountability* (Milton Keynes: Open University, 1997), pp. 47.

4. T. McIntosh, 'A Price Must be Paid for Motherhood: The Experience of Maternity in Sheffield, 1879–1939', unpublished PhD thesis, University of Sheffield, 1997, pp. 45, 220.

5. M. Freeden, 'The Stranger at the Feast: Ideology and Public Policy in Twentieth Century Britain', *Twentieth Century British History*, 1 (1990), pp. 9–34; H. Eckstein, *The English Health Service: Its Origins, Structure and Achievements* (Oxford: Oxford University Press, 1959), p. 102; C. Webster, 'Labour and the Origin of the National Health Service', in N.A. Rupke (ed.), *Science Politics and the Public Good* (London: Macmillan, 1988), pp. 184–202; C. Webster, 'Conflict and Consensus: Explaining the British Health Service', *Twentieth Century British History*, 1 (1990), pp. 115–51.

6. Municipal socialism in this context refers to an ideological vision for the city implemented by self-identified socialists and based on a redistribution of profits from municipal enterprise to fund services rather than lower the rates. Late Victorian and Edwardian 'municipal socialism' is perhaps better termed 'municipal trading'.

7. In the mid-nineteenth century, A.J. Mundella commented: 'I see a pretty state of things in your municipality. Everything is mean, petty and narrow in the extreme. What a contrast to Leeds! Sheffield would do well to spend half a million on improvements. A better Town Hall might be followed by better Town Councillors and more public spirit.' Quoted in D.E. Fletcher, 'Aspects of Liberalism in Sheffield, 1849–1886', unpublished PhD thesis, University of Sheffield, 1972, p. 91.

8. J. Cass, 'Water Supply', in C. Binfield (ed.), *The History of the City of Sheffield, vol. 2 Society* (Sheffield: Sheffield Academic Press, 1993), pp. 119.

9. A. Briggs, *Victorian Cities* (Harmondsworth: Penguin, 1968), pp. 237.

10. Neighbourhood or township democracy in the form of public meetings was encouraged as a bulwark against the tyranny of the municipality by Chartist leaders such as Isaac Ironside. B. Barber, 'Sheffield Borough Council, 1843–1893', in C. Binfield (ed.), *The History of the City of Sheffield, vol. 1, Politics* (Sheffield: Sheffield Academic Press, 1993), pp. 25–52; Dennis Smith, *Conflict and Compromise. Class Formation in English Society, 1830–1914* (London: Routledge, 1982), pp. 160–72

11. A. White, 'Class Culture and Control: The Athenaeum Movement and the Middle Class, 1847–64', in J. Wolff and J. Seed (eds), *The Culture of Capitalism: Art, Power and the Nineteenth-Century Middle Class* (Manchester: Manchester University Press, 1988), pp. 113–15.

12. See S. Pollard, *A History of Labour in Sheffield* (Liverpool: Liverpool University Press, 1959).

13. P. Abercrombie, *Sheffield: A Civic Survey and Suggestions Towards a Development Plan* (University Press of Liverpool, Hodder and Stoughton, 1924), p. 6.

14. R. Burns, 'The City as Not London', in M. Fisher and U. Owen, *Whose Cities?* (London: Penguin, 1991), pp. 62–70.

15. G. Tweedale, *Steel City: Entrepreneurship, Strategy and Technology in Sheffield, 1743–1993* (Oxford: Clarendon Press), p. 15.

16. W. Hampton, *Democracy and Community: A Study of Politics in Sheffield* (Oxford: Clarendon Press, 1970), p. 43.

17. A.D.H. Crook, 'Population and Boundary Changes, 1801–1981', in C. Binfield (ed.), *The History of the City of Sheffield, vol. 2, Society* (Sheffield: Sheffield Academic Press, 1993), pp. 482–3.

18. J.A. Banks, 'The Contagion of Numbers', in H.J. Dyos and M. Wolff (eds),

The Victorian City: Images and Realities (London: Routledge and Kegan Paul, 1973).

19. M. Savage, 'Urban History and Social Class: Two Paradigms', *Urban History*, 20 (1993), pp. 61–77; G. Rose, 'Imagining Poplar in the 1920s: Contested Concepts of Community', *Journal of Historical Geography*, 16 (1990) pp. 425–37.

20. Morris has suggested that 'the British towns of the industrial revolution were substantially the creation of the middle class and in turn provided the theatre within which that middle class sought, extended, expressed and defended its power', R.J. Morris, 'The Middle Class and British Towns of the Industrial Revolution, 1780–1870', in D. Fraser and A. Sutcliffe (eds), *The Pursuit of Urban History* (London: Arnold, 1983), p. 286. Savage has argued for a more neutral interpretation of the relationship between social class and place, where classes make places theirs through a process of struggle: Savage, 'Urban History', p. 72.

21. Despite incorporation in 1843 and achieving city status in 1893, Sheffield has a long tradition of being referred to as the biggest village in England. A report into smallpox in the late nineteenth century stated that 'the population of Sheffield is for so large a town, unique in its character, in fact it more closely resembles that of a village than a town, for over wide areas each person appears to be acquainted with every other person, and to be interested with that others concern': *Report on an Epidemic of Smallpox at Sheffield During 1887–8*, (Parliamentary Papers LXV, 1889), p. 286. Early twentieth-century developments towards organisation at the urban level included the merger of Sheffield's two Poor Law Unions, the Ecclesall Union and the Sheffield Union, into one city-wide body in 1925. See B.J. Elliot, 'The Last Five Years of the Sheffield Guardians', *Transactions of the Hunter Archaeological Society* (Sheffield: 1977), pp. 132–7.

22. *Sheffield Independent*, 23 October 1926.

23. *Sheffield Independent*, 3 November 1919.

24. Labour won 22 seats in 1923, 24 seats in 1925, and 38 in 1926: *Sheffield Yearbook* (Sheffield: 1923–26), *passim*.

25. S. Pollard, *A History of Labour in Sheffield* (Liverpool: 1959), p. 265.

26. Labour's adoption of municipalisation schemes was such that for a short time the party supported a policy for the introduction of a municipal currency: *Sheffield Independent*, 10 December 1919.

27. *Sheffield Co-operator*, November 1926.

28. *Sheffield Telegraph*, 11 March 1921.

29. A. Thorpe, 'The Consolidation of a Labour Stronghold, 1926–1951', in C. Binfield (ed.), *The History of the City of Sheffield, vol. 1 Politics* (Sheffield: Sheffield Academic Press, 1993), p. 88.

30. *Sheffield Mail*, 19 October 1923.

31. *Sheffield Year Book* (Sheffield: 1921). *Sheffield Independent*, 3 November 1923.

32. F.B. Smith, *The Retreat of Tuberculosis, 1850–1950* (London: Croom Helm, 1988), p. 15.

33. The MOH for Sheffield from 1897 to 1904, John Robertson, was responsible for establishing the pioneering tuberculosis notification scheme in Sheffield. Described as a 'great lab man', his MD thesis was concerned with the conditions governing the cause and distribution of consumption in England and Wales: Obituary, *Journal of the Royal Sanitary Institute*, 57 (1937), pp. 170–72.

34. S. Sturdy, 'The Political Economy of Scientific Medicine: Science Education and the Transformation of Medical Practice in Sheffield, 1890–1922', *Medical*

History 36 (1992), pp. 125–59.

35. Sheffield Labour Party, *Six Years of Labour Rule in Sheffield* (Sheffield: 1932), p. 18. On hospital appropriation see C. Webster, 'Health, Wealth and Welfare During the Depression', *Past and Present*, 109 (1985), pp. 204–30. The majority of beds were still operated under the Poor Law by 1937. B. Abel-Smith, *The Hospitals in England and Wales, 1800–1948* (Cambridge, Massachusetts: Harvard University Press, 1964), p. 371. On practicality versus ideology, M. Powell, 'An Expanding Service: Municipal Acute Medicine in the 1930s', *Twentieth Century British History*, 8 (1997), pp. 334–57.

36. William Asbury was chairman of the Health Committee as well as Deputy Leader of the City Council 1926–42; he was also chairman of the Regional Smoke Abatement Committee, and a subscriber to the Sheffield Women's Welfare Clinic. William Hart the Town Clerk in the 1920s was also clerk to the Sheffield National Health Insurance Committee. Ernest Rowlinson, Leader of the City Council 1926–41, was Chairman of the Education Committee and six other Committees; he was a also a member of the Nuffield Provincial Hospitals Trust. George Fletcher, Communist Organiser for Sheffield and Master Baker, was also a Poor Law guardian for the Darnall area of Sheffield. Sheffield City Council Minutes of the Health Committee, 1926–42, *passim*; *Annual Report of the Sheffield Women's Welfare Clinic* (1933); W.E. Hart, 'Hospitals as Affected by the Local Government Act, 1929', *Journal of the Royal Sanitary Institute*, 50 (1930), pp. 469–80; J. Bellamy and J. Saville, *Dictionary of Labour Biography*, vol. 6 (London: Macmillan, 1982), p. 235 and vol. 9 (London: Macmillan, 1993), pp. 83–91.

37. Sheffield and District Association of Hospital Contributors, *Record of the Penny in the Pound Scheme, 1919–1948* (Sheffield: 1949).

38. Sheffield and District Association of Hospital Contributors, *Penny in the Pound Scheme* (Sheffield: 1949), p. 12.

39. Sheffield and District Association of Hospital Contributors, *Record of the Penny in the Pound Scheme*, p. 21.

40. Ibid.

41. The majority of subscribers to the voluntary society, the Sheffield Women's Welfare Clinic, were local Co-operative Societies and ward Labour Parties. *Annual Reports*, Sheffield Women's Welfare Clinic (1933–39), *passim*.

42. Sheffield City Archives, LD 1638 M.F. A.159 Sheffield Trades and Labour Council, minutes of the Executive Committee, 29/11/1920.

43. Trades Union Congress and Labour Party, *Preventive and Curative Services* (London: 1922). See series of articles by Somerville Hastings (Surgeon, MP for Reading in the 1920s and Barking in the 1930s, Chairman of the London County Council Hospital and Medical Services Committee, Socialist Medical Association Delegate to Labour Party Conferences). Hastings condemned voluntary hospitals as undemocratic and workers' contributory schemes as objectionable and called for a national health care system administered by local authorities, financed through the rates and from exchequer grants. This was Labour Party policy for the 30 years prior to the NHS Act. 'Labour and the Hospitals', *Labour Magazine*, 2 (1924), pp. 54–6; 'Nationalisation of Hospitals', *Labour Magazine*, 4 (1926), pp. 489–500; 'The Hopeless Position of the Hospitals: Why a National System is Necessary', *Labour Magazine*, 4 (1926), pp. 535–7. See, J. Stewart, 'Socialist Proposals for Health Reform in Inter-War Britain: The Case of Somerville Hastings', *Medical History*, 39 (1995), pp. 338–57.

44. By 1937 Labour had gained control of 77 English and Scottish municipalities.

E. Taplin, Review of S. Davies, *Liverpool Labour: Social and Political Influences on the Development of the Labour Party in Liverpool, 1900–1939*; *Labour History Review*, 63 (1998), pp. 221–2.

45. Political and Economic Planning, *Britain's Health* (London: Pelican, 1939), p. 121. For a contemporary critique by an MOH of the haphazard pre-1948 hospital system see D.C. Lamont, 'The Hospital Services', *Journal of the Royal Sanitary Institute*, 66 (1935), pp. 9–16.

46. B. Crick, Review of A. Etzioni, *The Golden Rule: Community and Morality in a Democratic Society, Independent on Sunday*, 5 July 1997.

47. *Sheffield Independent,* 15 October 1926.

48. Sheffield Labour Party, *Six Years of Labour Rule in Sheffield 1926–1932* (Sheffield: 1932), p. 3.

49. 'Co-operative Labour Policy of Civic Government: A Progressive Charter for Sheffield Ratepayers', *Sheffield Co-operator*, November 1926.

50. *Sheffield Independent*, 23 February 1927, 5 May 1927.

51. Sheffield Labour Party, *Six Years*, p. 11.

52. E.G. Rowlinson, 'Why Sheffield is a Labour Stronghold', *Labour Magazine*, 6 (1926), p. 355.

53. Arthur Greenwood speech at Special Conference of the Labour Party, Montgomery Hall Sheffield 1927: *Sheffield Independent*, 11 April 1927.

54. Even prior to 1926 the distinction between the Labour Group on the City Council and the Trades Council had become blurred as Ernest Rowlison was leader of both between 1922 and 1926.

55. George Fletcher – Communist Organiser for Sheffield, local businessman, Trades Council delegate, and Poor Law guardian – stated: 'We should accept that we do control the affairs of the city. While we cannot do it constitutionally through our own body we can delegate men to do it for us. We don't need these men there in order that they may have Councillor before their name but because they should carry out the policy of the Trades and Labour Council': *Sheffield Independent*, 23 February 1927.

56. D. Massey, 'Places and their Pasts', *History Workshop Journal*, 39 (1995), pp. 182–92.

57. Ibid., p. 186.

58. Sheffield Labour Party, *Forty Years of Labour Rule* (Sheffield: 1966), p. 28.

59. Sheffield and District Association of Hospital Contributors, *Record of the Penny in the Pound Scheme*, p. 19. The Penny in the Pound Scheme had 220,000 contributors by 1926: *Sheffield Year Book* (Sheffield: 1926), p. 233.

60. In 1993 the income of the Westfield Contributory Health Scheme, an authorised insurance company that gives cash benefits for health expenses, was over £13 million, with assets over £11 million: Westfield Contributory Health Scheme, *Westfield People Seventy Fifth Anniversary* (Sheffield: 1994), p. 4.

61. R. Earwicker, 'The Labour Movement and the Creation of the National Health Service, 1906–1948', unpublished PhD thesis, University of Birmingham, 1982, p. 288; J. Rowett, The Labour Party and Local Government: Theory and Practice in the Inter-war Years', unpublished DPhil thesis, University of Oxford, 1979, p. 342.

62. M. Savage, *The Dynamics of Working Class Politics: The Labour Movement in Preston, 1880–1940* (Cambridge: 1987), pp. 31–2.

63. Communist Party of Great Britain Sheffield Branch, *Sheffield: the People's Policy for the City* (Sheffield: 1938), p. 7.

64. Sheffield Corporation, *Firth Park Maternal and Child Welfare Centre: Opening Ceremony* (Sheffield: 1938).

65. Correspondence between Sheffield Women's Welfare Clinic and National Birth Control Association. FPA A4/A 14.1, Contemporary Medical Archive Centre, Wellcome Institute for the History of Medicine, London.

66. S.M. Gaskell, 'Sheffield City Council and the Development of Suburban Areas Prior to World War One', in S. Pollard and C. Holmes (eds), *Essays in the Economic and Social History of South Yorkshire* (Sheffield: 1972), pp. 187–202.

67. P. Dickens, S. Duncan, M. Goodwin and F. Gray, *Housing, States and Localities* (London: Methuen, 1985), p. 166.

68. A.D.H. Crook, 'Needs, Standards and Affordability: Housing Policy After 1914', in C. Binfield (ed.), *The History of the City of Sheffield, 1843–1993, vol. 2 Society* (Sheffield: Sheffield Academic Press, 1993), pp. 76–99.

69. The council held a referendum on each of the new housing estates to gauge public opinion over the 'dry' estate policy. Of nine estates polled the five largest voted for licenced accommodation. The council refused to build the pubs leasing the land for one pub on each estate to developers and imposing restrictive licences: Thorpe, 'Consolidation', p. 103.

70. *Medical Officer of Health Report for Sheffield 1928* (Sheffield: 1929), p. 1.

71. Ibid.

72. A. Thorpe, 'Consolidation', p. 118.

73. E.P. Hennock, 'Vaccination Policy Against Smallpox, 1835–1914: A Comparison of England with Prussia and Imperial Germany', *Social History of Medicine*, 11 (1998), pp. 49–71.

74. C. Shaw, 'A Review of Infectious Diseases in Sheffield' typescript, (Sheffield Central Library Local Studies Library, 1993).

75. *Medical Officer of Health Report for Sheffield*, 1927.

76. S.M.F. Fraser, 'Leicester and Smallpox: The Leicester Method', *Medical History*, 24 (1980), pp. 315–32.

77. W. Asbury, 'The Case Against Vaccination', *The Journal of the Royal Sanitary Institute*, 48 (1927), pp. 140–50.

78. Ibid., 145.

79. *Sheffield Forward*, December, 1926.

80. Obituary, *Journal of the Royal Sanitary Institute*, 50 (1930), pp. 747–8.

81. F.E. Wynne. 'The Present Condition of the Milk Supply', *Journal of the Royal Sanitary Institute*, 49 (1928), pp. 3–12. Evidence of F.E. Wynne, Medical Officer of Health For Sheffield, House of Lords Select Committee on Sheffield Corporation Bill, 1928, HMSO, Parliamentary Papers, F 384.

82. Wynne's views on smallpox vaccination and on the links between the transfer of tuberculosis to humans through milk, were likely to have been shaped during his training and early working life in Lancashire. For the close association between university medical students, MOsH and clinicians in Manchester and its region see J.V. Pickstone, *Medicine and Industrial Society: A History of Hospital Development in Manchester and its Region, 1752–1946* (Manchester: Manchester University Press, 1985), pp. 226–7.

83. *Sheffield Independent*, 20 January 1927.

84. F.E. Wynne, 'The Administrative Control of Smallpox', *Journal of the Royal Sanitary Institute*, 48 (1927), p. 122.

85. Smallpox infection was reported to have been spread along tram routes. *Medical Officer of Health Report for Sheffield*, 1927.

86. *Sheffield Independent*, 31 January 1927.

87. *Medical Officer of Health Reports for Sheffield* (1922–26), *passim*.

88. Wynne, 'Smallpox', p. 120.

89. *Annual Reports of the Medical Officer of Health*, Sheffield, *passim.*; S.M.F. Fraser, 'Leicester and Smallpox: The Leicester Method'.
90. Obituary, *The Times*, 27 May 1961; *Who Was Who?* (London: Black, 1972), p. 35.
91. Wynne, 'Smallpox', p. 121.
92. One Sheffield firm reported 250 female staff absent due to vaccination. *Sheffield Independent*, 2 February 1927.
93. *Sheffield Independent*, 3 February 1927.
94. Sheffield City Archives SCA 582 2/1, Proofs of Evidence to House of Commons Committee Sheffield Corporation Bill, 1937.
95. G.W. Jones, 'Local Government or Local Governance?', *Government and Opposition*, 27 (1998) pp. 532–7.

CHAPTER TEN

French local authorities and the challenge of industrial pollution, *c.* 1810–1917

Geneviève Massard-Guilbaud

In the nineteenth century, British and French towns had different governance schemes.[1] Whilst British ones had considerable autonomy *vis-à-vis* the central state and could implement significant by-laws of their own, French cities remained, throughout the whole century, with some variations over time, under the supervision of an agent of central government, the departmental *Préfet*. The fight against industrial pollution provides an ideal focus for an exploration of this schematic account of the distribution of local government powers in France and the relationships maintained by different authorities, as well as an understanding of the actual distribution of power in the government of French towns. Compared to better known fields in which local authorities intervened in urban development, such as schools and street construction,[2] this theme of pollution, very important for the towns, both for public health and the control of the urban ground, is an ideal angle from which to address these questions of governance and the distribution of power. Exploring this theme provides a good idea of the relationship not only between the different public authorities but also between public authorities and industrialists, important protagonists of the local life. The question of the role of the latter is generally set in terms of representation in the local assemblies, but there is no proof that their power only went through this official channel. Hence the importance of studying a field where they play a prominent role, which was directly related to their interests.

Analysing the way things were conducted in France, I aim to provide some comparative elements with the British situation. This chapter covers the period which separates the first French law concerning the pollution (1810) from the next one (1917), which was voted in a rather different spirit, as we shall see. To examine the role of the different players, we first need to understand this legal arsenal, that is, the place the law assigned to each of them in the process of fighting pollution and the tools they had at their disposal to grapple with it. I shall then analyse the way the different types of actors behaved throughout the proceedings, evaluating how far their view was swayed by their position in the decision-making process, before trying to evaluate who really controlled the situation.

Although the elected authorities (municipal councils and mayors) were remote from the decision-taking powers held by the central state representatives, nevertheless such elected authorities played a significant role. This chapter will examine the manner in which the city-dwellers took the law progressively away from its originally intended path; the manner in which the prefects were confronted both with often insoluble contradictions, and with private economic interests which sometimes imposed their power. Finally, I shall offer an assessment of the willingness of the authorities to tackle industrial pollution and the effects of their actions, one which somewhat differs from that which has until now been assumed to have been the case.[3]

The fight against industrial pollution: whose responsibility?

Let us come back to the first question: on which authorities did the management of industrial pollution rest, at the local level, and which legal means were at their disposal to act against it? The first thing to notice is that legislation with regard to the so-called 'dangerous, unhealthy and unpleasant' factories was voted very early in France (1810), especially if one bears in mind the difference of chronology between French and British industrialisation processes. The French concern for pollution did not date from the nineteenth century. The harmful effects of industry had begun to attract the attention of the authorities as early as the third quarter of the eighteenth century, long before French industry took off. Drawing their inspiration from Pringle and MacBride's works, scientific authorities such as the Académie royale des Sciences, the Société royale de Médecine and the Institut, turned out writings warning against putrefying matter. At the same time, public opinion began to denounce the nuisance effects of different kinds of industry. In the early nineteenth century, odours were by far the most frequent subject of complaints, as they were supposed to carry fatal miasmas. But as time passed, people complained more and more about other problems such as water pollution, smoke and even noise.[4] Between 1790 and 1809, consideration of how best to control industrial pollution became more widespread. Attempts to classify industries with regard to the degree to which they polluted were carried out. Legislation was drawn up, but the first acts were not applied. In October 1810, an important Act (to be more accurate, a royal *décret*) which was to remain in force until 1917 was eventually passed.

It is not the intention here to analyse in detail the content of this Act, but it is necessary to have an idea of it to understand the way things occurred at the local level and to stress the main interests which were at stake. The main provision of this Act was to classify the 'dangerous, unhealthy or unpleasant' factories into three categories. Those in the first and second categories, or the worst, would be obliged from then onwards, to obtain a licence before beginning their unhealthy manufacturing processes. Those in the third would be forced to advise the authorities of their opening. For the first category, the licence had to be given by the Conseil d'Etat (the highest judicial court in France) and for the second category, by the prefect. From 1852 onwards, the prefect was entitled to give licences to both categories. The Act forbade the establishment of harmful and unhealthy factories (first category) near existing dwellings (but no distance was stated) and specified that once a factory had been authorised, no more complaints could be accepted from people who settled in its neighbourhood.

Although the decree had been issued, among other reasons, due to pressure of public opinion, paradoxically it did not aim at protecting the people from industrial pollution. Nor on any account was it a public health measure, even if the Ministre de l'Intérieur (counterpart of the Home Office minister) insisted, during its preparation, on the fact that 'both the general interest and that of neighbours ought not to be sacrificed to the manufacturers' one'. In spite of this rhetoric, the decree's main objective was to protect industrialists from the complaints of their neighbours. It was an objective rooted in an age of scientific optimism, as the small number of industries classified in the first category bore witness. This was an act based upon the philosophy of *laissez-faire* and of economic liberalism.[5]

Before trying to evaluate the impact, let us first examine the procedures involved in issuing the licences to the manufacturers, which show the nature of the powers respectively granted to the different local authorities. Prefects had the responsibility of issuing the licences. To gather information, they took two different steps. They first entrusted the mayor with undertaking an inquiry. A civil servant, whose title and identity varied according to place and time, was sent by the mayor to the factory concerned in order to initiate a technical inquiry. It might have be an *ingénieur des Mines* (inspector of mines)[6] or an *agent-voyer* (surveyor of highways).[7] The mayor had also to undertake a public inquiry called 'inquiry of *commodo vel incommodo*'. This inquiry involved the opening of a register where people from the district, informed in the usual official ways – posters and public announcements at the end of Mass – could record their opinions for or against the intended factory. In big cities, the mayor generally handed over his powers to a police superintendent or to a prominent local citizen of his choice. Petitions and letters from neighbours were appended to the file. Finally, the mayor had to give a considered opinion, which remained a consultative one until 1917.

Concurrently with this step being taken by the mayor, the prefect asked for another investigation to be undertaken by the Conseil départemental d'Hygiène et de Salubrit (Departmental Board for public Health) which also depended on his authority. The first board for public health had been created on 18 Messidor Year XI (7 July 1802) in the department of Seine, as a consultative authority composed of appointed members. It was twenty years before such boards began to spread to other French departments, and still longer before they were all actively involved. In the department of Loire-Atlantique, a board was created as early as 1817. With the exception of Paris this was the first in France. By contrast, in the Puy-de-Dôme, the board does not seem to have existed much before the 1840s, or at least to have done any real work though its activity increased with time. Departments which still had no board in 1848 were obliged to create one at this date.[8]

Made up of members appointed by the prefect, they were composed of 'experts'. The board of Puy-de-Dôme, for example, contained the following full members in 1893: three chemists, a General Inspector of the *Ponts-et-Chaussées*,[9] an *ingénieur des Mines*, a Departmental architect, three professors of the School of Medicine, one professor of obstetrics, a *chef de clinique* in the School of Medicine (the rank below that of professor) and the Departmental veterinary surgeon. The assistant members comprised an Inspector of the *Ponts-et-Chaussées*, the Director of Health for the Clermont-Ferrand Army Corps, a Captain in the *Génie* (Military Engineers), and two heads of department in the *Préfecture*. The composition changed little over the next 15 years, although two new members had appeared, the departmental *Inspecteur du travail* (Factory inspector) and the Director of the Municipal Laboratory. These boards for public health generally sent a group of two or three members to the factory and drew up a report, including concrete proposals, which was sent to the prefect.

Analysing these official proceedings, we can make two different observations. First, we can notice the significant place granted to the 'experts' (health experts, engineers and technicians) in the decision-making process. It is necessary, then, to pay some attention to the fact that the decision-making power was given to the prefects and not to the mayors. From 1800 until 1882, the French mayors were not strictly elected by the populace, but generally appointed by the king or the imperial or republican government through the agency of the prefect.[10] But the latter had to choose the mayor within the municipal councils which, until 1848, were elected on the basis of a tax-paying franchise and, thereafter, on male universal suffrage. The mayors had been elected in the sense that they were selected from amongst the alderman who were elected by the citizens, or, until 1848, by the wealthiest among them. Thus the mayors can be seen as representatives of their city, although the fact that they were also appointed made them simultaneously agents of the central state. The only elected local authority – the municipal council and its mayor – was thus officially deprived of any decisive power in matters of industrial pollution. Complete official power was given to the prefects, who embodied the central state in every French department. As holders of high political office, appointed by the central executive power, the prefects did not represent public opinion in any way. Neither had they theoretically to cope with its pressure, as they did not draw their power from it.

Perspectives on industrial pollution

During the years immediately following the passing of the decree, the procedures described above were usually not fully applied. The *commodo* survey was not always held. The licence generally confined itself to that which was strictly necessary: three lines on a simple scrap of paper. No particular conditions were imposed on the manufacturers. But as the century progressed, the working of the system generally improved. The *commodo* survey became customary. It was not just a formality but was generally carried out with great seriousness. The opening licence became a four-page preprinted form, on which a special space was provided for restrictive conditions: an indication of the improvement of the prefecturial bureaucracy but also evidence that it henceforth seemed normal to dictate conditions to the industrialists. From 1858 the prefects were supposed, when sending their statistics to the minister, to state clearly, for each factory to which they had given a licence, the conditions which had been dictated to it, and the motives which had determined them. At the beginning, the prefects' comments were quite formal ('measures have been taken in the interest of the public health') but they became progressively more serious.[11]

Very often, especially at the beginning of our period, the factories which asked for an authorisation had already begun their production. They often came to ask for a licence under pressure from local people. These, indisposed by the stench, the smoke or the noise, complained about them to the mayor or the prefect. A police superintendent was sent to the premises and, if the manufacturer had no licence, he was ordered to apply for one. In other cases, manufacturers asked spontaneously for the licence but only after having begun their activity. For these situations the *rapporteurs* therefore described in their reports industries and manufacturing plants which already existed and not just those which were planned.

These reports say a great deal not only about the factories but about the opinions and perspectives of their authors. The reports of the *ingénieurs des Mines* were, as we might expect, very rich in technical details. The conclusion of their reports was often favourable to the industrialists, asserting that the industry concerned was or would be very useful to the town rather than being harmful to the inhabitants. It was as if solidarity between men whose technical competences were more or less the same (manufacturers or engineers of the factories on the one hand, and engineers of the public office on the other) overrode all other considerations. Their connivance even extended to deliberate lies, as in Clermont-Ferrand, where an *ingénieur des Mines* was obviously lying by omission to protect the industrial chemist Kessler, in the 1880s.[12] Of all the protagonists, the engineers were surely the most biased. As they had no financial interest in the factories, their behaviour can probably be attributed to blind trust in modern technology and a strong conviction that the trouble caused by the industry had to be borne for the sake of progress.

The reports made by the police superintendents were totally different. They were generally shorter, as their authors, who were not qualified to discuss production, could only describe the general state of the factory or estimate their distance from the nearest dwellings. Unlike those of the engineers, these reports were rather stereotyped and showed the lack of interest of their authors in industrial processes. When their opinion was requested, they often took into account the potential trouble that the intended factory could cause to public order by giving rise to protests. They were, therefore, not systematically favourable to the manufacturers.

But what about the mayors? Were they ready to accept any type or degree of pollution as long as work and wealth were created in their towns? Their reports were generally careful; we would be wrong to believe that the mayors were systematically biased towards the manufacturers. We can, of course, find mayors so convinced by the need for industrial growth that they came to forget their role as protectors of public health. Here are, for instance, the words of the mayor of Clermont, in 1838, about a pipe factory whose neighbours had complained about it:

> If complaints from neighbours had to be heard, then this would extend equally to all the other enterprises in the neighbourhood, and with all the more reason. Yet the real issue is the reverse, that is to say to ensure that we promote and facilitate the establishment of all sorts of industries.[13]

This kind of view can be found especially during the first decades of our period. But times were changing and the Act of 1810 was no longer applied in 1910 in the way that had been conceived a century earlier. The pressure exerted by the inhabitants became greater and greater as the century progressed. In the Puy-de-Dôme, for example, of the total number of complaints lodged between the beginning of the nineteenth century and 1914, only one-third date from the first half of the century whilst a half came from the 30 years splitting 1884 and 1914.[14] Because they were answerable to their electors and probably also because of the strengthening under the Republic of their consciousness about playing a significant political role, the mayors became more sensitive to the complaints and to the public interest. They felt more and more concerned with public health and anxious to play the role of arbitrator between industry and city inhabitants. Having no power of their own, the mayors sometimes sharply pressed the prefect to act, as in this letter that the mayor of Nantes sent to the prefect of Loire-Inférieure in November 1910:

> One thing is certain: the requirements which have been imposed up to now have had no effect. Either it has proved impossible to monitor the application of the measures required in law, which means that they are illusory and must be replaced by others, or the measures themselves are inoperative. Either way, the same conclusion follows. My fellow citizens will not understand if the authorities appear powerless in the face of facts which not only undermine their material well-being but are also by their very nature damaging to their health. I earnestly pray that you summon the Board of Health as a matter of urgency, and that you obtain from it not some palliative measure that is ineffective and inapplicable, but a forceful measure that can be immediately put into operation. If recourse to radical measures is necessary, then it is in my judgement the responsibility of the Board of Health to identify them. The property and the health of an entire neighbourhood of Nantes must surely be more dear to us than the interests, however respectable they might be, of a handful of factory owners.[15]

This type of attitude was not rare and should not be obscured by opinions favouring industrial development which lost ground throughout the century.

Generally speaking, the boards for public health were probably the least susceptible to pressure coming from the manufacturers. While the reports of the *ingénieurs des Mines* only took into account the technical point of view, those coming from the boards were much more sensitive to the well-being and the health of the inhabitants. Within the boards, the engineers were probably balanced by the 'health specialists'. Over the century as a whole, the Boards of Health should not be regarded as sleepy or useless bodies. They often took a point of view favourable to industry but did not always do so. The membership of the boards was internally divided between the more or less liberal, the conservative and the innovative. In 1901, in Clermont-Ferrand, the *rapporteur*, in an account of the poor state of sewage management, proposed that the practice of spreading sewage should be stopped and industrialists obliged to use other methods. He was promptly disowned by the board.[16] Yet in other cases the work of the boards could be impressive. The board of Loire-Atlantique, for instance, immediately following the first decades of its existence, did an astonishing amount of very progressive work.

Although the decision fell solely to the prefect, he nevertheless took very much into consideration, the opinions which were given to him. When the prefect disagreed with the reports he had received, which was in very few cases, he did not take a conflicting decision but rather asked their authors to study the file again (which had the consequence of prolonging the procedure, irritating the industrialists even more). That was, for instance, the case in 1909 with a piggery in Nantes, situated in a densely populated neighbourhood which was already foul and noisy because of the proximity of the numerous pigs. The mayor had pronounced a negative point of view, but the Board of Health had given a positive one. The prefect noted that the latter had made proposals intended to improve the problem of the odour but had not taken into account the question of the noise. He asked it to consider the question again.[17]

It is generally admitted that the Act of 1810 was passed in a spirit favourable to industry. For my part, I do not contest this interpretation. But purpose and effect are two different things: if the Act of 1810 protected the manufacturers so well, why did they try to get round it, as they did throughout the whole century? Several factors can explain this attitude. First, and in accordance with the spirit of that time, the manufacturers found the imposition of any sort of administrative control or limitation unacceptable. Next, they were obviously not ready to spend money in setting up equipment whose sole aim was the improvement of public health. Furthermore, from the middle or the third quarter of the century, the context had changed so much that the law could no longer be implemented in the spirit in which it had been passed. As we have seen, the Act foresaw that no factory could be driven away once it had been authorised. This measure had been taken at a time when the size of the cities was quite stable, but most cities soon began to spread outside their original boundaries. And as nothing could prevent them from growing, factories initially built in wastelands (which, for this reason, had obtained their licence without problem) found themselves surrounded by dwellings a couple of decades later. Despite the law, the authorities can often be found following public opinion in arguing that a factory should leave its existing location and in attempting to drive it out. It tended to be easy, in the first decades of the century, to establish a factory in a remote and deserted part of the suburbs. Finding such a place had become far more difficult by the end of the century. A more radical change of location was a solution which only increased overheads. It is not rare to meet cases in which an industrialist agreed to leave a place as soon as the prefect had proposed a new site. But the prefect was everywhere faced with the opposition of the mayors and the residents of the town.

Case law had evolved to such an extent throughout the century, in favour of the inhabitants, that industrialists were sometimes obliged to 'remind' the prefect the initial sense of the decree.[18] Although it had been passed to protect them, the industrialists had never co-operated in enforcing it. On the other hand, as no Act had been passed to protect the city-dwellers, the latter used it to put pressure on their leaders to shoulder their responsibilities. Their petitions often quoted the Act as proof of their right. One can thus say that the Act of 1810 was paradoxically used to defend the opposite cause from the one it had been intended for and that, as the concern for public health progressively grew, it worked more and more as an Act of protection of the city-dwellers against industrial pollution. The next episode of the story supports this thesis, since the Act which followed, in 1917, would come to be considered a public health law.

Public authorities, manufacturers and the struggle for control

The third and last set of questions involve the degree to which the prefects were convinced of the necessity of fighting industrial pollution. What relationship did they have with the manufacturers whose attitudes were generally uncooperative? And, finally, how far were they able to impose their views?

The few historians who have taken an interest in questions such as these consider that the role of the public authorities, and even their commitment to reducing pollution, was limited.[19] It is indeed easy to offer (as has been done above) quotations favouring industrial development, even at the end of the century. However, a more cautious approach is needed to this question, namely one which stresses the significant evolution which took place during the course of the century – leading to a more nuanced assessment. For several reasons that we must consider, the task of the public authorities, and especially that of the prefect who had to settle issues once and for all, was a complex one.

First, the speed at which the industrial processes were changing created significant difficulties for the authorities. We must bear in mind that the prefects were, in fact, confronted with problems they had never met before and which they simply did not know how to address. The archives contain many letters from the prefects to their counterparts in other departments asking what they authorised, or what conditions they imposed on manufacturers before authorising particular processes. These letters give evidence of their disarray. Increasingly, the minister produced formulae which they could draw upon when in need of inspiration. But the national instructions often arrived long after new problems had appeared, and the local authorities remained without help for long periods. So, instead of smiling when we see a prefect ordering the planting of trees to combat an odour or the heightening of a wall to block sulphurous vapours, as once occurred in Clermont-Ferrand, we should rather ask: 'what could he have done better with the knowledge he had at the time?' Insoluble problems sometimes led the prefects to unsatisfactory solutions, which created still more problems in their wake. This was, for instance, the case in Nantes where the prefect, thinking he could neither ban – because they were useful – nor authorise – because they polluted – several factories which transformed dry sewage into fertiliser, allowed them to locate 'at their own risks', in other words without a licence, in the so-called island of the Prairie-au-Duc. These half-illicit factories attracted many others, which all settled without a licence. Several decades later, with the city sprawling well beyond its walls, a full neighbourhood had been built on the island and nobody knew how to turn out all these factories which had become a serious source of complaint. On the eve of the First World War, much had been written about the problem but it was still not resolved.[20]

Arbitrating between protagonists of different interests was another problem for the authorities. How to give satisfaction to the members of the middle class who asked for cleaner air without depriving the workers of their jobs? Moreover, conflicts about pollution not only arose between inhabitants and manufacturers or between working class and middle class. They often divided employers themselves, especially with regard to water problems. In February 1906, for example, the Fishermen Union of Loire-Atlantique asked the prefect to prevent factories discharging acid water in the river Loire.[21] It was difficult to grapple with the pollution caused by a particular industry when the whole town was making a living from it, as in Thiers with its highly polluting cutleries industry. These questions, which might be rhetorical if applied to the present day, were vital for an understanding of the nineteenth century.

Finally, and here was the thorniest question, even when a decision was taken and some measures imposed on manufacturers, how to oblige them, especially the large ones, to accede to the orders? It is an open secret that the decisions of the prefects were often circumvented. Evidence of their non-application is abundant until the end of our period. I shall only quote, amongst a hundred possible others, the example of a departmental veterinary surgeon's letter to the prefect of the Puy-de-Dôme, dating from November 1897, speaking of the general state of cleanliness of the dairy farms:

> Prescriptions of the prefectural by-laws have generally not been abided. Time has come to act energetically vis-à-vis the interested parties if we do not want them to go on trifling with the public health.

City-dwellers knew perfectly well that the conditions required by the prefects and supposed to fend off problems of pollution were not always respected. This was why such inhabitants always demanded the closure or removal of the polluting factories. As in the case of labour law, which began to be respected only when a corps of inspectors was created, the problem of enforcing prefecturial authority with respect to pollution began to be solved only when special inspectors, with the power to impose penalties, began to go round the factories. Even in the most advanced departments, however, such inspectors appeared only around the turn of the century, becoming more general after the 1917 law which required prefects to create such a body of inspectors in every department.

Another clue to the weakness of the prefects with respect to the manufacturers is their attitude towards the factories which were already in production when requesting a licence. I have never come across a case where this fact was considered by the authorities as a reason to give a negative answer to the plaintiff. It was only from 1917, again, that the lack of licence at the outset became a case for preventing the issuing of one.

There is no doubt that the local authorities were much more effective in dealing with small factories than large ones. The latter were protected by their economic weight, their social utility and the complexity of their manufacturing processes which made technical control difficult to assess for the layman. If the preferred means of opposing the prefect's authority was passive resistance, whether in refusing to ask for legal authorisation, or in 'forgetting' to abide by the imposed prescriptions, another means of pressure was to launch a campaign. In Rezé, the town facing Nantes on the southern bank of the river Loire, for instance, an industrialist who wanted to settle a blood processing factory organised a massive delivery amongst the population of tracts praising, with blatant exaggeration, the supposed beneficial effects of the factory he was trying to open:

> The creation of a factory in this part of the town will bring workers and households, which will find there regular work. This factory will be able to attract other ones, which will give work to every corporation: masons, harness makers, cartwrights, roofers, publicans (*débitants*), bakers, grocers etc. Within some years you will have a wet dock where ships can arrive at any time. These ships, which will discharge on your side of the river Loire, will need warehouses and stores, there will be enormous opportunities for carriage and haulage.[22]

Attempts to bring politic pressure to bear, through appeals to the *député* (MP), to the minister, or to the Conseil des Arts et Manufactures (the authority which advised the minister on industrial questions) were made to contest the prefect's decision, although this tended to be rare. But, generally speaking, the firm and sometimes even mocking tone in which the large manufacturers addressed prefects was a good indicator of the real balance of power which existed between them.

It is therefore obvious that the prefects faced considerable resistance from large manufacturers. This does not indicate that the prefects were idle or failed in their attempts to implement a public health policy. An attentive reading of the archives supports a contrary conclusion. Although the prefects might have reacted too slowly to the problems and were not omnipotent, they did at least strive to be effective and had a steady and positive effect. I am convinced that it would be a manichean vision to conclude that they were indifferent to the problem and did not try to improve the air and water quality, even in working class areas. Admittedly, the archives reveal great scandals created by some influential manufacturers who refused to comply with laws and by-laws. But there is a danger of not seeing the wood for the trees: we must not forget all the other cases when the administrative conditions were somehow implemented. Sometimes losing, in the short term, the arm-wrestling match which pitted them against manufacturers, the prefects nevertheless counterbalanced them in the long term, preventing the most flagrant abuses. In spite of all the failures and delays, the idea that the authorities had the right and even the duty to intervene to protect the health of the population gained ground. At the turn of the century even the manufacturers no longer had the unselfconsciousness which characterised them some decades earlier.

Conclusion: fragmented responsibility, increased efficacy

The French law concerning polluting industries, passed in the early part of the century, defined whose responsibility it was to manage the problem. Allowing the intervention of many parties, it deprived the elected authorities of any decision-making power, but trusted the prefects and gave a significant power to the 'specialists', technicians and doctors. Even if they had no official power, the mayors nevertheless succeeded in playing a significant role in the process. Pressurised by the will of the citizens, and progressively more aware and convinced of the necessity of driving a real public health policy, the mayors represented an important link in the decision chain, generally pushing the prefects towards greater strictness and taking into consideration the health and comfort of the inhabitants.

For their part, city-dwellers seized on the 1810 decree, using it as a tool to get their point of view heard. Even though the fact that they operated in the long term means that it is difficult to show the effectiveness of the complaints, one must none the less conclude that they played a significant role in the decision-making process. Their repeated insistence on the right to be protected against industrial pollution without doubt made the case law evolve in favour of the inhabitants.

Industrialists also played an important role in the management of pollution problems, not by taking part in the elected councils but by putting pressure on them. Their attitude throughout the century prevents us from believing that they felt protected by the decree which had been passed in their favour. On the contrary, the industrialists regularly threw a spanner in the works, deploying passive as well as active resistance to the public authorities. If they were often strong in the face of the prefect, they progressively lost ground and had to comply with restrictions imposed on them.

At the end of the period, this evolution informed the main characteristics of the law of 1917, which reversed the priorities of 1810. Priority was now given to an affirmation of the necessity of fighting industrial pollution to protect public health, the right of veto for the mayor, a more efficient means of enforcement obliging industrialists to comply with the law; and the creation of a specialised corps of inspectors. The war, which generally had the effect of strengthening the role of the state in the economy, allowed considerable enforcement of the law, in spite of the strength of the industrialists' pressure.

Notes

1. I am very grateful to Victoria Martin for the time which she has generously spent improving the imperfect English of my original text. Thanks also go to Geoffrey Crossick for valuable advice and to Christoph Bernardt for his very helpful critical reading of a draft of this chapter. It goes without saying that any errors which remain in the text are my responsibility alone.
2. Although British readers should appreciate that urban history is much less developed in France than in Britain, and its impact has been less significant.
3. French social historians have paid little attention either to the problem of urban pollution or to that of the exercise of power in the town, at least in nineteenth century. This chapter, based on primary sources, rests on the very rich archives of the *Préfectures*, kept in the Archives Départementales. In view of the extensiveness of these archives, I first chose to explore those of three very different departments: the Loire-Atlantique (at the time the Loire-Inférieure), a department which includes the two harbours of Nantes and Saint-Nazaire, with an industry specifically geared towards the sea (sugar refineries, fish canning factories, oil industry); the department of Rhône, including Lyon and its agglomeration, a large industrial city, the second in France after Paris; and also the Puy-de-Dôme, a rural department in Auvergne, characterised at the time by an industry scattered over many little workshops and where the tyre industry, which would make Clermont-Ferrand 'Michelin-city', in the twentieth century, had still not taken off.
4. For more details, see G. Massard-Guilbaud, 'Les citadins face aux nuisances urbaines en Auvergne au XIXe siècle, *Recherches contemporaines*, 3 (Université de Nanterre, 1997) pp. 5–48.
5. On this decree, see A. Corbin, *Le Miasme et la Jonquille* (Paris: Aubier-Montaigne, 1982); English translation: *The Foul and the Fragrant. Odour*

and the French Social Imagination (Leamington Spa: Berg, 1986); and, by the same author, 'L'opinion publique et la politique face aux nuisances industrielles dans la ville préhausmanienne', in A. Corbin (ed.), *Le temps, le désir et l'horreur, Essais sur le XIXe siècle* (Paris: Aubier, coll. historique, 1991), pp. 185–98. More generally, on industrial pollution, see A. Faure, 'Autorités publiques et implantation industrielle en agglomération parisienne (1860–1914)', in D. Voldman (ed.), *Région parisienne, approches d'une notion (1860–1980)*, *Cahiers de l'IHTP* no. 12 (October 1989), pp. 93–104 and A. Faure, 'L'industrie à Paris: La Villette', in J.M. Jenn, *Le XIXe arrondissement, une cité nouvelle*, Délégation à l'action artistique de la ville de Paris: Archives de Paris (1996), pp. 91–112. *Ch. Mayet, L'hygiène et les pollutions industrielles, un exemple de règlements sanitaires appliqués à Aubervilliers*, Mémoire de maîtrise, Université Paris X, 1994. P.F. Claustre, 'Une ville saisie par l'industrie: nuisances industrielles et action municipale à Argenteuil (1820–1940)', *Recherches contemporaines*: Université Paris X Nanterre no. 3 (1995–96), pp. 91–119.

6. A French *ingénieur des Mines* is an engineer trained in the state college called *Ecole des Mines* and working as a government official in the field of public works. The term refers here to a post rather than an occupation, hence the choice to translate it as 'inspector'.

7. In the nineteenth century, the term *agent-voyer* indicates an employee responsible for departmental roads and ways (and, as we can see in the case studied here, for other tasks as well). On the *voyers*, see A. Guillerme, *Corps à corps sur la route* (Paris: Presses de l'Ecole Nationale des Ponts-et-Chausses, 1984).

8. Décret of 1848, 18th December. The French boards of health were conversant with problems of cleansing and drainage, endemic and epidemic illness, vaccines, poor relief, sanitary conditions of towns, schools, hospitals and workshops, demographic statistics and so on.

9. Bridges and highways service. The *ingénieurs des Ponts*, like the *ingénieurs des Mines*, were trained in a special state college before working as government officials.

10. Except for short periods in 1815, 1848, 1871. See Jocelyne George, *Histoire des maires, 1789–1939* (Paris: Plon, 1989), p. 17.

11. There were exceptions, for example, in the Loire-Atlantique, where the board of health acting during the 1830s and 1840s worked more diligently than its successors.

12. Archives départementales du Puy-de-Dôme (ADPDD) M 1024.

13. ADPDD M 1017.

14. For more details, see Massard-Guilbaud, 'Les citadins face aux nuisances urbaines en Auvergne au XIXe siècle'.

15. Archives départementales de Loire-Atlantique (ADLA), 1M1550. For another detailed example of the way a mayor could manage industrial pollution, see my article 'Urbanisme, spéculation foncière et pollution industrielle. Solidarités et rivalités entre élites clermontoises, 1870–1914', *Siècles*, 3 (Clermont-Ferrand: 1996).

16. ADPDD, M 10361.

17. ADLA, 1M 1436 bis.

18. See the letters of the industrial chemist Kessler to the Prefect of the Puy-de-Dôme in M 1025.

19. See, for instance, A. Faure, 'Autorités publiques'.

20. ADLA, 1M 1550.
21. ADLA, 1M 2879.
22. ADLA, 1M 2901.

CHAPTER ELEVEN

A paradigm of inaction? The politics and un-politics of smoke abatement legislation in Stockport, 1844–56

Jean Adams

The issues

The issue of air pollution has been thrust onto the main political agenda. Acid rain in particular has been discussed as if pollution were a new and recently discovered concept. In reality, the problems of smoke pollution have been lamented since Roman times.[1] Yet the few modern works on smoke pollution in Britain concentrate on the scientific aspect of pollution control rather than its politics.[2] While air pollution has loomed large in northern industrial towns for over 200 years, smoke abatement is missing from most historical overviews of these urban places. Still the literature of the time is full of references to the central role that pollution played in everyday life by authors such as Engels, De Tocqueville and Gaskell. Engels in particular singled out Stockport for criticism; he awarded the town the dubious honour not only of being one of the 'smokiest duskiest holes' but also of being 'excessively repellent'.[3] Stockport has been chosen for this case study not only because it suffered some of the worst smoke pollution in the nineteenth century, but also because it typified the northern industrial town in its industrial development and its economic and political experiences.

This case study will draw on the community power debates of the 1960s and 1970s, and apply the theories and concepts about power, agenda control, and non-decisions to the nineteenth-century debate on smoke pollution in Stockport. M.A. Crenson's *The Un-Politics of Air Pollution*[4] explores this non-decision making process by examining why some issues are given political salience and some are not, and why these categories are subsequently acted upon differently. Following this approach, a study of nineteenth-century Stockport will allow a micro study of the issues of governance in an archetypal nineteenth-century mill town through an examination of how those in positions of power and influence responded to the increasingly urgent consequences of smoke pollution created by rapid urbanisation and industrialisation.

Smoke pollution is an appropriate subject for a study of nineteenth-century community power. As the century progressed, calls for action for smoke abatement grew, and the national press, local pressure groups and landed interests in Parliament increasingly pushed for reform. The issue of smoke abatement was always a contentious one in the nineteenth century, nowhere more so than in industrial mill towns. Initial attempts at introducing smoke abatement could be thwarted by a few powerful individuals who had vested interests, usually industrial. The first parliamentary select committee to inquire, 'how far it may be practicable to compel persons using steam engines to erect them in such a manner less prejudicial to public health'[5] took place in 1819. Many other attempts via select committees were made in the following years to introduce smoke abatement. It was accepted by Parliament that smoke could be abated, but it was concluded that present knowledge was not sufficient to introduce national legislation. Thus smoke abatement came under local improvement legislation and was subject to private bill procedure, which was expensive and perilous especially when local opinion was divided. The smoke issue then, involved many aspects of power, both within localities and between them and central government.

But how can a study of these themes be structured? Dahl's *Who Governs?*[6] argues that nineteenth-century New Haven politics were distinguished by 'cumulative inequalities' of political resources and were therefore élitist. This evidence is contrasted with the town's more pluralistic politics of the 1950s. Unfortunately, Dahl does not back his evidence of nineteenth-century power with the case studies with which he supports his twentieth-century evidence. Bachrach and Baratz, however, formalise a model in which the determinants of both decision- and non-decision-making can be appraised. Further, they provide a methodological structure for such a case study, taking full account of the concepts of power, force, influence and ability.[7] John Garrard's *Leadership and Power in Victorian Industrial Towns*[8] shows that historical study of power in northern industrial towns is practicable, and an earlier paper[9] suggests a foundation for the comparative analysis of the political context in which nineteenth-century urban municipal leaders operated. By discovering how effective was the practice of limiting the scope of decision-making through manipulation of the dominant political institutions and powers, it will be possible to measure the power and influence of these municipal élites.

Context: Stockport and the smoke abatement issue

Stockport was a prototypical mill town of the north-west of England in the nineteenth century. The availability of water made the town an ideal site for the industries of the time. Just as corn and logwood mills had previously taken advantage of this powerful natural resource, so did the newer industries of silk and cotton. Stockport's potential for development was further enhanced by the construction of tunnels through the soft sandstone to points upstream of the meanders of the River Goyt. This greatly expanded the land suitable for the development of factories dependent upon water to power their engines.

The conversion of Stockport into an industrial town began in 1736 through the establishment of silk throwing. The subsequent decline of the silk trade and the development of cheap materials and new spinning machines saw the rise of the cotton trade. Until then, cotton spinning had been confined to a domestic industry: early inventions in most industries were on a small scale and designed to improve the efficacy of the home worker. The invention of steam power increased the development of factories, but it was not until the application of water to power machinery and the consequent increase in the size of the machinery that the large-scale factory became a feature of the landscape of Stockport. The period of maximum growth in Stockport was between 1780 and 1840. By 1795, four of the 23 factories in Stockport were steam-powered; in 1822, there were 47 cotton factories in Stockport in which 5,730 power looms were worked by steam.[10] By the late 1830s cotton spinning, bleaching, printing, dyeing and Christys felt and hat manufacturing industries had been joined by engineering, chemicals and metal working. The population expanded to match the rise of industry increasing from 15,000 in 1794 to 20,000 in 1816; by 1841 it had reached 30,000.

With large-scale industry came smoke pollution. The population of the Greater Manchester area was described by the Manchester Board of Health in the 1840s as 'surrounded on every side by large factories whose chimneys vomit forth dense smoke which hangs heavily'.[11] This view of Stockport as an increasingly smoky and densely crowded town also appeared in a critical editorial in the local paper, the *Stockport Advertiser*, in March 1853.[12]

> The smoke nuisance has long been a reproach and byword of contempt upon its inhabitants. Strangers have for years pointed to Stockport as the smokiest town between London and Manchester, and those that travel over the line of the London and North Western railway invariably put up the window as in the hope of keeping out the smoke.[13]

Manufacturers no longer needed to seek their power where there was fast running water but found it instead near the canals which brought coal to them directly and cheaply. Wherever there was a mill, there was also an industrial hamlet of which the mill formed the centre. Workers were based in streets of terraced houses that had been built rapidly and cheaply on the vacant ground.

Throughout this period political and religious tensions remained high, with the ever rising population vying for work and accommodation in an increasingly close packed and smoky industrial town where social and environmental problems were exacerbated by the constant inflow of a poor, largely Irish migratory population Following the incorporation of Stockport in 1835, the conflict between the Tories and the Liberals spilled over into council debates. The lack of clear political direction worsened Stockport's many social problems. The undoubted underlying Liberal, Nonconformist predisposition was faced with the hostile, mill-owning Tories and the militant Protestant working class. Their innate Protestantism, coupled with resentment towards the moral and social concept of respectability favoured by the Liberal Nonconformists, was whipped up by Tories who clouded the arguments for social reform in anti-Irish and anti-Catholic rhetoric. Throughout this period, the Tories and Liberals vied for control of the Council. Father and son sat on opposite sides of the council and even of the House of Commons. This division between the political élites made effective reforming and improvement legislation more difficult and complex.[14]

The limited conception of local government originated in the individualism of the age. It stood in sharp contrast to the magnificent contributions made towards the voluntary institutions and to the lavish investments of capital in factories. The tradition of the Nonconformists towards thrift ensured that the councillors' role as trustees of rate funds transcended their duty to improve conditions. The membership of council committees in Stockport was dominated by the local industrial elite such as mill owners Henry Marsland, Joseph Orme, John Gouldthorpe and Cephias Howard. They had great influence on policy-making and policy formulation. The full council generally passed committee reports *nem con*, further diluting both access to debate and discussion of proposed legislation.

Crenson[15] argues that political activists could be the victims as well as the wielders of power. By monopolising their town's civic energies for their own favourite issues, they could deprive other issue areas of the political resources necessary for decision-making. He gives the example of how a vigorous effort by local decision-makers to enact an air pollution ordinance could deter other decision-makers from launching a programme to develop heavy industry. In his study of the town of Gary, Crenson quotes the mayor commenting that although he was not opposed to pollution control, the sight of smoke rising from the stacks meant that the town was prosperous. Similarly, in Stockport smoking factory chimneys meant work, and smoking domestic chimneys meant wealth and properly cooked food. The very presence of all the factories, the employment linked to them and the backward linkage effect of the wages on other industries and businesses had a restraining influence on the desire to introduce pollution controls.

Stockport's experience of smoke abatement can only be judged by understanding the general context in which the nineteenth-century debate on the issue took place. There were significant obstacles to effective legislation. First, the scientific community were not agreed on how to respond to the problem. Second, those in favour of smoke abatement were unorganised and politically isolated. Thirdly, the underlying political philosophy of *laissez-faire* and retrenchment in imperial finance acted as a restraining influence on proposed legislation. Finally and, as we shall see most importantly, industrial élites could act in their own interests to thwart attempts to introduce meaningful legislation.

Between 1840 and the passing of the first smoke abatement clause in the 1854 Stockport Amendment Act there was a great deal of argument and political activity around this issue. There were struggles for power within the local elite and between central and local government. It will become evident that, until central government decided to take a strong lead – and to a significant extent, even afterward – smoke abatement was effectively marginalised.

The struggle over smoke abatement clauses in Stockport

The first moves towards improvement legislation began in 1844, when a bill for the further regulation and improvement of the Borough of Stockport was proposed. This general improvement bill included clauses in relation to the provision of public baths and public walks as well as the abatement of the smoke nuisance. Two clauses would have had economic consequences for most millowners and other industrial outlets.

> 65. Ovens and furnaces to have protective walls at least nine inches thick.

> 66. All furnaces or other chimneys within four miles of the boundary to consume their own smoke after the first of January 1845. A penalty of 40 shillings for every week such furnaces or annoyance shall be continued after a month's notice.[16]

These clauses were initially expunged at the behest of the mill owners during debate in the council about a prospective improvement Act. They complained that such clauses were unjust and would place an intolerable burden upon them. It was agreed, however, to instigate a committee for public baths, pleasure walks and a town hall which would examine the prospect of introducing an improvement bill that would not cover smoke abatement. The town council accepted the findings of the committee and secured a loan of £19,700 from outside the borough to finance the proposed bill, the passage of which depended on expensive lawyers and, ultimately, on the private bill committees of the Lords and Commons.[17] The high cost and uncertain prospects of such bills partly explains why councils were reluctant to refer bills to Parliament that were contentious, or at least did not have a measure of all-party support. In turn, this helps to explain why smoke abatement fell at such an early stage and why it was prevented from becoming an issue worthy of debate and decisive action.

As the content and the costs of the proposed improvement bill became more generally known, there was uproar in Stockport. Ratepayers demanded a public meeting to discuss the bill. The disproportionate burden placed on the ratepayers for funding improvement legislation, added to the underlying doctrine of *laissez-faire*, ensured that such proposals were anathematised. Surprisingly, and in some ways contradictorily, the content of the proposed bill was also criticised for failing to improve the conditions of the mass of the population. The plans for grand buildings, for public baths and a town hall were particularly criticised by the shopocracy and the millocracy. They considered the burden placed upon them to fund such measures unfair, particularly as there was no tangible benefit to themselves. The failure to address the smoke nuisance problem was singled out for criticism by all except the mill owners. There was a flurry of anonymous critical letters in the *Stockport Advertiser* calling for urgent action to address the smoke problem. This anonymity of those in favour of smoke abatement reduced their influence while reflecting the power wielded by the mill owners. The *Advertiser* criticised members of the council for acting in a way which served their own interests, particularly with regard to smoke abatement.

> those who have dictated the bill, have interfered to prevent expense to themselves, seeing that nearly every member of the council of the corporation is directly or indirectly interested in saving expense to himself.[18]

Also, the fact that Manchester already had a smoke abatement clause, and yet Stockport was to be denied one, added to bitterness of the debate.

Despite repeated calls by the ratepayers, the mayor continually refused to convene a meeting to discuss the implications of the proposed bill. In frustration, 300 ratepayers convened their own meeting, where it became known that the Town Clerk, Henry Coppock, had already submitted a bill to Parliament, which was now about to get its third reading. A heated discussion followed in which it was claimed that the Town Clerk was guilty of corruption and of acting without consultation or agreement. The improvement bill, far from bringing benefits and improvements to Stockport, would – it was claimed – greatly reduce the position of the middle classes, the ratepayers and small business owners. The meeting agreed to oppose the third reading of the improvement bill. To that end, a petition signed by 4,000 ratepayers was sent to the House of Commons calling for the bill to be rejected.

Stockport Town Council, at the behest of other council members, held an urgent meeting to discuss the actions of the Town Clerk. It became clear that Coppock, frustrated with the slow progress of the council, had decided to submit the proposed improvement bill without reference to other members of the council. He was accused of duplicity, his conduct being 'inconsistent with his profession'. Enjoying 'a position of almost unlimited power and influence',[19] Coppock was Clerk not only to the Borough Council, but also to the magistrates, the Board of Guardians, the Reform Association, the Overseers of the Poor, the Police Commission and was also secretary to the library! Yet this decided Liberal, unsparing in his efforts to secure triumph for his friends, was detested by the Tories. At the meeting, it was reported to council that Joseph Brotherton, MP for Salford, on moving the bill in the House of Commons, had stated that 'there was no town in England which required more improvement than Stockport and that there was no serious opposition to the Bill in Stockport'.[20] Such was the anger created amongst Stockport's councillors, middle class and ratepayers, that all attempts to reach an agreed plan of action failed. The mayor decided to hold an official enquiry into the proposed bill in an attempt to defuse the situation.

This investigation became an argument about the inclusion of a smoke burning clause. J. Hamer opposed smoke regulation on the grounds that it would increase the burden on the mill owners and thus reduce the position of working men; Councillor Hamer argued that a smoke-consuming chimney would cost 120 guineas per boiler. Alderman Cheetham, a Liberal mill owner, proposed that, although smoke from furnaces could not be entirely consumed, the nuisance could and should be abated by focusing attention on the stoker, who could mitigate the smoke. Cheetham stated that he had seen from Mr Gouldthorpe's factory smoke so opaque that you could almost feel it. Gouldthorpe, a Conservative, claimed that smoke was in fact an antidote for all evils. He proposed that Stockport should advertise the health of its population and encourage people to come to Stockport to take the air! On being put to a vote the motion to remove the smoke nuisance clause was carried by 24 votes to 12.

The rejection of the smoke clause again stimulated a run of letters of complaint in the *Advertiser*. There was great dismay that, although Stockport was renowned as one of the smokiest towns in the country, it was still not to receive relief. The fact that it had not been conclusively proved that smoke abatement was effective did not prevent other towns from trying to improve conditions. It was argued in a leader that improvement Acts including smoke clauses were beginning to be adopted by many towns, and yet those who were supposed to act in the best interests of the population of Stockport failed to act. Whilst councillors and mill owners managed to live outside the town's boundaries and thus escaped the smoke, they were happy for others to suffer.

> Few of our readers will dispute the great importance to a community especially in crowded and densely populated towns of securing the preservation of public health ... We cannot calculate how much human life might be improved ... of still greater importance is the knowledge of how much the living conditions of our species may be improved by legislative interference.[21]

The efforts of the *Advertiser* to promote smoke abatement, and public criticism of the council's failure on the issue, unfortunately came to nothing. The Stockport Improvement Bill was sent back to Parliament bereft of the smoke abatement clause and was passed into law in September 1845.[22]

In 1853 the Town Council proposed an Amendment to the Improvement Act, including a modified smoke abatement clause which specified that chimneys should be constructed so as to consume smoke arising from the combustion of fuels. In addition, all other chimneys should be adapted within two years or the owners would be fined 40 shillings per day. When the draft bill came before the council on 4 May 1853, the clauses in regard to the smoke nuisance were once again expunged at the bidding of the mill owners Henry Marsland and Cephias Howard. They argued that the cost of introducing any smoke abatement clause was prohibitive and that the council had already intervened excessively in the affairs of the people of Stockport. The improvement committee was dominated by Conservative mill owners who attempted to remove any mention of smoke abatement in the proposed legislation. However, the Liberal members argued against its exclusion and demanded the proposal be put to a vote. Despite the Liberal majority on the council, the motion to include an abatement clause was expunged as the Liberal and Conservative members who had vested interests in preventing the proposal voted together.

Again correspondence and critical leaders appeared in the local press, and again the *Advertiser* took up the smoke abatement cause. Whether for partisan reasons or otherwise, the criticism was forthright:

> We are sorry to perceive that the very clause, which might have placed Stockport in the category of well regulated towns, has been rejected by a majority of 18 to 12 votes. Whatever could the motives of the eighteen gentlemen who voted for the rejection of the smoke nuisance clause be it would be difficult to divine, but of this you can be assured, that for the majority of the burgesses it has been a great disappointment and will not be readily forgotten.[23]

Despite the attempts of the *Advertiser*, the Stockport Amendment Improvement Bill was sent to Parliament unchanged. However, when the Stockport bill came before the Committee on Private Bills, its chairman, Lord Redesdale, reacting to the increasing concerns of smoke abaters and his own desire to reduce smoke pollution, would not pass the bill without the inclusion of a smoke prevention clause.

On 1 April 1853 the town clerk, at a special meeting held in the Court House, read to the full council the report of proceedings and Lord Redesdale's comments in respect of the smoke nuisance clause. The insistence of Lord Redesdale on including a smoke nuisance clause created even greater objection to its inclusion. Alderman Cheetham complained that, when the council agreed that another improvement bill was to be applied for, it was never intended that penalties upon mill owners, mill occupiers or any other parties should be incurred. He was incensed at what he saw as Stockport being singled out for special treatment. In an attempt to conciliate, the mayor argued that the object of the clause could be gained as long as the smoke was lessened rather than abated. Alderman Walmsley objected to the smoke clause stating that he knew of no constitutional power that allowed Lord Redesdale to enforce a clause for the burning of smoke; it was after all, he claimed, a moral impossibility! Dr Turner, a local physician, advised that the high death rate, and the need for the majority of the population to spit, showed the effects that the smoky atmosphere was having on the health of the population. Turner argued that:

> the smoke in Stockport was so dense that one could not see one's watch. The natural effect of the reduction in smoke would be to reduce the incidence of chest disease. It is a great disappointment that our great firms continue to pour forth volumes of black smoke into the air, heedless of the social mischief they are causing.[24]

It was eventually agreed without a vote to support a smoke clause only if the bill would be lost without it.

These attempts at evasion failed. Lord Redesdale, who had himself introduced an unsuccessful proposal for smoke abatement legislation in 1848, refused to pass the bill without the inclusion of a smoke abatement clause. Arguing that Stockport was the town most in need of a smoke clause, he inserted the Manchester Clause into the amendment bill. The selection of this particular clause further irritated the council, in part because the clause stipulated the appointment of an inspector for the suppression of smoke, in part because Manchester, a looming predatory presence, was held up as an example. When the council attempted to replace the Manchester Clause with a more ambiguously worded version, Redesdale – perhaps reflecting the landed élite's dislike of the new monied élite and of burgeoning industrial towns – reinstated the Manchester Clause. The Stockport Improvement Amendment Bill received Royal Assent on 17 June 1853.

Yet enforcement of the long-resisted clause was neither immediate nor frequent. It was not until December 1856 that the Inspector managed to bring a successful prosecution against smoky chimneys, when Thomas and George Cooke of Oxford Road Twist and Co. and R. Birley and Co. of Chorlton Mills were each fined 40 shillings. Their prosecutions brought forward complaints in the *Advertiser* and the beginning of a new campaign for smoke abatement legislation in Stockport. However, the number of prosecutions against smoky chimneys dwindled and no new legislation was adopted for 30 years.

Smoke abatement and non-decisions

Whilst it is evident that political action and conflict occurred, and decisions were made, in relation to smoke abatement more detailed analysis will show how Stockport Council manoeuvred smoke abatement into a political non-decisional state.

In the nineteenth-century urban arena, the visible philanthropic and social role of the 'urban squirearchy' created a municipal élite who enjoyed a considerable and cumulative political advantage.[25] Whilst more open than the rural élite, it was still exclusive and the symbiotic relationship between social and political leadership pervaded municipal politics at every level. Thus in Stockport council incorporation in 1835 limited the number of popular access points. None the less, there were limits to the power of the municipal élite – quite apart from its internal divisions - from groups like the ratepayers, small property owners and traders. These groups managed to exert influence by extracting pledges or significant inaction from members. More serious limitations came from Parliament, particularly in relation to improvement legislation, by imposing high costs and affecting outcomes. Still, the debates on Stockport Council show how for years the town's industrial, economic and political élites acted in their own interests and thwarted attempts at introducing a smoke abatement clause in Stockport's proposed bill. Stockport's municipal élites achieved this lack of action by successful issue management and agenda manipulation. Similar tactics subsequently limited the effectiveness of smoke abatement clauses once these were centrally imposed.

Issue emergence generally involves two processes – issue attention and legitimation – the key variables in getting decision-makers to take up problems. Issue emergence, as Hogwood and Gunn suggest, is a process of recognition, 'assuming not only threats and a problem but also the opportunity for positive action'.[26] Public policy theorists have argued that legitimacy in the context of agenda setting depends initially on an issue gaining attention and also to a considerable degree on the value systems of policy makers and the position within a society of the individuals or groups promoting an issue.[27] For an issue to be considered legitimate, there has to be a compatibility between the issue and its proposed solution. If a proposed solution challenges perceived beliefs and ideologies it is likely to be ignored or considered disruptive. In Stockport, the disproportionate financial burden placed on the ratepayers for the funding of improvement legislation, added to the underlying doctrine of *laissez-faire*, ensured that improvement proposals such as smoke abatement were spurned and, once enacted, thwarted.

Agenda-setting theory suggests that the legitimacy of issues and groups is often determined by those already regarded as legitimate. Thus in Stockport smoke abatement legislation would have meant mill owners and council members introducing penalties upon themselves. Berhout argues that legitimation is the active negotiation of authority by those in authority.[28] There was no benefit of smoke abatement legislation for those in authority in Stockport because they usually lived outside the town and did not suffer the effects of their inaction.[29]

Lukes[30] argues that it is wrong to see such activity in the one-dimensional terms of agenda setting and legitimation. Rather than being reactive, the activity we have seen in Stockport council should be seen as proactive. The mill owners acted upon the issue of smoke abatement to render it ineffective. Danziger's[31] 'second face of power' argues that this process of rejecting an issue by sustaining a mobilisation of bias against it is a non-decision and not a question of legitimation. Thus by failing to take a decisive lead on the calls for smoke pollution, and by rejecting attempts at formulating legislation in favour of it, Stockport Council was involved in active non-decision-making: the setting up of committees and inquiries into the feasibility of smoke abatement implies that smoke abatement was a legitimate issue and was placed firmly on the agenda awaiting the formulation of policy. But, both the committees and the inquiries were undertaken by municipal élites who had vested economic and industrial interests in preventing legislation. The theory legitimising this policy-making role of the industrial élite was partly based on the assumption that the skills and acumen attained whilst running successful businesses meant that they were equipped to cope with the decision-making process.[32]

The proliferation of committees shows how an individual élite could attain influence in many areas of policy-making. By relegating issues to committees, access was limited to a smaller and more powerful élite. The millowner and anti-abater Gouldthorpe sat on the watch, finance, improvement and sanitary committees. The increasingly complex nature of the subjects of some legislation meant that it was ever more necessary to have a detailed understanding of issues. We see at the beginning of the 1850s in Stockport how in some council debates 'experts' like the medical officer Dr Turner were called to give evidence. John Garrard[33] shows that this was increasingly the case after 1850 and that expertise rather than economic weight began to be the determining factor in appointing members to committees. Most reports were passed *nem con*, and the proliferation of committees meant that access to them and the ability to influence them became more difficult and more complex. The activity of the committees in Stockport fit Bacharach and Baratz's definition of non-decision-making, as the means by which demands for change in the existing allocation can be suffocated before they are even voiced, or kept covert or killed before they gain access to the relevant decision making arena.[34]

The non-decision regarding smoke abatement may have been due to several factors. First, it could have been due to a lack of understanding of the causes and effects of smoke or technological ignorance of methods of control. While there was a well-recognised problem of smoke pollution, it was not clear whether the effect of breathing smoke led to the development of chest disease or premature death. Conflicting scientific and medical evidence was presented. It has to be remembered that there were many conflicting and contrasting ideas on the cause of disease and disease prevention. The competing theories and paradigms for action weakened the strength of this argument and opened the way for the more dominant economic and political interests.[35]

Second, smoke could simply not have been an issue seen as requiring urgent action. Attempts by the *Advertiser* to instigate a campaign for abatement were hindered by the amorphous nature of its readership and the lack of political support from within the council. Likewise, the number of those calling for change was unknown, and as such remained economically and politically weak.

Third, as an issue smoke abatement may have been removed from the agenda of debate because of financial costs and the burden placed on ratepayers. Blowers[36] argues in his study of brick works in Bedfordshire that non-decision-making rests primarily upon economic concerns. Evidence in the *Advertiser* supports this view:

> Those who have dictated the (improvement) Bill, have thus far, interfered to prevent expense to themselves, seeing that nearly every member of the council of the corporation is directly or indirectly interested in saving expense for themselves.[37]

For the pluralists, the decentralisation and heterogeneity of local politics illustrate the penetrability of the political stratum. Yet, as Dahl says, 'diversity does not mean that any dissatisfied group can find a spokesman in the political stratum'.[38] The specific emphasis of the pluralist upon political activists overlooks the power of obstruction, of enforcing inaction and thereby making the political process impenetrable. Garrard argues that the agenda of local institutional politics may have been controlled or manipulated by individuals in strategic positions, either from within or by influencing access to those institutions to those outside.[39] Lukes argues that:

> bias in the system can be mobilised, recreated and reinforced in ways that are neither consciously chosen nor an intended result of particular individuals' choices ... the bias of the system is not sustained simply by a series of individually chosen acts but also, most importantly by socially structured and culturally patterned behaviour of groups and practices of institutions.[40]

The mass of the population was faced by conflicting interests. Smoke pollution affected their health, but they wanted and needed employment. Stockport's élites so dominated the perception of the mass of the population who believed that their interests were the same as the elites, that no real debate took place. As Crenson[41] has shown, the mere presence of a dominant employer can be sufficient to render opposition to its activities mute, but in Stockport the élites discussed and acted upon the issues of smoke abatement and neutralised it into a non-decisional state.

If we accept Lukes's theory of political socialisation, we must seek to fix responsibility for the consequences of inaction. It would be easy to see the inaction on smoke abatement purely in terms of a municipal, industrial and economic élite acting entirely in its own interests, but this would be far too simplistic. Crenson argues that the issues that are neglected, the non-decisions, are not politically random oversights but instances of politically enforced neglect. Similarly, arguing that 'All forms of political organisation have a bias in favour of the exploitation of some forms of conflict and the suppression of others, because organisation is the mobilisation of bias', Schattschneider suggests that pluralist policies in reality restrict the scope of the political process to a limited range of 'acceptable' issues and political demands.[42] In short, some issues are organised into politics and some are organised out. Pluralists argue that this is because of the rivalry among issues. If this were so, the prominence of one issue should be negatively related to the prominence of another. In Stockport, however, the council was hostile to most forms of improvements that incurred costs and eroded the freedom of the individual. During this time, no one improvement issue gained prominence at the expense of another.

The process of decision-making in improvement legislation was not only the responsibility of Stockport Council; it was a dual process between local and central government and, as such, depended on the vagaries of two socially, economically, culturally and politically distinct institutions. This significantly complicates Dahl's notion of pluralist power relationships, not least because Lord Redesdale's decision to introduce smoke abatement was partly in response to calls from ratepayers and smoke abatement pressure groups which had previously been marginalised within the town. What this shows is how decisions and non-decisions are multifarious. The issues discussed have successfully to gain access to several agendas.

Danziger[43] offers an explanation of this dynamic by presenting power and powerlessness in terms of power distribution. She argues that a group (Q) is politically powerless to the extent that it is unable to promote or defend its interests within authoritative processes of value allocation within a particular community. Yet in the Stockport case the dominant industrial elite within the council was both powerful (*vis-à-vis* dissident interests within the town) and weak (*vis-à-vis* the parliamentary private bills committee). Moreover, for a time there was an influential interaction between minority interests inside the elite and strong forces in central government. But ultimately the balance of power on the issue lay with those members of the local élite who opposed smoke abatement; they kept effective enforcement off the 'agenda' of local government even after it was nominally in force.

Nevertheless, for Baratz and Bacharach power in itself cannot be possessed because the exercise of power is dependent upon the relative importance of conflicting values in the minds of the recipients in a power relationship. Power is, therefore, relational rather than possessive or substantive. It is relational first because, in order for a power relationship to exist there must be a conflict of interests or values between two or more persons or groups. Power is, according to Lasswell,[44] the process of affecting policies with the help of (threatened) deprivations. The threat of sanctions differentiates power from influence; force is when an objective is pursued in the face of non-compliance.

The political activity involved in the process of introducing smoke abatement legislation in Stockport between 1844 and 1856 shows that both the decision-making process of Stockport Council and central government were subject to conflicting pressures. Stockport Council faced pressure from the ratepayers, the *Advertiser*, peer groups, those fearful of economic consequences and central government. Stockport Council put pressure on local residents by a combination of mediated and actual deference, by weighting committees in favour of its members and manipulating the political agenda to conserve its own interests. John Garrard[45] sees these 'pressures' in terms of conflict. He concentrates on the outcome of disputes between individuals and groups at different social-economic levels, between large and small property owners and between differing geo-economic areas. Central government and in particular Private Bill committees had pressure from landed interests, pressure groups in favour of reform, deputations from local councils, and calls from the intelligentsia to act responsibly on public health issues. The private committee and, in particular, Redesdale put pressure on local councils to act and he increasingly became paternalistic and authoritarian in his demands.

Conclusion

This chapter shows both that the whole local political system was open to pressures and constraints from central government and that the power of local leadership was dependent on the extent to which the local political system was open to pressures from within the locality. Neither a simple élitist model nor a simple pluralist model of nineteenth-century urban politics explains Stockport's experience with smoke abatement. The undoubted power of Stockport's political elites was limited by the growing power of the parliamentary private committee and in particular Lord Redesdale.[46] The process discussed was not pluralist; the final policy was not the result of a bargaining process between several competing power centres of which Stockport Council was one. Neither does the political action or decision-making process fit any of the previously discussed community power debates. The successful agenda manipulation by Stockport's élites ensured that despite Lord Redesdale's efforts, smoke abatement was effectively manoeuvred from the agenda into a non-decisional state for over 30 years. Analysis of such patterns over a larger time period and for other towns will determine the applicability of these conclusions to the study of urban governance more generally.

Notes

1. For instance, J. Evelyn, *Fumifugium* (London: Methuen, Bedel and Collins, 1661).
2. See, for example, P. Brimblecombe, *The Big Smoke* (London: 1987). Among the few broad historical treatments is C. Flick, 'The Movement for Smoke Abatement in Nineteenth Century Britain', *Technology and Culture*, 21 (1980), pp. 29–50.
3. F. Engels, *The Conditions of the Working Class in England* (London: Penguin, 1987; first published 1842), p. 84.
4. M.A. Creason, *The Un-Politics of Air and Pollution* (Baltimore, MD: The Johns Hopkins University Press, 1971).
5. E. Ashby and M. Anderson, *The Politics of Clean Air* (Oxford: Clarendon Press, 1981), p. 2.

6. R.A. Dahl, *Who Governs?* (New Haven, CT: Yale University Press, 1966).
7. P. Bachrach and P. Baratz, 'Decisions and Non-Decisions: An Analytical Framework', *American Political Science Review*, 57 (1962), pp. 632–42.
8. J.A. Garrard, *Leadership and Power in Victorian Industrial Towns* (Manchester: Manchester University Press, 1983).
9. J.A. Garrard, 'The History of Local Political Power: Some Suggestions for Analysis', *Political Studies*, 25 (1977), pp. 252–69.
10. A. Redford and I.S. Russell, *The History of Local Government in Manchester*, vol. 1 (London: Longmans Green, 1939).
11. H. Heginbotham, *Stockport Ancient and Modern*, vols 1 and 2 (Stockport: 1882), p. 247
12. First published in 1822, the paper played a major part in calling for the abatement of smoke. Whilst it generally adhered to the principles of Toryism it managed on this issue to take a more independent line.
13. *Stockport Advertiser* (*SA*), 25 Mar. 1853.
14. For analysis of working-class politics in Stockport during the period see N. Kirk, *The Growth of Working-Class Reformism in Mid-Victorian England* (London: Croom Helm, 1985).
15. Crenson, *Un-Politics*.
16. Stockport Improvement Bill, 1844.
17. The costs of introducing and guiding an improvement bill through Parliament acted as a restraint on local councils which feared losing (Garrard, *Leadership and Power in Victorian Industrial Towns* [Manchester: Manchester University Press, 1983] p. 101) shows that the cost of introducing Bolton's Bill was £9,000 in 1854.
18. *SA*, 21 Nov. 1845.
19. Heginbotham, *Stockport*, p. 252.
20. *SA*, 31 July 1846.
21. *SA*, 25 Mar. 1847.
22. The Act had little impact on other aspects of improvement. The provision for a public park was taken up in the following year when Lord Vernon gave 1783 square yards of land (including the site of the Court House) to the council for a chief rent of £50 per annum. He also dedicated the 14 acres of Stringer's fields for public use, land valued at £3,300. In return Lord Vernon obtained the Cheese House at a nominal rent of £5 per annum and a strip of land reserved for industrial development. The public park was not opened until 1858. Attempts to address the inadequate water supply were equally ineffective: only 4,013 out of the 14,311 tenants were supplied with water by the water company. A token nod in the name of improvement was made when the town purchased a swooping machine which mechanised the collection of sewerage in 1846.
23. *SA*, 25 Mar. 1853.
24. *SA*, 8 Apr. 1853.
25. J.A. Garrard, 'Urban Elites 1850–1914: The Rule and Decline of a New Squierarchy?', *Albion*, 27 (1995), pp. 583–621.
26. B.W. Hogwood and L.A. Gunn, 'The Dynamics of Policy Change', *Policy Sciences*, 14 (1982), pp. 225–45.
27. S. Ward, 'The Politics of Environmental Agendas; The Case of UK Local Authorities', unpublished thesis, University of the West of England, 1994.
28. F. Berhout, *Radioactive Waste, Politics and Technology* (London: Routledge, 1991).
29. For contemporary recognition of this point see *SA*, 12 May 1848.
30. S. Lukes, *Power: A Radical View* (London: Macmillan, 1974).

31. R. Danziger, *Political Powerlessness* (Manchester: Manchester University Press, 1988).
32. Cf. E.P. Hennock, *Fit and Proper Persons: Ideal and Reality in Nineteenth Century Urban Government* (London: Edward Arnold, 1973).
33. Garrard, *Leadership and Power*.
34. Bachrach and Baratz, 'Decisions and Non-Decisions?'
35. C. Flick, *Movement*; B. Lightburn (ed.), *Victorian Science in Context* (Chicago: University of Chicago Press, 1997).
36. A. Blowers, *The Policy Process: A Reader* (London: Harvester-Wheatsheaf, 1993).
37. *SA*, 21 Nov. 1845.
38. Dahl, *Who Governs?*, p. 93.
39. Garrard, *Leadership and Power*.
40. Lukes, *Power*, p. 16.
41. Crenson, *Un-Politics*.
42. B.E. Schattschneider, *The Semi-Sovereign People* (London and New York: The Dryden Press, 1960), p. 42.
43. Danziger, *Political Powerlessness*.
44. H.D. Lasswell, *Politics: Who Gets What, When and How* (New York: Whittlesey House; London: McGraw-Hill Book Company Inc. 1936).
45. Garrard, *Leadership and Power*.
46. The centralising of improvement legislation was to grow with the development of the Local Acts Office and the Local Government Board in 1871, further diluting the power of the élites.

CHAPTER TWELVE

Industrial conciliation, class co-operation and the urban landscape in mid-Victorian England

Donna Loftus

Introduction

The urban and the industrial were two sites of anxiety in the reform projects of the mid-nineteenth century. Proliferating inquiries into the health of towns and the industrial workplace mark attempts by contemporaries to order and define the boundaries of the social and the economic, the moral and the environmental. On the one hand, the urban and the industrial were seen as overlapping sites of community and market; on the other, they were realised as distinct locales subject to specific laws and forms of governance. The industrial relation and the workplace had a particular and complex impact on urban governance in the mid-nineteenth century. Work emerged as one of the central paradigms for imagining and regulating the industrial community and, as such, provided a site for the wide-ranging attentions of liberal commentators. In official investigations, journalism and novels, industrial relations and working conditions were perceived as impacting on the prosperity and order of the wider community. As the history of factory legislation has chronicled, the location of the workplace within urban space was central to competing claims as to its regulation.[1] Arguments for factory reform often claimed rights to regulation on the basis of wider community interests beyond strictly economic criteria. Often articulated around the bodies of women and children, workplace regulation was seen as central to moral order and the social and physical health of the working population. Employers themselves often presented the workplace as the centre of community relations in terms that defined their own civic identity.[2] Such claims could be used to defend the workplace as subject to an employer's own private authority and beyond local or state governance.

In the aftermath of the factory question, a number of debates went on to consider the social organisation of capital in the community.[3] Schemes of industrial co-operation including limited liability companies, Christian Socialist workshops and local trade boards provided a forum for a complex debate and negotiation of urban governance and industrial relations in the mid-nineteenth century. Out of these debates in the 1850s formalised systems of industrial conciliation emerged as a 'panacea' for urban social ills and an arena for industrial harmony.[4] *Ad hoc* bodies, composed of employers and workers for the negotiation of trade interest, had long since existed in certain local trades but, at a time of increased liberal interest in local voluntary agencies of regulation and reform, conciliation took on a renewed significance. Its promotion drew on three distinct images of urban industrial space and governance. First, boards of conciliation, composed equally of employers and workers in the local trade for the negotiation of trade issues, were presented as vistas of cross-class communication. Conciliation was promoted as a local arrangement which might produce consent through the realisation of mutual interests and shared goals. Second, conciliation was argued to provide a 'neutral space', beyond sectional interests, for capital and improved labour to discuss issues of trade rationally and democratically.[5] Third, conciliation was promoted, by reformers such as R.A. Slaney and A.J. Mundella, as a scheme for the further improvement of the skilled working man, and as an appeal for the leadership of enlightened local capital.[6] Boards were considered as educating an improved stratum of working-class men in the nuances of the local market and the process of democratic negotiation which would consequently reveal the futility of strikes and the superiority of conciliatory discussion. The combination of communication, negotiation and education was considered as a means of instituting local industrial harmony, a state which would promote the prosperity and social order of the wider community.

This chapter will discuss the emergence of conciliation, its visualisation of local space, industrial relations and urban governance. Analysis of debates about conciliation contributes to a wider understanding of urban governance in a number of ways. The promotion of boards, composed equally of employers and workers for the negotiation of local trade questions, can be seen as part of wider schemes to manufacture consent through the designation of public space for private negotiation.[7] Such arrangements were felt to inform the greater legitimacy of capital in the locale through the democratisation of participation and through revealing the mutual interests of the market. These debates focused on a stratum of skilled workers in local trades whom promoters of conciliation hoped would become reformed co-operators in the local market and thus self-regulating individuals in their communities. Conciliation potentially offered employers civic leadership, based on notions of enlightened capital, whilst maintaining their authority for the regulation of the workplace. At best, however, employer attitudes to conciliation can be largely characterised by ambivalence. Employer interest in schemes often appeared to fluctuate with conditions which might threaten their local authority and leadership, such as trade cycles, trade union activism and suggestions of legislative intervention. Employers could use conciliation to support claims of local trade specificity and enlightened production methods, emphasising their own professionalism, local knowledge and leadership. At the same time, the legitimacy of such authority was closely linked with perceptions of the market and its boundaries. Whilst some employers welcomed conciliation as a form of local trade self-regulation, many resented in practice having to impart their knowledge of prices and accounts on boards. Whilst work might be promoted as a central part of the community in discourses of conciliation, employers often considered the workplace and its accounts to be to be their own private property.[8]

As might be expected, given such uncertainties as to the boundaries of the workplace, the experience of boards was contentious and fraught. Most conciliation boards were called to settle disputes about wages, an issue on which employers often declined to negotiate. Consequently, third parties or arbitrators, usually lawyers, were needed to defuse conflicts.[9] At the same time the discourses that placed the market at the centre of the local community led to competing claims on the autonomy and authority of employer leadership. With the increasing prominence given to the damaging effects of poor industrial relations in both the local and national economy, boards and their decisions were presented as requiring some form of compulsion. In the 1860s the need to enforce decisions made trade union membership a prerequisite to negotiation, whilst associations of employers were required to ensure prices were not undercut. The desirability of local voluntary self-regulation conflicted constantly with the need to make conciliation an effective mechanism of industrial co-operation in the mid-century. The passing of Mundella's Act in 1872, giving power to both parties to enforce decisions by the legal process, symbolised the subjugation of local trade interest to these national legal requirements.[10]

The next section of this chapter will locate debates on conciliation in the context of a wider discourse on urban and industrial regulation in the mid-century. Afterwards, particular attention will be given to the Nottingham lace industries whose boards of conciliation, comprised equally of employers and skilled unionised working men, were publicised in the 1860s as a model of enlightened industrial organisation leading to urban reform. The experience of Nottingham is both typical and particular.[11] The Nottingham manufacturer, A.J. Mundella, the figure most associated with conciliation, promoted his measures with reference to the transformation of Nottingham's urban relations as a result of conciliation. After helping to establish conciliation boards in Nottingham lace and hosiery in the 1860s, Mundella travelled the country bringing to liberal audiences practical advice on their formation. In this respect, conciliation was a central factor in both Nottingham's civic identity and Mundella's national liberal career, helping to define the town, the lace and hosiery industries and Mundella himself as progressive and modern. Mundella's advocacy of conciliation was based on his particular experience of Nottingham industries, yet his speeches emphasised how trade-specific arrangements could uniformly improve urban and industrial order. Mundella staked a claim to liberal prominence with his argument that voluntary and flexible conciliation, based on rational and respectful negotiation, would provide the best mechanism for industrial regulation and social peace given the peculiarities of trades and localities. However, the experiences in Nottingham's lace boards, as with other trade boards, revealed the counter-claims and trends that resulted in the passing of Mundella's Act in 1872.

Industrial harmony and social peace: conciliation, 1850–60

Social inquiry in the mid-century often mapped the urban and the industrial together as sites of concern. Enquiries into public health referred to industrial relations in the same way that inquiries into work referred to the health of the community. Within the terms of these interlinking concerns enlightened capital was often designated as partly responsible for urban governance. Similarly, it was not uncommon to identify employers, in various capacities, as responsible for urban social relations. Whether motivated by the duty of wealth, Christianity or liberal principles, the enlightened and locally involved employer was associated with a healthy town in which civic amenities and individual well-being were linked to harmonious social relations and political civility.[12] Examples of such mapping are evident in many accounts of the period. Charles Knight in his descriptions of English towns emphasised the link between work and public health. Focusing on the new town of Birkenhead, Knight referred to the provision of churches, parks and drainage organised by a small knot of commercial improvers and employers as an illustration of the potential of enlightened capital to urban reform. The notion of the new town was significant here. Knight stated that as a creation of 'our own day' Birkenhead could avoid the mistakes of Liverpool and Manchester.[13] In contrast, the 'moral degeneration of Manchester' was linked to employer absenteeism, 'thus at the very moment when the engines are stopped and the counting houses closed, everything which was thought – the authority – the impulsive force – the moral index of this immense industrial combination, flies from the town and disappears in an instance'.[14]

Enlightened capital could civilise in other ways beyond urban improvement schemes. Large modern factories were in themselves associated with the physical and political health of the town and its workforce. The simple presence of the employer could be enough to improve the working classes. The *Morning Chronicle* investigations into manufacturing districts, which were commissioned in 1849–51, reported on the improved environment of towns where employers lived amongst workers, providing a check on drunkenness and vice. In comparison, small manufacture in towns devoid of an enlightened employer could be associated with filth and political radicalism. Bolton was described as a 'bad specimen of a cotton town', made up of 'old' forms of production, 'old' houses and 'old' men with 'old' ideas, a 'population which in a great degree preserves the hurtful prejudices and filthy old fashions, which have little hold in the more modern seats of industry'.[15] Oldham's structure of production, with its small capitalists renting spaces in factories, was also linked to the appearance of the town as 'filthy and smouldering'.[16] This interest in the social arrangements of industry within communities fed into a debate in the period on the associated roles and responsibilities of capital and labour. Such debates identified two key characters of progressive modern industries and towns, the enlightened employer and the respectable worker; they were perceived to share interests that would be revealed through communication.

This link between urban reform, health, and social and industrial relations was a feature of early interest in conciliation. Along with the reform of company law to free up the mechanisms for limited liability, conciliation was perceived as a simple reform of the organisation of the market allowing for the local association of capital and labour. Limited liability and conciliation were often seen as combined measures for including the more 'improved' members of the working classes in the local market and schemes of civic improvement, under the leadership of enlightened industrial capital. Liberal reformers, such as R.A. Slaney and J.S. Mill, promoted limited liability and conciliation as ways of communicating the legitimacy of market to the urban 'improved' working classes through share ownership schemes and trade boards.[17] Such reforms of capital were seen to combine commercial and moral rewards for local communities. Whilst freeing up capital for schemes of urban improvement, such reforms were also promoted for their potential to make the urban industrial working man a 'tranquil and conservative citizen', whose association with enlightened capital would strengthen the 'social fabric'.[18] Yet, as Mill noted, even if schemes of industrial co-operation failed 'the attempt to make them succeed would be a very important matter in the way of education to the working classes, both intellectually and morally'.[19] The value of limited liability and conciliation in the 1850s was that, whether successful or not, they would reveal to working men the skills and qualities required for business, and would thereby legitimise the profits of the capitalist and industrial forms of production.

In the 1850s the case for conciliation took on its own rationale. Its cause benefited from a disenchantment with the increasingly complex and legalistic nature of debates on company law reform and limited liability. At the same time, the rising tide of publicity given to the damaging effects of strikes on the local community made conciliation a more pressing issue. The importance of harmonious industrial relations to community welfare was emphasised in the association of strikes with wider social and political disorder in the 1850s. The issue was deemed important enough to warrant two select committee inquiries, in 1856 and 1860.[20] The inquiry reports recognised the damaging impact of strikes on the local community:

> These strikes, it is evident, are injurious to the employers, the employed, and to the small retail dealers in the district where they occur, and, it may be added, to the interests of all in the vicinity, and if extended or becoming general, might endanger the social order of society.[21]

Both identified strikes as a social problem with social causes and consequences. In particular, poor communication between masters and men was noted as leading to unrest. The 1856 report blamed a 'want of confidence' between employers and workers caused by 'the difficulty of access and the separation of caste, feeling and goodwill', as primarily leading to strikes. Again, both reports acknowledged that a mutual sympathy might be fostered through a 'more intimate acquaintance with each others' views'.[22] In effect, this acquaintance was often envisaged as little more than informing workers of those laws of political economy rendering managerial prerogatives essential. In the context of the Preston strike, noted for employers' refusal of conciliation, evidence from 'good' employers was amassed. Those employers – Henderson of Durham, Crossley of Halifax and Howard of Leeds – who had recently formed an Association of Carpet Manufacturers of the North of England explained how they peacefully secured a reduction by explaining to the workers why it was necessary. Their collective workers, they claimed, drafted an address to the striking cotton operatives of Manchester explaining the good feeling in their trade as a result of this simple communication and the 'bond of union' it had produced.[23] Conciliation was thus promoted as a cheap but effective measure of industrial and social reform.

Both inquiries, like other social narratives of the period, recognised the importance of communication to industrial and social harmony. As well as informing parties of their presumed mutual interests, communication was perceived to humanise industrial relations and clarify conditions of employment. At the same time, the reports recognised that personal communication was not always possible in the large modern workplace.

Whilst the civilising qualities of modern manufacture might be acknowledged, the anonymity of its relations was feared. Responding to such fears, the Royal Society of Arts and the National Association for the Promotion of Social Science (NAPSS) organised conferences of capital and labour, in a bid to carve out a public arena for the negotiation of class positions.[24] The consequence of local class isolation was explored in terms of dark spaces, hidden agendas and political sedition. At a conference on strikes in 1854, the Royal Society of Arts noted how workers, unable to talk in the workplace, were driven to debate in public houses and disorganised rallies in town halls whilst employers could argue their interests in private.[25] In contrast, working-class improvement was associated with the incorporation of a respectable working class into a disciplined and rationalised public space. Henry Fawcett argued that strikes resulted from the growing intelligence of certain sections of the working classes who would no longer submit to the authoritarian and antiquated arrangements of capital in which decisions on prices were made by employers in private and later imposed on the workforce.[26] Likewise, Slaney referred to 'angry passions' as the result, not of workers' ignorance, but of their frustration with the denial of space for rational and moderate debate on questions of trade.[27]

Such arguments informed a growing tide of support for institutionalised conciliation. At the same time, however, debates faltered on whether or not social and industrial peace was important enough to warrant legislation making conciliation compulsory. The NAPSS noted that the welfare of the community did have a claim to make on industrial arrangements:

> Employers and employed have no right to manage their affairs so badly as to cause inconvenience to third parties. Every man who pays poor rates has a right to complain at their being increased in consequence of avoidable distress; not to mention the still more direct inconvenience caused by all considerable strikes to large bodies of men totally unconcerned, on either side, with the cause of the dispute.[28]

Both select committee reports also concluded that the failure of industry to prevent strikes was a matter of public concern given its disastrous consequences on the locality. Still, the reports stopped short of recommending legislation to make boards of conciliation compulsory. Official debate was limited by some uncertainty as to the legitimacy of parliamentary involvement in matters of markets and working men. As such, there was little subsequent parliamentary debate on the select committee reports. The question of compulsory conciliation was dismissed by the House of Commons as a debate that might encourage workers to think they could 'expect things' from government.[29]

Employers themselves appeared to be largely absent from public debates on conciliation. When they were present many attempted to distinguish the value of communication as a managerial strategy from questions of the public accountability of industrial practices. In turn, employers could present the local market as a particular sphere, independent of social questions. Edmund Potter and Henry Ashworth both applauded the placing of the workplace in the wider community, but both determined that labour was a purchasable commodity whose price was to be determined by the market alone.[30] Employers were interested in conciliation as a broader system of local justice, wresting commercial decision-making from lawyers and legislators. The Association of Chambers of Commerce, established in 1860, saw conciliation as one part of a broader campaign for local commercial courts, to be formed out of mercantile and manufacturing expertise. The Nottingham manufacturer, A.J. Mundella, was a central figure in the promotion of industrial conciliation and a key campaigner for such commercial courts within the Associated Chambers of Commerce. For him conciliation and commercial courts were part of a vision of local, flexible market regulation.

Industrial regulation and urban reform: conciliation in Nottingham, 1860–72

Like many towns, Nottingham did not fit easily into an image of progressive industrial urban centres. Local civic leaders and enlightened employers, such as William Felkin and Mundella, emphasised Nottingham's modern industry and skilled core of 'labour aristocrats' employed in the process of lace making in large modern factories. Certainly, such representations were acknowledged in the parliamentary inquiries of 1833, 1843 and 1863 in which the modern lace factories and warehouses were identified as progressive. There was, however, another aspect to Nottingham's urban and industrial landscape noted in these inquiries. Many women and children were employed in the processes of lace finishing in small workshops and homes throughout the region which fell outside of the existing factory acts. The mass employment, of unregulated female workers, was emphasised in reports of immorality, drunkenness, sexual licentiousness and high rates of infant mortality in the city.[31] The lace industry, like the local hosiery trade, was also considerably unstable and volatile. This instability was blamed partly on the nature of a trade, dependent on fashion, in which goods could not be stockpiled and, partly, on a number of small masters joining the trade causing overproduction and price reductions.[32] Despite the identification of a core labouring aristocracy, Nottingham workers were not without a radical reputation; both lace and hosiery workers had been active in Chartism. The lace market in the centre of the town symbolised these multiple identities. It was a site of industrial progressiveness with its large warehouses given over to modern industry. At the same time, the market-place was often crowded and chaotic, used for fairs, political rallies and protests.

The conciliation movement in Nottingham was a factor in negotiating these competing civic and industrial claims. As with other trades in other locales, conciliation had a long history in Nottingham, but the famous Arbitration and Conciliation Board emerged in autumn 1860 from a long-running dispute over the payment of out workers.[33] Mundella, a pioneer of factory production in Nottingham often associated with radical liberalism, continued to employ men at the higher rate of wages. Eventually Mundella negotiated directly with working men, explaining that a reduction was the only way to guarantee employment. Mundella's apparent successes led to the formalisation of conciliation boards in the hosiery and lace trades. Mundella then went on to promote his schemes in lecturing tours around the country and through his association with the NAPSS and the Associated Chambers of Commerce. Typically such advocacies drew on the representation of conciliation as a scheme of urban improvement that was familiar to the inquiries of the 1850s. Conciliation was presented as carving out a public space for the association of enlightened capital and respectable labour. Seen as mutually improving, this public space for private negotiation was presented as promoting class consensus, economic prosperity and social peace. At the same time, Mundella also emphasised conciliation as a locally specific and voluntary arrangement which appealed to the specific and particularised experience and knowledge of local employers in matters of trade.

The particularities of Nottingham's lace and hosiery trades were a central aspect of the support for conciliation from large employers and skilled workers. The early 1860s were a period of quite intense instability, of rising output, falling prices and increasing competition.[34] Evidence from the 1861 inquiry into lace factories would seem to imply that both employers and skilled working men, organised in the powerful Lace Makers Society, were concerned with overproduction. The Lace Makers Society supported factory legislation as a means to limit production, whilst employers looked to voluntary means to regulate output. In this context, boards of conciliation were presented as the unification of skilled men and employers to regulate local trade, as an alternative to state intervention. The Nottingham manufacturer, former mayor and self-proclaimed 'expert' in the lace and hosiery trades, William Felkin, certainly thought that boards of conciliation would make parliamentary intervention in business unnecessary.[35] A union of masters and men would, he argued, police bad employers, overproduction and the quality of goods in the locality.[36] Likewise, Mundella envisaged conciliation as a scheme of local trade regulation uniting workers and employers against unscrupulous manufacturers. Such arrangements were, however, carefully presented not to usurp the claims of political economy. Mundella argued that the market price of lace and hosiery was often forced by the undercutting of small masters in the trade. In turn, he argued that conciliation would actually promote the legitimate regulation of political economy as interpreted by 'good' employers and respectable workers. The benefit of local and institutional price controls would result in a stabilising of the market, enabling employers to stock up and offer workers permanency of wages and work. Such arrangements, Mundella argued, would eventually impact on local prosperity and peace.

As Mundella's arguments revealed, the revived interest in conciliation in the 1860s was informed by the persistence of trade cycles of industrial unrest that might otherwise appear beyond human control. In his evidence to the Royal Commission on Trades Unions, Mundella argued that the experience of industrialisation had taught capital and labour that it needed to work together to contain unrest in the continuing cycles of boom and bust. Explaining the take-up of schemes in 1868, rather than when they were promoted in the 1850s, Mundella noted the growing intelligence of employers and workers with the realisation that the 'old system', where masters could drive down prices in bad times and workers would drive them up in good, was injurious to both parties and the wider community.[37] This he compared to the civilised negotiation of conciliation in which an awareness of shared interests, cultivated consensus and collective action in the interests of peace and prosperity. Again the anonymity of modern production methods, consequential misunderstandings and employer arrogance were perceived as the cause of industrial unrest. Reflecting on the place of employment relations in the wider community Mundella noted:

> In the old time, when I was an apprentice, my master knew every man he employed and knew his circumstances. When his wife was sick he helped him, or lent him money, or helped to send his boys to school. Now we employ thousands; we do not know their faces; they are 'hands' to us, they are not men; there is no mutual sympathy, and that is the top and bottom of all the mischief.[38]

In turn conciliation was promoted as a mechanism for knowing the industrial worker. The rhetorical image of masters and men meeting as joint producers on boards was often invoked to restore legitimacy and authority to the market and employers. Mundella, like other advocates of conciliation, was adamant that manners rather than money were the cause of strikes. Stories in which the consequences of employer arrogance were seen to result in the 'public calamity' of strikes achieved almost mythical status.[39] The iron employer David Dale talked of strikes as the result of 'the adoption by foremen and managers of a tone toward the men under them inconsistent with those men's self respect'.[40] By such definitions, however, conciliation was not appropriate to all forms of production and all workers, and the failure of conciliation was often seen as an indictment of working men.[41] Women were by definition excluded. The lack of boards in the woollen and worsted trades of Yorkshire was explained by the fact that 'the majority of workers, more than 70 per cent, are women and children'. The wholesale exclusion of women and children was about more than their presumed ability to negotiate. The worsted spinner and manufacturer W.E. Foster argued that conciliation was not appropriate to trades employing women and children as 'Their chief business is already done by other parties'.[42] In Foster's trade, as protected workers, women and children were represented by the state. The conciliation movement of the 1860s addressed itself specifically to working-class male self-representation and particularly to unionised working men. In the context of the Reform Act of 1868 and campaigns for trade union reform, forums of local trade self-regulation might be considered as one way for capital to circumvent a direct link between organised labour and the state. Boards were certainly seen as mechanisms for the civilising of urban space and public manners through the incorporation of respectable working men into a disciplined and democratic local space.[43]

The argument that workers themselves became civilised through the experience of conciliation was central to its apparent progressive qualities. Prior to boards, lace and hosiery prices were bargained in a public exchange of handbills and proclamations which in turn rejected strikes and lock outs. Instead, conciliation claimed to settle prices in a private and civilised negotiation in which union representatives were treated as equal representatives of trade. With such arrangements Mundella spoke not only of the civilised negotiation of industrial relations but also of the disciplining of public space. Furthermore, he talked of the political unrest of pre-conciliation Nottingham, in which inflammatory handbills were posted on the street, noting that since the establishment of the conciliation boards 'not one has been published'.[44] In a rhetoric redolent of the reform campaigns, working men were presented in conciliation as reasoned and rational individuals able to represent themselves and their class. With employers they had the requisite knowledge to represent the trade.

The recognition of local trade peculiarities within the promotion of universal principles of progress was a central facet of conciliation as a reform project. Whilst admitting the need for some governance of industry in the interests of the community, conciliation legitimised only the self-regulation of trade interests. Whilst Mundella talked of 'reason and humanity' and the laws of political economy, he also claimed 'Engineers cannot legislate for tailors, nor tailors for engineers; each industry must legislate for itself'.[45] For similar reasons Mundella was opposed to outside arbitration, and within trades and localities attention to separate and legitimate interests often resulted in the complicated and elaborate structure of boards. In the Nottingham hosiery and lace boards, standing committees were made up of two workers and two employers from each branch of the trade as a means to settle issues for each branch. If disputes continued they were then sent to a meeting of the full board of 12 employers and 12 workers, drawn proportionately from the differing branches of the trades. Finally, provision was made for a referee if disputes continued. Despite such elaborate structures and democratic discourses, the experience of conciliation did not manufacture consensus through the realisation of mutuality and the legitimacy of the market. Indeed, most boards exposed the limits of liberal consensus and political economy.

Despite such progressive and optimistic promotions and the elaborate structure of boards, the history of Nottingham conciliation was fraught. Interviewed by the Webbs in the 1890s, one of the workers' representatives on the lace board argued that it was forced on the men in 1868. He claimed discussions were mostly about prices and that workers felt employers always asked for a greater reduction than they required in a false compromise.[46] The vision of localised and voluntary self-regulation was in practice difficult to achieve. Issues of compulsion made trade union membership a prerequisite to negotiation, whilst associations of employers were required to ensure that decisions on prices were maintained. Despite such arrangements prices were still undercut by small masters. Most disputes after 1868 were effectively about wages, the settlement of which employers often declined to negotiate. The most significant complaint about the boards, one echoed in boards across the country, was the refusal of employers to impart their full knowledge of accounts and profits. As boards were formed in various trades throughout England, third parties or arbitrators, usually lawyers, were often needed to defuse conflicts, an intervention that was often resented by employers. The authority of the market or the mutuality of capitalist production was of little consolation. One arbitrator, Judge Ellison, questioned by the Webbs on his experience as a referee on the Board of Arbitration for the South Yorkshire Collieries, summed up the problem:

> It is for (the employers' advocate) to put the men's wages as high as he can. It is for (the men's advocate) to put them as low as he can. And when you have done that it is for me to deal with the question as well as I can; but on what principle I have to deal with it I have not the slightest idea.[47]

The lace board, like others in the 1870s, folded when workers refused to accept reductions without first seeing the figures. Employers refused to share this information, the board collapsed and a strike ensued.

In spite of the promotion of conciliation as the local regulation of trade interests, Mundella passed his Conciliation Act in 1872, giving power to boards to fix wages and power for either party to force decisions by the legal process. Although largely inoperative, the Act was considered as subjugating local trade peculiarities to national legal systems. Mundella's reasons in passing this Act are difficult to ascertain and, perhaps, may have stemmed from his wish to represent working men's interests. Still, the same arguments that fed into conciliation – the implications of labour relations for local economic and social harmony, the disciplining of capital and labour and the need to build consensus – could easily be asserted to support legislation. Equally, although conciliation was premised on voluntary regulation of a democratised local market, the need to enforce decisions necessitated a state response and a legal framework. A system which was initially perceived to institutionalise the local leadership of enlightened capital in the local market, in practice, challenged this authority. The authority of employers to interpret local trade was in effect challenged by workers themselves and the activity of lawyers on boards. Similarly, the legitimacy of the mutually beneficial market was often exposed as the separate interests of capital and labour were revealed on boards.

Conclusions

Embodying the mid-Victorian emphasis on local and voluntary self-regulation and improvement, conciliation was seen as a social panacea, a mechanism uniting the employer and the improved worker in the interests of industrial progress. Like other mid-Victorian concerns, however, the practice of conciliation raised tensions over the boundaries of local and national governance. Initially, conciliation was promoted as a scheme for working-class improvement under the direction and leadership of local employers. The idea of a local neutral space for capital and labour to meet, to put the principles of political economy into practice, was threatened by the practical evidence and experience of conciliation. In practice, the separate organisation of employers and workers was often required to discipline members to obey decisions. Similarly, the legal status of decisions was awkward; as voluntary arrangements they could be and were usurped by statutory legislation. The passing of Mundella's Act in 1872, giving power to either party to enforce decisions legally marked a shift in the conceptualisation of local class co-operation, from voluntary and self-regulatory to legal and national. The Act also highlighted the power that an enfranchised working class might exercise to regulate trade. In turn, organised employers in the 1870s distanced themselves from conciliation. In the context of a renewed parliamentary interest in industrial legislation, Factory Act consolidation and extension, and trade union recognition, organised employers presented the workplace as an abstract site, whose management required distance from the broader social and political issues of the day.

Notes

1. R. Gray, *The Factory Question and Industrial England, 1830–1860* (Cambridge: Cambridge University Press, 1996); S. Rose, 'Protective Labor Legislation in Britain: Gender, Class and the Liberal State', S. Rose and L. Frader (eds), *Gender and Class in Modern Europe* (Ithaca, NY: Cornell University Press, 1996), pp. 193–210.
2. A.H. Yarmie, 'British Employers' Resistance to Grandmotherly Government', *Social History*, 9 (1984) pp. 141–69.
3. These concerns with the social arrangements of capital coincided with a revived interest in *laissez-faire*ism in the 1850s, after the legislative activity of the Whig governments of the 1830s and 1840s. See P. Mandler, *Aristocratic Government in the Age of Reform: Whigs and Liberals, 1830–1852* (Oxford: Clarendon Press, 1990), pp. 275–82.
4. L.L.F.R. Price, *Industrial Peace: Its Advantages, Methods and Difficulties* (London: Macmillan, 1887), p. 5.
5. *Journal of the Society of Arts*, 6 January 1854, p. 113.
6. P. Richards, 'R.A. Slaney, the industrial town, and early Victorian social policy', *Social History*, 4 (1979), pp. 85–101; W.H.G. Armytage, *A.J. Mundella 1825–1897: The Liberal Background to the Labour Movement* (London: Ernest Benn, 1951).
7. For a discussion of broader attempts to reorder public space and reform manners see J. Belchem and J. Epstein, 'The Nineteenth-Century Gentleman Leader Revisited', *Social History*, 22 (1997) pp. 174–93.
8. A. McIvor, *Organised Capital: Employers' Associations and Industrial Relations in Northern England, 1880–1939* (Cambridge: Cambridge University Press, 1996), p. 3.
9. J.R. Hicks, 'The Early History of Industrial Conciliation in England', *Economica*, 10 (1930), pp. 26–37.
10. An Arbitration Act was passed in 1867 which gave power to the Home Secretary to license permanent councils of conciliation. The Act was limited to the interpretation of existing contracts of employment and not the fixing of wages. No licences were applied for. Mundella's Act gave boards the power to fix wages and prices and legally to enforce decisions. Both Acts were repealed in 1896.
11. R.A. Church, *Economic and Social Change in a Midland Town: Victorian Nottingham, 1815–1900* (London: Frank Cass, 1966).
12. See J.S. Mill, 'The Claims of Labour: An Essay on the Duties of the Employers to the Employed', *Edinburgh Review*, 81 (1845); A. Helps, *The Claims of Labour: An Essay on the Duties of the Employers to the Employed* (Manchester: John Harrison, 1846).
13. C. Knight, *The Land We Live In. A Political and Literary Sketch Book of the British Empire* (London: Charles Knight, 1847–50), p. 100.

14. Ibid., p. 175.
15. 'Labour and the Poor in England and Wales 1849–1851, *The Morning Chronicle*, 29 October 1849.
16. *The Morning Chronicle*, 12 November 1849.
17. R.A. Slaney, 'On Limited and Unlimited Liability in Partnerships', *Journal of the Society of Arts*, 2 June 1854, pp. 476–85. See also J.S. Mill's evidence in the *Select Committee Report on Investments for the Savings of the Middle and Working Classes* (1850) [508] pp. xix, 80–85.
18. See, 'Partnership Law', *Quarterly Review*, April 1852, p. 407 and 'Partnerships with Limited Liability, *Westminster Review*, 6 (1853), p. 414.
19. J.S. Mill in *Investments for the Savings of the Middle and Working Classes*, p. 85.
20. *Select Committee Report on Masters, Servants and Workmen* (1856) [343] p. xiii and *Select Committee Report on Masters and Operatives* (1860) [307] p. xxii.
21. *Masters, Servants and Workmen*, p. XV.
22. Ibid.
23. *Masters, Servants and Workmen*, p. 100, Q.1150/2.
24. See the respective reports from these conferences: Supplement to the *Journal of the Society of Arts*, 3 February 1854; *Trades Societies and Strikes* (J.W. Parker and Son, 1860).
25. Supplement to the *Journal of the Society of Arts*, 3 February 1854, pp. 193, 196.
26. H. Fawcett, 'Social Economy', *Transactions of the National Association for the Promotion of Social Science* (1859), p. 635.
27. *Masters and Operatives*, p. 46, Q.476.
28. *Trades Societies and Strikes*, p. xvii.
29. *Hansard*, third series, CLVI, 29 February 1860, p. 2015.
30. *Trades Societies and Strikes*, pp. 595, 606.
31. For greater exposition of these issues see, R. Gray and D. Loftus, 'Industrial Regulation, Urban Space and the Boundaries of the Workplace: Mid-Victorian Nottingham', *Urban History*, forthcoming.
32. Inventions in lace making machines had been so rapid in the first half of the nineteenth century that new machines soon became obsolete and could be bought fairly cheaply – as such there were an increasing number of men setting up workshops in their own homes and outhouses.
33. J.H. Porter, 'Wages Bargaining Under Conciliation Agreements, 1860–1914', *Economic History Review*, 23 (1970) pp. 460–75.
34. Church, *Economic and Social Change in a Midland Town*, pp. 287–90.
35. Felkin published his *History of the Machine Wrought Hosiery and Lace Manufactures* in 1867.
36. *Masters, Servants and Workmen* (1856), pp. 87, 97, especially Q.1029.
37. See Mundella's evidence to the *Royal Commission on Trades Unions, Tenth Report*, 1867–68 [3980–VI] 39, especially p. 97, Q.19693/4.
38. Ibid.
39. R. Kettle, *Strikes and Arbitration* (London: Simpkin, Marshall, 1866), p. 10.
40. D. Dale, *Thirty Years Experience of Industrial Conciliation and Arbitration*, (Leeds: Labour Association, 1899), p .7.
41. The failure of miners in North Wales to accept conciliation was recalled in evidence of their ignorance and simplicity. H. Crompton, *Industrial Conciliation* (London: Henry S. King, 1876), p. 76.
42. *Masters, Servants and Workmen*, p. 110, q.1243.

43. Belchem and Epstein, 'The Nineteenth-Century Gentleman Leader Revisited', p. 186.
44. *Royal Commission on Trades Unions*, Tenth Report, p. 76, Q.19377.
45. *Bradford Review*, 8 February, 1868.
46. Webb Collection, E, Vols A. and B., London School of Economics Library.
47. S. Webb and B. Webb, *Industrial Democracy* (London: Longmans, Green and Co., 1897), p. 229.

CHAPTER THIRTEEN

The search for legitimacy: universities, medical licensing bodies and governance in Glasgow and Edinburgh from the late eighteenth to the late nineteenth centuries[*]

Campbell F. Lloyd

The issues

In the eighteenth and nineteenth centuries Scottish cities, especially Glasgow and Edinburgh, experienced complex interactions between rival medical élites (in university medical faculties and in medical licensing bodies), and between medical élites and 'lay' leaders (notably in local government). These relationships had implications for control of medical practice, standards of medical education and – not least – urban governance. Also, as the medical elites of these cities interacted with each other, and with counterparts elsewhere in the UK and abroad, these relationships had consequences beyond the boundaries of Glasgow and Edinburgh. Historians have produced work relevant to this subject, especially with regard to changing patterns of medical education and to the nineteenth-century reform of the medical profession. Yet, Newman,[1] Loudon,[2] Waddington,[3] and Digby[4] – amongst others – have mainly dealt with the situation in England and Wales. Much of the relevant work which deals with Scotland has focused on the prominent position of Edinburgh as a centre of medical learning,[5] reflecting the greater attention traditionally given to Edinburgh as the Enlightenment hub in Scotland.[6] Concentration on Edinburgh and on medical education *per se* has resulted in less consideration being given to the maintenance of specialist legitimacy, and place in urban governance, of the universities and medical licensing bodies in Glasgow and Edinburgh from the later eighteenth to the nineteenth centuries.

An underlying problem of Scottish medicine was a negative image south of the border. This difficulty, still a problem in the later nineteenth century, extended back into the eighteenth century, and recurred in pamphlet literature through the early nineteenth century.[7] Reasons behind this anti-Scottish stance were many and complex. Throughout the nineteenth century a Scottish medical education was less expensive to students than that available in the rest of the UK.[8] This cheaper education fuelled the notion that students taught in Scotland were from an inferior social background. Given the issues surrounding the view of physicians as gentlemen, this promoted resentment against those educated in Scotland when they sought work in England. Resentment was exacerbated in the highest English medical circles by memories of those Scots prominent in attempts to reform the Royal College of Physicians in London in the 1760s.[9] More generally, the negative legacies surrounding Scottish links to Jacobitism, especially after 1745–46, resulted in distorted caricatures of Scots and cartoons such as 'Sawney in the Boghouse' which developed the idea of the 'barbarian' Scot.[10] Hangovers of Jacobite sympathies to absolutism in later debates over ideas of knowledge, in what Fissell notes as 'polite and vulgar behaviours', were linked also to disdain for religious 'enthusiasm' and diversity.[11] Thus Scots and their institutions could be damned on various levels.

While the reputation of the Scot could be maligned, practical problems for Scottish trained practitioners and the legitimacy of their qualifications appeared with the 1815 Apothecaries Act. Covering England and Wales only, the 1815 legislation was used to limit automatic rights to work there for both Scottish and Irish medical graduates. Such exclusions fed on anti-Scottish rhetoric, especially in the form of pamphlets laced with false information, by organisations and individuals. A picture was painted of Scottish institutions as backward or lax in their teaching and standards, sometimes in tandem with criticism of that other 'abode of backwardness', Ireland. In 1845 a pamphleteer quoted Dr Wakely, MP to the effect that Dublin was in 'gradual decline' and that the course at Glasgow for medical degrees was 'very deficient'.[12] This type of propaganda occurred even in the face of evidence of improvements to curricula and requirements by Glasgow University and the Faculty of Physicians and Surgeons of Glasgow (FPSG). Evidence shows that their curricular demands were at a level of study generally equal to that of the other major medical teaching institutions of the UK.[13]

Another issue that Scottish medical education had to confront was its autonomy. The latter, for Freidson and Elias, is crucial. For Freidson, a profession is a group where 'a high degree of autonomy', 'free from lay control', is developed. Elias notes the importance of the professional group's struggles to reform its institutional frameworks. Waddington, however, recognises two important limitations to such ideas. First, it was the growing 'medical market' that helped in the 'emancipation of medical men from a variety of forms of lay control of medical practice'. Second, and more fundamentally, a profession's ability to control change is limited by more general social factors.[14] Such issues are important when considering the maintenance of legitimacy by medical teaching and licensing bodies in Glasgow and Edinburgh. While medical professionals were involved in attempts to influence change, wider lay interests impinged significantly.

Consideration of legitimacy and relationships in these cities can also be enhanced by some of the issues raised by Anne Digby's socio-economic analysis of the medical profession, notably the use by medical practitioners of public positions to enhance their social status and incomes. Such positions often interlinked with lay support and possible direct lay participation in management and in financial backing. Digby also notes the importance of the medicalisation of medical institutions and the place of patient-centred medicine. Thus value was placed on medical knowledge which medical professionals could use to influence institutional developments. Knowledge also increased in value as the basis for appointments at the expense of social status and family connections.[15] In a case study, Fissell displays such changes in direct lay input to medical and institutional management for eighteenth-century Bristol.[16]

Relating some of these ideas to the universities and medical licensing bodies in Glasgow and Edinburgh, this chapter hopes to appraise the standpoints of these institutions, especially their changing attitudes to lay input from their urban areas. By showing how medical academics and medical licensing bodies utilised lay connections in their communities, the chapter also aims to show that their continued legitimacy rested on these broader links as well as on public perceptions of specialist legitimacy.

The need for effective links among élites

In his controversial study of Edinburgh's medical education Chitnis argued that medical teaching methods and the work of graduates from the early nineteenth century had a major impact in allowing Victorian society to overcome some of the worst aspects of urban and industrial development.[17] One danger of the Chitnis approach is that while it can be seen that the individuals involved had an impact on their local community, there is little emphasis on the reciprocal impact of the community on these medical educators and their effectiveness. In their work these medical academics – who overlapped heavily with the leaders of the licensing bodies – often relied on public esteem which depended on their involvement in the community, including medical societies, most of whose members were neither academics nor leaders of the licensing authorities. In Glasgow, for example, members of the FPSG acted as district surgeons and Medical Officers of Health.[18] Others such as James Adams, Donald Campbell Black,

Sir William Tennant Gairdner and James Burn Russell published widely
on contagious diseases, fevers, germ theory and public health issues.
Through these public involvements and as members of numerous medical
societies in the Glasgow area, FPSG members and academics enhanced the
legitimacy they derived from their roles in the faculty and the university.[19]
The idea of professional autonomy based on the exclusion of lay input,
therefore, is not very helpful in the context of Glasgow and Edinburgh
universities and medical licensing bodies.

The increasing prestige of Glasgow and Edinburgh medicine, to which
these élite–lay interactions contributed, was also reflected in Scottish,
British and imperial contexts. In terms of the shift from more localised
connections to the wider national view, the dynamism of the economies
of Glasgow and Edinburgh allowed their élite groups to sustain and
develop their influence both at home and abroad.[20] The broader influence
of these elites in local and national governance and in the development
of the economy impinged on medical professionals. Thus, for example,
the FPSG corresponded with medical lecturers in Belfast about course
requirements and other FPSG members held summer classes there.[21] The
rising standing of Scottish medicine occurred despite the fact that the
British Medical Association, emerging in 1832, had only three Scottish
members by 1842 and did not have a Scottish branch for a considerable
period after that.[22]

Yet a difficult prerequisite for the rising local and wider standing of
Glasgow and Edinburgh medicine was the effective co-ordination of key
institutions in each city. Ideally, the medical faculty needed good links to
its university's authorities, and each, in turn, required effective working
relationships with the local licensing body (or bodies, Edinburgh having
separate organisations for physicians and surgeons) and with the city
council and other major civic bodies. Given the complexity of the
institutional frameworks and the difficult issues besetting medicine and
civic affairs alike, these were significant obstacles to overcome.

Disputes and their resolution

There were clear differences between the two cities from the late
eighteenth century in the legal and formal links between the town councils,
the universities and the medical licensing bodies. The University of
Edinburgh was legally linked to Edinburgh town council. The council
had founded the university, was patron of various chairs, owned the
university property and invested university funds. Through the council
the university had less formal links to the Edinburgh Colleges of Surgeons
and Physicians, and had negotiated access to the Edinburgh Infirmary. In

contrast, Glasgow University had formal links neither to Glasgow Town Council nor to the FPSG. Also, the university did not have free access to the Infirmary. Moreover, from 1796 the University of Glasgow faced competition from Anderson's Institution which, in stark contrast to the university, had a strong lay input to its board of managers appointed under John Anderson's will.

These structural limitations had negative consequences for medicine in Glasgow. For example, the university bitterly complained in the 1830s that not only had it given £500 to the infirmary in the expectation that it would be used for teaching, but that 'every effort is made (by the FPSG) to oppose the university which is determinedly shut out from all aid for teaching either in or from the Hospital'.[23] Nor was the FPSG well linked to the council. The FPSG had broken its formal ties with the council in the 1720s when the surgeons finally ended any links to the Incorporation of Barbers. The level of autonomy pursued by the FPSG was such that they were exempt even from the militia ballot in 1812.[24] In an early attempt to emphasise their legitimacy and equality in the urban space the FPSG proposed to build a new hall beside the town council chambers.[25]

In Edinburgh, despite but in some ways because of better formal links, similar problems arose for academic medicine. The university Senate's attempt to have complete autonomy over the curriculum, met firm resistance from lay patrons. Commencing in 1825 the town council sought in the Court of Session to uphold their 'exclusive right of prescribing regulations for study, more especially with a view to degrees, in the College of Edinburgh'. In asserting their position as patrons the town wanted attendance at lectures in midwifery to be required for a medical degree. The Senate objected but lost in the Court of Session decree of 1829. In 1845, the town wanted a reluctant Senate to accept that the extramural medical schools in Edinburgh should share rights of recognition with medical Schools in Dublin and London. This case also went to the Court of Session where, ultimately on appeal to the House of Lords, the Senate lost in 1854. The Senate had sought to have put aside the town council's rights, especially to interfere in educational matters. But the Court of Session took the view that 'men of learning have not been always the best judges for directing the course of university study'.[26] The Senate might have thought that the legal profession would have been on their side as a commission on local government in 1833 found that the town council were 'not a body well fitted to discharge the duty of Patrons of the University'.[27] But Edinburgh University was forced to work with the town council College Committee which then remitted information to the Colleges of Surgeons and Physicians and to the extra-academical lecturers in the Edinburgh School of Medicine for their comments.[28] Prior, then, to the 1858 Medical Act and the 1858 Universities (Scotland) Act,

Edinburgh University and its medical professorship failed in its attempt to create autonomy for itself by breaking the control of urban government; despite the claims of medical knowledge the concept of lay influence was reinforced for the future.

The disputes at Edinburgh point to the institutional rivalry which was apparent in the Scottish medical world of the period and had parallels throughout Scotland and elsewhere in the United Kingdom. Aberdeen experienced disputes over funding and facilities for medical education between the two universities of King's and Marischal.[29] The institutions in Aberdeen were criticised by the *Lancet* as an unsuitable place to spend government grants.[30] These attacks on Aberdeen are symptomatic of the activities of interest groups during a period of contentious medical reform. As Waddington has shown, both the *Lancet* and the British Medical Association (BMA) attacked the licensing bodies in London over their exclusivity and incompetence. Institutions in Scotland were also open to criticism not only from reformers but also from each other. Edinburgh University, eager to promote its place in medical reform legislation, refused to recognise non-Senate-based medical lecturers from Aberdeen.[31] Similarly, the FPSG was often ignored in proposed medical legislation, and in the 1840s the Edinburgh colleges attempted to make themselves national licensing bodies for Scotland to the detriment of the Glasgow faculty.[32]

Within Glasgow, where the legal links between the University, the Faculty and the Council were weaker than in Edinburgh, dispute also flourished. The rights of Glasgow University 'College' professors were challenged by some of the Crown-appointed medical professors in the early nineteenth century. Then Glasgow University was involved with the FPSG in two legal cases before the Court of Session, where the university interest lost in 1819 and again in 1838.

Both cases revolved around the rights of Glasgow University graduates in surgery to practice within the jurisdiction of the FPSG without a licence. In effect the jurisdiction of the FPSG extended to the counties of Lanark, Renfrew, Ayr and Dumbarton. The College of Surgeons of Edinburgh and the College of Physicians of Edinburgh had jurisdiction over eight other counties.[33] Medical graduates holding an MD could present themselves to the FPSG or to the College of Physicians of Edinburgh and had an automatic right to practice as physicians in their areas of jurisdiction. To practise surgery was, however, different and both the FPSG and the College of Surgeons of Edinburgh could exclude anyone who had not fulfilled their requirements and passed their examinations. In a regulatory role they could take irregular 'practitioners' to court but this was costly, especially given the expenses entailed by other functions required to sustain their legitimacy.

Clearly in these jurisdictions the FPSG and the College of Surgeons of

Edinburgh were involved in urban governance through regulation. This regulation relied on their incorporated status, which – with their members' adherence – provided this legitimacy. In this they differed from the universities which had no regulatory functions and whose graduates had no say in their affairs until after 1858. As part of the various strands of prereformed local government in Scotland,[34] the medical licensing bodies were required to provide some medical advice gratis in their areas. In Glasgow the anti-smallpox vaccination policies of the FPSG were part of its willingness to introduce 'the only specific prophylactic measure which existed against disease during this period'.[35] This was continued, even though indifference by the public to follow up treatment limited its effectiveness. Their members were often related to the commercial and landed élites within their localities, who had an interest in local government.[36] The same relationships could sometimes be seen amongst the professors of the universities.[37] The latter and the medical licensing bodies wanted to keep or enhance their statutory rights within their area. The teachers at the university and at the Andersonian were all members of the FPSG and used this to legitimise their courses. Indeed any FPSG member was recognised as having a right to teach courses which counted in the 'examination of candidates for diplomas'.[38] The licensing bodies were linked to local government through the development and management of local medical institutions. Such liaison can be seen in Glasgow where the FPSG Preses wrote to the Lord Provost about the building of the fever hospital.[39]

In a broader arena the licensing bodies and the universities wished to extend their rights in Scotland, Great Britain, Ireland and later the Empire. Glasgow University sought recognition by the military forces in the 1820s,[40] and the FPSG sought recognition in the Irish Medical Charities Bill and the Irish Poor Law Bill in 1838.[41] In this latter involvement the FPSG's recognition of Belfast lecturers can be viewed as part of a widening of its sphere of influence and legitimacy. In such areas of expansion the licensing bodies and universities had ambiguous relationships with central and local government on whom they often had to rely. On the one side the colleges and the universities wanted to retain all the rights to protect their unreformed status, yet on the other they eagerly sought enhanced positions outside their statutory remits. The dependence of these organisations on the civil authorities produced expressions of allegiance. The FPSG illuminated their hall in February 1810 to celebrate the fiftieth anniversary on the throne of George III, but to be politically 'on side' they also sent an address of loyalty to the Prince Regent, attesting to the 'unalterable reverence entertained for the constitution as by law established but also the unabated confidence we continue to repose in the mild and truly legitimate sway of the house of Brunswick'.[42] Similarly, Glasgow University sent an address to the King in 1820 in support of George IV and the Protestant succession.[43] Yet the colleges and the universities remained jealous of their local immunities. Glasgow University objected to a clause in the 1821 Police Bill and petitioned Parliament, through the Lord Provost, pointing out that the university was free by statute from 'all tributes, duties, exactions, taxations, contributions, watchings, wardings and tolls'.[44] The FPSG claimed similar immunities.

Partners in urban governance

Yet in many respects members of the licensing bodies and the universities worked with the urban administration, often in voluntary and unpaid positions. While they lacked Edinburgh's formal institutional tie, for Glasgow University and the FPSG these activities enhanced professional prestige and the deference paid to them by their local communities. Despite their disputes in the civil courts both the FPSG and the university were seen to have representatives working as directors of the Glasgow Royal Lunatic Asylum alongside, for example, the Lord Provost, members of the town council, the Merchants House and the Trades House. In some respects both prior to and after the 1858 Medical Act, Glasgow medical institutions relied on the legitimacy of local government. They worked to provide it with services and gained prestige from it.

Thus medical professionals working in the universities and licensing bodies provided additional medical services to their cities more generally. In Edinburgh, John Thomson, who lectured on the eye as a surgical professor, established an eye dispensary in 1824.[45] In Glasgow William MacKenzie lectured at the university and founded the eye infirmary in the city by the 1820s. The FPSG regularly examined women as midwives for the surrounding counties, occasionally employing future professors of the university.[46] Despite institutional rivalry, members of the universities' medical schools were invariably also members of the licensing bodies in the cities for fundamentally these communities were small enough to overlap albeit in an informal manner. Such overlapping profited from the much less sharp distinctions in Scotland than in parts of England between physicians, surgeons, midwives, and apothecaries.

The tie to urban governance increased after the 1832 Anatomy Act. The universities and the extramural medical schools depended on the local authority Poor Law institutions for acquiring pauper cadavers. While deeply unpopular with the mass of the population,[47] this institutional association diminished part of the distrust of the medical community in the eyes of those of the public who perceived themselves as 'free of the fear' of a pauper's end. Both the 'professionals' and the lay bureaucracy were involved in designating the paupers' bodies as objects in the pursuit of knowledge, though at Glasgow students were still abused as 'doctor' and 'Burker' well into the 1850s,[48] their 'knowledge' still tinged with crime.

Moreover, both Glasgow and Edinburgh were important centres of extramural medical teaching in private schools and classes from the early nineteenth century; these classes were recognised towards qualifications and licences in medicine. In Glasgow the university faced competition from Anderson University Medical School from the 1790s. By the 1870s Glasgow University took legal action to stop Anderson's using the title of University. Other medical schools in the city also provided competition, such as the anatomy classes run by the Burns brothers John and Allan. Like Andrew Duncan in Edinburgh, John Burns, when Professor of Surgery at Glasgow University, thought that the competition from local extramural schools was good for the university in maintaining standards.[49] Within this competition the FPSG and the College of Surgeons in Edinburgh played a part as examining bodies maintaining professional competency. Both university and licensing body could legitimise knowledge but the universities did not have to regulate it.

The competencies of universities and medical licensing bodies were recognised in the Medical Act of 1858. The aim of some medical reformers to have a single statutory body controlling all entry to, and examination in, medical education followed by registration was compromised. As Waddington has demonstrated,[50] the compromise was very much due to the activities of the College of Surgeons of London, which lobbied hard to fend off the BMA and *Lancet* ideas of a single medical governing body. In this lobbying the universities and other licensing bodies across Britain and Ireland concurred, although they might deliberately try to undermine each other in the process. Their mutual agreements by 1857 created a sustained defence of traditional corporate rights which fended off monopoly by the few. The General Medical Council had to work in a framework where the universities and the licensing bodies all continued and this led to sustained criticism. The *Lancet*, in its continued attacks on the 'abuses' of the medical corporations, attacked the Royal College of Physicians of Edinburgh, over the permissive section of the 1858 Act, where it was allowed to join with the FPSG and the College of Surgeons of Edinburgh to grant a double licence in medicine.[51] The General Medical Council, while creating a national British organisation, retained levels of self-government under the auspices of state input through legislation.

The issues of free trade and institutional rights continued, but in Scotland the Universities (Scotland) Act of 1858 meant that lay input into the development of medical education and university-based services was enhanced. In some respects even the language used reflected the Medical Act. Scottish university graduates were to form general councils and have a representative on the newly created University Courts, themselves dominated by lay representatives.[52] The universities were to send representatives to the General Medical Council where they could influence policy. Thus again in Scotland layer behind layer of lay input prevailed in professional development.

Through these University Courts – which also reflected student, graduate, and professional input – changes in medical education, standards and practice were enhanced and legitimised through lay co-operation. This was extended by the use of university staff as public health officers.[53] In many respects the universities and their lay representatives became involved in educational standards in their localities and in governing science and medical institutions. By the late 1870s the University Courts of Glasgow and Edinburgh were being extensively asked for recognition of medical and public health courses by other universities and colleges in Britain and the Empire.[54] In this process both informal and formal lay input helped by pulling together the medical institutions in these two cities. In combination with the public and associational links of medical specialists this greater unity enhanced both how they were seen locally and how their legitimacy was recognised across Britain and the Empire. Where Glasgow had been described in a London-based pamphlet of 1797 as being in Lanark and the FPSG was only noted as having to give free medical advice to the poor,[55] the city had emerged as a recognised leading centre of medical education in Britain and the Empire by the 1890s. Edinburgh's position, too, was enhanced though from a higher base.

Conclusion

Overall the incorporated structures and legal links at Edinburgh did not stop the disputes over autonomy which were also seen in Glasgow. In each city the university, the licensing authorities and local government had to work out a viable division of labour which depended as much on the increasingly broad involvements of medical specialists – which enhanced their standing with the local political elite, ordinary medical practitioners and the general public – as on structural reforms. Edinburgh's medical pre-eminence can be more effectively explained by the greater initial size of its medical school and greater fee incomes for its professors than by the concept of a unified medical establishment.

A major issue for both Glasgow and Edinburgh was that early in the period the universities and the medical licensing bodies formed part of an unreformed service sector based on statutory, but increasingly outdated, rights. In this they were in parallel with urban government structures in Scotland which were under increasing pressure for change in the nineteenth century. Like unreformed local government itself, the medical academics and the medical licensing bodies at first sought autonomy from outside influence, but in each case an accommodation with 'lay' interests was crucial to enhanced legitimacy, both locally and (in the face of opposition to their very existence) throughout the UK and beyond. The 1858 Medical Act and the 1858 and 1889 Universities (Scotland) Acts drew the Universities, the medical licensing bodies and the town councils together in Scotland. Each was stronger than they had been 100 years before, not only because they were better linked to each other but also because they were more effectively connected to their surrounding communities more generally.

Notes

* This chapter has arisen out of work undertaken as part of a Glasgow Wellcome Unit for the History of Medicine project for a four-hundredth anniversary history of the Royal College of Physicians and Surgeons of Glasgow. I take this opportunity to thank Dr J. Geyer-Kordesch, the project fundholder, for the opportunity to work on the material. I should also like to thank other members of the department for their advice and comments.

1. C. Newman, *The Evolution of Medical Education in the Nineteenth Century* (London: Oxford University Press, 1957).

2. I. Loudon, *Medical Care and the General Practitioner 1750–1850* (Oxford: Clarendon Press, 1986); I. Loudon, 'Medical Education and Medical Reform', in V. Nutton and R. Porter (eds), *The History of Medical Education in Britain* (Amsterdam: Rodopi, 1995).

3. I. Waddington, chapter 3 in John Woodward and David Richards (eds), *Health Care and Popular Medicine in Nineteenth Century England* (London: Croom Helm, 1977); I. Waddington, *The Medical Profession in the Industrial Revolution* (Dublin: Gill and MacMillan, 1984).

4. A. Digby, *Making a Medical Living* (Cambridge: Cambridge University Press, 1994).

5. For example, J.B. Morrell, 'The University of Edinburgh in the Late Eighteenth Century: Its Scientific Eminence and Academic Structure', *Isis*, 62 (1971), pp. 159–71. Edinburgh's reputation and the size of its student body have helped to produce this emphasis. However, this has meant that less has been said on the situation and impact of institutions in Glasgow, partly because Glasgow institutions were seen as being less unified than those in Edinburgh. This chapter partly aims to address this issue in comparison to Edinburgh.

6. A.C. Chitnis, *The Scottish Enlightenment and Early Victorian Society* (London: Croom Helm, 1986); N. Phillipson, *The Scottish Whigs and the Reform of the Court of Session* (Edinburgh: Stair Society, 1990).

7. J. Bradley, A. Crowther, and M. Dupree, 'Mobility and Selection in Scottish University Medical Education, 1858–1886', *Medical History*, 40 (1996), pp. 1–24, esp. pp. 1–3; I. Waddington, 'The Struggle to Reform the Royal College of Physicians, 1767–1771', *Medical History*, 17 (1973), pp. 107–26; C.F. Lloyd, 'Educational Debate in the Public Eye', in M. Hewitt (ed.) *Scholarship in Victorian Britain* (Leeds: Centre for Victorian Studies, 1998).

8. *Report on the Increase in the Teaching and Examining Work of the Professors of the Medical Faculty* (Edinburgh, 1874), p. 9.
9. I. Waddington, 'Struggle to Reform the Royal College', *Medical History*, 17 (1973), pp. 107–26.
10. M. Lynch, *Scotland: A New History* (London: Pimlico, 1991), p. 234.
11. M.E. Fissell, *Patients, Power, and the Poor in Eighteenth century Bristol* (Cambridge: Cambridge University Press, 1991), p. 198.
12. *Remarks on Medical Reform and on Sir James Graham's Bill by Lucius* (London, Dublin and Edinburgh, 1845), p. 8.
13. *Statutes of the University of Edinburgh, Relative to the Degree of M.D. 1845*, p. 9 indicates the recognition of courses at other U.K. institutions. For a list of course requirements across the UK in 1838 see RCPSG 1/1/7, Faculty minute book, pp. 150–51.
14. I. Waddington, *Medical Profession*, pp. 177–9.
15. Digby, *Medical Living*, pp. 299–301.
16. Fissell, *Patients, Power, and the Poor*, ch. 7.
17. A.C. Chitnis, 'Medical Education in Edinburgh, 1790–1826, and some Victorian Consequences', *Medical History*, 17 (1973), pp.173–85.
18. F.A. Macdonald, 'Vaccination Policy of the Faculty of Physicians and Surgeons of Glasgow, 1801–1863, *Medical History*, 41 (1997), pp. 291–321, esp. pp. 292–7.
19. For outline descriptions of these see J. Jenkinson, *Scottish Medical Societies 1731–1939: Their History and Records* (Edinburgh: Edinburgh University Press, 1993).
20. R.H. Trainor, 'The Elite', in W.H. Fraser and I. Maver (eds), *Glasgow Vol. II* (Manchester: Manchester University Press, 1996); I. Sweeney, 'The Municipal Administration of Glasgow', PhD thesis, University of Strathclyde, 1990.
21. Royal College of Physicians and Surgeons of Glasgow (RCPSG) 1/1/7 Faculty minutes, p. 65.
22. P. Bartrip, *Themselves Writ Large: The British Medical Association 1832–1966* (London: BMJ, 1996), p. 29. For instance, the Glasgow and West of Scotland branch was only founded in 1876.
23. Glasgow University Archives (GUA) Sen 1/1/5, 26 April 1830.
24. RCPSG 1/1/5, 6th January 1812.
25. *Extracts from the Records of the Burgh of Glasgow A.D. 1739–59* (Glasgow, 1911), p. 509.
26. *Reports of Scotch Appeals and Writs of Error ... in the House of Lords* (Edinburgh, 1855), pp. 485–512.
27. *Report by the College Committee of the Town Council, on the subject of the Memorial to Lord Melbourne from the Senatus Academicus of the University of Edinburgh* (Edinburgh, 1839), pp. 4–5.
28. *Report of the College Committee of the Town Council of Edinburgh Patrons of the University regarding the Statutes of the University Relative to the Degree of M.D.* (Edinburgh, 1846), pp. 3–4.
29. C. Pennington, *The Modernisation of Medical Teaching at Aberdeen in the Nineteenth Century* (Aberdeen: Aberdeen University Press, 1994), p. 4.
30. Ibid, p. 5.
31. Ibid, p. 6.
32. RCPSG 1/1/8, 27 May 1848. The President of the FPSG reported to the committee that the College of Surgeons of Edinburgh had admitted that it wanted to become a College of Surgeons for all Scotland.
33. Neither Glasgow nor Edinburgh institutions had any rights outside these areas

across the rest of Scotland, so that beyond their jurisdictions medical licensing and regulation was an apparent 'free for all'.

34. For a fuller account of the state of Scottish local government structures to the early nineteenth century see R.M. Sunger, *Patronage and Politics in Scotland, 1707–1832* (Edinburgh: John Donald, 1986) and A.E. Whetstone, *Scottish County Government in the Eighteenth and Nineteenth Centuries* (Edinburgh: John Donald, 1981).

35. F.A. Macdonald 'Vaccination Policy', pp. 229–321.

36. The President of the FPSG in 1871 was the grandson of a Glasgow timber merchant.

37. In the late eighteenth century, the sister of William Hunter, the celebrated anatomist, had married the Reverend James Baillie, who later was appointed Professor of Divinity at Glasgow University. John Burns, Professor of Surgery at Glasgow University from 1816, was related to owners of the Cunard Shipping line and to David MacBrayne, who also had shipping interests in the West Coast lines.

38. Strathclyde University Archives OB/1/1/3. p. 12.

39. RCPSG 1/1/7, p. 79.

40. GUA Sen 1/1/4, pp. 142–3.

41. RCPSG 1/1/7, 6 March 1838.

42. RCPSG 1/1/5, 10 February 1817.

43. GUA Sen 1/1/4, pp. 29–31.

44. GUA Sen 1/1/4, p. 70.

45. Chitnis, *Scottish Enlightenment*, p. 13.

46. RCPSG 1/1/5, 2 May 1808.

47. R. Richardson, *Death, Dissection and the Destitute* (London: Routledge and Keegan Paul, 1987), p. 263.

48. G.Buchanan, AM, MD, 'On the Effects of Mr. Warburton's Anatomy Bill, and the Facilities for the Study of Practical Anatomy in Glasgow', *Glasgow Medical Journal*, 2 (1855), pp. 431–43, 438.

49. *Evidence to the Universities Commission Vol. II* (London, 1837), pp. 126–132.

50. Waddington, *Medical Profession*.

51. *The Licence of the Royal College of Physicians of Edinburgh* (Edinburgh, 1870), p. 8.

52. For the development of the courts with their lay membership see C.F. Lloyd, 'Relationships between Scottish Universities and their Communities c.1858–1914', unpublished PhD thesis, University of Glasgow, 1994. In Edinburgh the 1858 Act provided for the continued role of the town council members in appointing a number of the professors and in having a place, by right, on the Edinburgh University Court. The Act brought courts, with lay members, to all the Scottish universities, and from 1889 all shared the Edinburgh court's earlier representation of local government. These reforms recognised the complexity of the changing nature of representation and legitimacy in urban governance and helped defuse conflicts.

53. I owe this information, which relates to Aberdeen, Glasgow and Edinburgh, to Mrs Brenda White of the Department of Economic and Social History, University of Glasgow.

54. C.F. Lloyd, 'Relationships', appendix 4.2, pp. 356–60.

55. T. Champney, *Medical and Chirurgical Reform proposed from a review of the healing Art, throughout Europe, particularly Great Britain* (London, 1797).

CHAPTER FOURTEEN

Ownership of the place of burial: a study of early nineteenth-century urban conflict in Britain

Julie Rugg

Local government during the first half of the nineteenth century may be characterised by the delivery of services and utilities by a range of different agencies as diverse as improvement commissioners, vestries, joint-stock companies and charitable boards. The period was one of transition: the eighteenth-century 'parish state' system of oligarchic control centred on church administration was buckling under the multiple pressures borne of increasing urbanisation,[1] but England was yet to see the domination of the late-Victorian, all-powerful municipality.[2] During the first half of the nineteenth century, decisions had to be made about the appropriate agency by which necessary services should be delivered. The choices were not always clear-cut, and this chapter explores an issue of particular complexity: the provision of land for burial. Histories of both cemetery development and urban government have tended to overlook the fact that the supply of land for burial could be a contentious local issue.[3] However, examination of the provision of this last, essential service offers a fresh perspective on both local–central relations with respect to urban improvement and on the apparent dichotomies between business involvement in service provision and the ownership and management of amenities on a non-profit basis.

From the 1820s, a challenge was presented to the virtual monopoly on burial provision that had been held by the Church since the eighth century. Communities increasingly made recourse to space in new cemeteries – large, often attractively landscaped tracts of land – which the Church neither owned nor controlled. The possibility of establishing secular cemeteries meant that provision and ownership of the space of burial became contested issues. Deciding which agency should most appropriately own and manage burial ground involved protracted negotiation and in some cases conflict between two or more of five major agencies: the State, the Church, local government, Nonconformist communities, and financial markets. The battle to control burial space took place at both local and national levels, and continued for much of the century. However, this chapter focuses on the early period, from the foundation of the first cemeteries in the 1820s to the passage of the Burial Acts in the 1850s.

This chapter contends that, in the early history of cemetery establishment, the principle of local control of burial provision tended to remain a constant. In exploring this issue, the chapter will illustrate the reasons why the Church lost its grip on provision that it had dominated for centuries. Increasing secularisation of this essential urban function did not mean the successful growth of state intervention in this area. In fact, state control of burial provision was never successfully proposed. Neither was it the case that early nineteenth-century communities were happy to let the market dictate a response to the need for new burial ground: speculative, profit-oriented cemeteries did not became a popular option. On the contrary, in the first half of the nineteenth century, new cemetery development was dominated by local, secular, essentially non-profit organisations that ensured that control of burial space would be retained by the community. This characteristic was safeguarded by the Burial Acts of the 1850s, and since that time has not been challenged.

Studying cemeteries and culture

The provision of space for burial is often considered as simply one of the range of services required by the rapidly growing urban centres of the early Victorian period, to be included in lists of amenities along with gas and water supplies. This tendency is understandable, given the relatively undeveloped nature of cemetery research in the UK. British historians have rarely addressed the broader meanings attached to cemeteries, and the concomitant issues relating to their ownership and management.[4] These issues are not unimportant: a community's place of burial carries substantial local significance. Indeed, work completed on nineteenth-century cemeteries in the United States draws a connection between cemetery establishment and emerging nationhood. Early settlers had buried as they travelled, or interred in tracts of land that they owned and farmed. The creation of stable communities could be achieved through the establishment of a common site for burial, where hitherto disparate people could acknowledge a linked ancestry and history.[5] The sense of history attached to cemeteries underlines their importance in expressing nationality. For example, the successive partitioning of Poland over the last three centuries was often accompanied by the destruction of that nation's cemeteries. Post-war reconstruction and the cemetery conservation movement in that country have iterated the principle, inscribed at the entrance to the Peksowe Brzysko Cemetery – Poland's Pantheon – 'homeland is soil and graves'.[6] Within nations, cemeteries can also serve to express political, religious and ethnic allegiances, and can constitute the battleground for the celebration or eradication of subcultural identity.[7] In these broader contexts, it becomes vital to understand which agencies appropriate ownership of the place of burial, and the means by which control is negotiated.

Before proceeding further, it is perhaps worth clarifying definitions of different types of burial space. Although the terms are generally used interchangeably, this chapter will differentiate between graveyards or churchyards and cemeteries. The term churchyard or graveyard will be used to refer to ground surrounding parish churches – areas that that for the most part have dominated burial provision since the eighth century. These areas are generally small in scale, usually not more than an acre or so – and through their use the Church held a virtual monopoly of burial provision until the 1850s. From the 1820s, Britain saw the increasing use of a new burial form – the cemetery. These were larger tracts of land – ten or more acres was common – located on the outskirts of town and generally not attached either to specific parish churches or the Church itself. It is through the introduction of cemeteries that the Church lost its near monopoly of burial provision although, as this chapter demonstrates, this transition was by no means a smooth one.

It was frequently the case before 1850 that these new cemeteries were laid out by joint-stock companies, that financed the purchase and laying out of the site through the sale of shares.[8] The use of, and meanings attached to, cemetery companies was not static, even in the relatively short time period from 1820 to 1850. Initially, during the 1820s and early 1830s use of the format was dominated by Nonconformist communities seeking burial space independent of the Established Church. The financial success enjoyed by these early companies provoked speculative interest, and during the mid-1830s and mid-1840s, joint-stock investment manias provided a fruitful context for the growth of profit-oriented cemetery companies. By the late 1830s, concern had grown about the supposed detrimental effects on public health caused by miasmas from overcrowded graveyards. As a consequence, by the 1840s the cemetery company was falling into more general use as a means by which communities could ensure the supply of sanitary space for burial. Thus, in the broad context of conflict and debate attached to which agencies should most appropriately supply a service, the agencies themselves could be subject to change and flux as they were constantly being reshaped by economic and political forces.

All these reasons underline the appropriateness of a detailed, local base for studying burial provision. This chapter is therefore based on an extended series of local historical studies of cemetery development in all the major towns in Britain in the first half of the nineteenth century. In particular, the chapter utilises cemetery company documentation including prospectuses, minute books and annual reports. Prosopographical work was also completed on some company directorates, to explore in more detail the possible factors motivating cemetery establishment. This material was supplemented with reference to other local sources such as newspapers and town guides. Town histories also provided immediate context for cemetery foundation. The use of these locally based sources is important, since it marks a departure from the usual approach to cemetery history, which is to rely wholly on London-based sources and in particular on the deeply flawed material collated by the sanitary reformer, Edwin Chadwick.

The Church's loss of control of burial space

Space for burial was, until the first half of the nineteenth century, usually a service provided at the parish level by the Church. As the Victorian period progressed, however, this tradition came to be questioned and by mid-century the Church had begun to lose its control of land for interment. For the most part, this change was connected with the changing nature of cities and their population. First, and most crucially, the dominant tradition of church provision of land for interments came under increasing attack from powerful provincial Nonconformists who wanted to establish their own independent burial space. Second, as the century progressed, the Church proved itself to be incapable of providing sufficient space for burial for the newly massing dead of a rapidly increasing population.

As with many other histories of urban change, the history of cemetery development began in Manchester. Here the first significant steps were taken to establish cemetery provision outwith the control of the Church of England, using the readily replicable model of joint-stock company foundation. The foundation of the Rusholme Road Cemetery in 1820 was built on conflict arising from the growing power of Nonconformity in the city, and the willingness of that community to take local action to tackle religious political grievances. Manchester in 1820 had seen the earliest church rate battle, in which Dissenters had successfully overturned the requirement to collect from all parishioners – regardless of religious affiliation – a local tax to finance the upkeep of the church. The need for Nonconformists to own and control their own burial provision was acutely felt. Indeed, George Hadfield – leading Dissenting agitator and one of the instigators of the church rate battle in Manchester – wrote of the particular importance of the need 'to get our own ministers enabled to preside at our funerals'.[9] In addition to this wish to use Dissenting ministers, Nonconformists also sought to be able to use an appropriate burial service and to have the option of interment in unconsecrated ground. The establishment of the Rusholme Road Proprietary Cemetery – which for the first time financed the laying out of a cemetery through the sale of shares – set a precedent for similar action in other towns and cities. During the 1820s and 1830s, Nonconformists in places including Liverpool, Birmingham, Leeds, Portsmouth, Great Yarmouth, Sheffield, Newport and Wisbech founded joint-stock companies that established cemeteries, where the advertising rhetoric declared the land to be 'for all classes of persons of what religious persuasion soever they may be' or 'established on the broad principle of religious freedom'.[10]

The growing confidence of provincial Nonconformity was only part of the reason why the Church began to lose its hold on burial space. By the 1840s, considerable alarm was being expressed at the failure of the Church authorities to respond to the need for more extensive burial provision, to match the heavily increasing demand from growing urban populations. It is perhaps unnecessary to rehearse the reasons for population growth that was particularly marked in the 1810s: other histories have given exhaustive detail.[11] It is also the case that other histories have described the ghastly consequences of overcrowding in inner city churchyards and burial grounds in London, drawing largely on the work of Edwin Chadwick and the burial reformer George Alfred Walker.[12] It should be stressed, however, that the situation could be equally bad in provincial towns and cities. Indeed, the General Board of Health produced a report to that effect in 1851. Evidence was collected from all over Britain of churchyards measuring no more than an acre, and that had been in use for centuries, being expected to accommodate hundreds of extra burials a year. It was found that 'throughout the length and breadth of the land all the old graveyards are most unduly crowded with interments'.[13] Burial had become a public health issue, and in this situation the spiritual claim of the Church on both the deceased and the grieving could feasibly be sidestepped. For much of the 1840s, the joint-stock cemetery format was being adopted by communities wanting to establish more sanitary burial grounds, to avoid having to use the inner-city graveyards. Burial was becoming secularised.

The precarious position of the Church in these developments was underlined by attempts made to frame national legislation on the issue of inner-city burials. Attention was first given to the need to regulate burials in London, and in this instance intensive conflict arose from the desire to maintain a church interest in any new provision. A principal player in the move towards regulation was W.A. McKinnon, Liberal MP for Lymington, whose apparent general interest in sanitary matters provoked him to move for a select committee on city interment in March 1842. The committee was clearly biased in favour of the Church. Clergymen were questioned about the losses in income suffered through the opening of private burial grounds. Indeed, the evidence presented by the Bishop of London was almost exclusively taken up with reference to the clergy's reliance on burial fees and funerary perquisites, which in some livings comprised over 50 per cent of clerical income.[14] Accordingly, McKinnon's Select Committee Report urged that reform be implemented without harm to existing interests, that all burial in the city be prohibited, and that 'modern' cemeteries be established outwith the city, managed by the parochial authorities and financed through the levying of a special type of church rate. By this means, the clergy would still be able to officiate at all parish funerals and suffer no loss of income.

McKinnon stepped into a storm of Nonconformist objection. The conciliatory recommendation that unconsecrated land should be provided was not considered satisfactory, since that land would still remain under the control of parish councils. Nonconformists were alarmed at the notion that parish councils may be empowered to take over control of Dissenting joint-stock cemeteries. Indeed, the recommendations looked set to establish a church monopoly over burials 'once more to establish her ghostly empire over the entire territory of the tomb'.[15] The proposals were 'of selfish origin and sectarian character' and McKinnon was derided as 'a cat's paw to the clergy'.[16] By June 1843 the outcry created by the proposals was enough to persuade the Home Secretary to withhold support for the McKinnon bill, with the comment that the subject was 'of extreme delicacy'.[17]

The inability to frame national or even metropolitan legislation to protect the Church's interest in burials did not mean that the Church remained inactive. The Church was in a good position to resist the wider implications of new cemetery establishment since it held one trump card: the need for both speculative and community-based public health companies to establish ground that was at least partly consecrated. It would appear that many bishops would only agree to consecration if the cemetery company was formally established through Act of Parliament. Close research is required on the legal aspects of this development to provide full clarity. However, it is certain that once an act was lodged it became possible – through the course of its passage through Parliament – for church supporters to ensure that the act contained clerical compensation clauses. In the capital in particular, the Bishop of London had exacted varying levels of payment from almost all the cemetery companies opened in the 1830s. For example, for each vault burial the South Metropolitan Cemetery Company was compelled to pay 7s 6d to the vicar of the parish from which the deceased came; the West London and Westminster Cemetery Company had to pay 10s, with an additional shilling's payment to the parish clerk.[18]

The Church could take further action outwith the legislative process, and indeed such strategies were required: church control of burial space was being contested in towns and cities throughout Britain. For example, the clergy in Oxford were successful in preventing the foundation of a cemetery company in the city, declaring:

> It has always been the practice of the Church to make provision for the interment of her dead as the last act of Christian fellowship ... This is the ancient practice, from which we do not feel at liberty to depart.[19]

Similarly, attempts to found a cemetery company in Shrewsbury were blocked at an exceptionally early stage. In a letter to the Leeds General Cemetery Company, Mr D. Watts, director of a proposed new company in Shrewsbury wrote that he was unable even to publish a prospectus in the newspapers – 'not one of them dare insert it', and any attempt 'to break in on the old restricted uses is cheated'.[20] In Hereford in 1847 the intervention of the bishop put an end to plans to form a cemetery, even though it was backed by the town's leading citizens, including the mayor and MPs.[21] However, despite successful rearguard action in some localities, in national terms the advent of the cemetery company proved to be the first decisive step away from church-controlled burial provision. Following the passage of the Burial Acts in the 1850s, the Church increasingly fell into the position of having to negotiate space for its congregations in cemeteries owned and maintained by secular authorities.

State control of cemeteries

The conflict between interventionist Utilitarian policy and the objection to any form of government centralisation was evident in a number of arenas in the 1830s and 1840s, particularly in the reform of the poor law and in attempts to establish public health legislation. Burial provision also features within this debate, in attempts to centralise control of burial provision and establish national cemeteries. However, the State never became an agency which directly established new cemeteries. Three factors undermined the success of a centralised response: the involvement of the ever unpopular sanitary reformer, Edwin Chadwick; the complexity of the concomitant religious political implications of state provision; and apparently justified faith in the view that the market would provide an adequate response.

In attempting to sidestep calls to implement McKinnon's evidently partisan recommendations for church control of new cemeteries, Sir James Graham had alluded to the completion of a report on interments by Edwin Chadwick. Historians often agree that Chadwick's Interment Report of 1843 constitutes the most characteristic of his work, in providing radical and broad-based solutions producing ripples of implication well beyond the anticipated boundaries of action. Had Chadwick directly addressed the need for new cemeteries, resolution of the issue of burials in favour of state control might have occurred. However, it was not in Chadwick's nature to propose half measures. His analysis of the burial problem began from the very moment of a death, and took into account the lack of any superintending health official in the event of a bereavement, the heavy reliance of the poor on burial clubs, and the excesses of the funeral industry. As a consequence, Chadwick's contribution to the interment debate was to propose that the State – through the Board of Health – take entire control in the event of a death, arranging collection of the body and providing funeral services. His was a 'comprehensive national plan', the 'great and cardinal point' of which was 'entirely to supersede the parochial system in the matter of city burial, and to put the whole management under the control of the Government'.[22] The 'disturbed interests' of the clergy would be compensated through profits made by the state-controlled national cemeteries, which would take over all burial functions following the closure of inner-city churchyards and private burial grounds.

As with McKinnon, Chadwick's plan met with the opposition of Nonconformists who objected to any system that included the State paying compensation fees to the Established Church. Indeed, Chadwick had anticipated this objection, and had attempted to persuade the leading Dissenter, Edward Baines Junior, to support the recommendations because of their basic secularising tendencies.[23] However, even with the support of Baines it was unlikely that the recommendations would garner widespread popularity: as with almost all of Chadwick's proposals, they were seriously out of step with the prevailing *laissez-faire* ethos. Panic attached to the cholera epidemic of 1849 had pushed Parliament into consideration of a metropolitan interment bill based on Chadwick's recommendations, but opposition remained heavy. According to Lord Stuart, speaking in debate on the bill in 1850, it

> violated many principles to which he was attached in a most unconstitutional way. Centralisation, now too much in fashion, and which threatened to overturn many ... institutions would be increased and extended by the Bill. It looked as though the whole business of the country would soon be transacted by boards and commissions ... the object in view might have been accomplished just as well without violating the constitutional principles of self government and liberty.[24]

Furthermore, it was objectionable that the State should interfere with the undertaking trade, by prescribing the boundaries of expenditure at a time of grief, and to degrade paupers by contracting out poor burials to the most competitive tenderer.

A further blow to measures to secure state control of burials was the apparent feasibility of a reliance on market forces to deal with the issue. A ready solution had already become evident. Even the Dissenters could find no objection:

> pass a law interdicting city sepulture, and there leave the matter. Let the public provide for itself. The principles of legitimate commerce have already constructed noble cemeteries on all sides of the metropolis.[25]

Sir James Graham considered that even this degree of state interference was unnecessary:

> Gradually, without force of legislative enactment, the inclination of the public led them to adopt burial places outside the towns rather than in the churchyards within them, and that ample facilities were given by private companies for that object.[26]

From the early 1830s, and particularly during the joint-stock investment boom of the middle of that decade, a string of joint-stock cemetery companies had established a number of cemeteries on the outskirts of London. This number included the cemetery of All Saints at Kensal Green, Highgate Cemetery and Nunhead Cemetery. However, Chadwick derided these cemeteries as a solution, considering that the added expense of travelling out of the town would mean that the poor would be forced to continue use of inner-city burial grounds. In addition it was thought that their charges, even without the additional travel expenditure, were already in excess of more usual fees, and their practices in sanitary terms did not constitute a real improvement on practice in the inner-city churchyards. None the less, despite Chadwick's reservations about the private sector cemeteries, reference to their operation was a major factor in undermining his call for a centralised response to the burial issue. Although the Metropolitan Interment Bill was passed, support for its implementation abated along with the cholera and the bill was withdrawn within months. The State never again proposed the notion of nationalisation of cemeteries and has, since the Burial Acts, tended only to take responsibility for framing regulatory legislation.

The burial crisis: a market response?

The establishment of joint-stock cemetery companies all over Britain in the 1820–53 period would seem to indicate that the faith in a market response to the need for new burial ground was justified. Entrepreneurs could be relied on to pinpoint demand for a particular commodity, and the success of Dissenting joint-stock cemeteries through the 1820s was clear demonstration that the format was financially viable. The high number of cemetery companies floated during the speculative booms of the mid-1830s and 1840s would also seem to indicate that the establishment of burial ground was viewed as a reasonable investment opportunity. However, it would be mistaken to contend on these grounds that the market provided a successful response to the need for new cemeteries. The incursion of business interests into the arena of cemetery provision was resisted at the local level by communities that simply withheld their support.

The speculative, entrepreneurial cemetery company had specific characteristics that distinguished it from its Nonconformist and public health-motivated counterparts: for example, the prospectuses rarely listed directorates, and aimed to raise a higher than average capital. In addition, these companies tended to emerge during the periodic joint-stock investment booms of the mid-1830s and mid-1840s.[27] The speculative cemetery company was restricted in locale to London, southern Scotland and Manchester, where cemetery company establishment on a particularly frenzied scale erupted in April, 1836. This month was especially notable for investment mania. Manchester saw the launching of many improbable schemes in April, including a zoological, botanical and public gardens company, which was to be combined with a coliseum and baths.[28] Attempts were also made to float a joint stock exchange buildings company, which was revealed to be a fraud, its directors 'well known speculators ... [who have] hitherto studiously avoided bringing their names before the public'.[29]

Cemetery establishment during April matched the fury of other joint-stock flotation. Two companies were founded early in the month – the General Cemetery Company and the Ardwick Cemetery Association. Both companies advertised their understanding of burials as a public health issue and as a required civic improvement. The Association in particular was undoubtedly a respectable concern. Included in its list of nine directors was Thomas Potter, founder of the *Manchester Guardian*, and later to be the first mayor of the city. Potter was a leading light in the Unitarian Cross Street Chapel, which was also attended by another of the directors, Henry Pershouse. Notwithstanding the fine sentiments expressed by the Ardwick directors, speculation in its scrip was immediate, and imitators sprang up within days. On 23 April the prospectus of the Manchester Necropolis was published, and mention was made of the massive oversubscription for the Ardwick shares. Further enterprises issued prospectuses in April. Notice of the Salford and Hulme Cemetery Company was also published on 23 April, its prospectus appearing one week later. The company's appeal was essentially territorial:

> The cemeteries recently contemplated, even when established, will necessarily from their distant situations, be ill adapted for the reception of interments from the densely populated towns of Salford and Hulme.[30]

The prospectus of the Salford, Pendleton and Broughton Royal Cemetery Company was issued the same day, its rhetoric limited to expressing similar sentiments – that although Manchester had three cemeteries, Salford had none.[31]

At the end of April, an amazed editorial in the local newspaper surveyed the number of cemetery companies which had been founded in the city and asked 'Are we about to be visited by the plague?'[32] In all, seven companies had been floated in Manchester in April 1836, only two of which survived to found cemeteries – neither overtly profit-making concerns. Local investors had withheld their support for the other companies, and they faded almost as quickly as they had arisen. The unwillingness of communities to hand over burial provision to speculators is further illustrated by company formation in Scotland. Both Stirling and Greenock were subject to the largely unwelcome attention of speculators. The attitude of locals towards speculators was perhaps most clearly expressed in Greenock. The *Renfrewshire Advertiser* carried the prospectus of the Greenock Cemetery Company in February 1845.[33] The notice was typically basic in its appeal, and carried no list of directors. Reaction to the company was heated. It was acknowledged that the town needed a cemetery, but it should not be one established by 'those who have no interest in the matter other than the opportunity which it affords for stock-jobbing and speculation'. Indeed, the company should be 'of a strictly local nature, to which the Provost and Magistrates ... and a portion of the clergy of all denominations should be parties ... Such a company would afford satisfaction and be a blessing'.[34] It seems that this particular sentiment held the day. The Greenock Cemetery Company failed, and in 1846 John Gray, a town councillor, successfully put forward plans for a cemetery which was backed by the town council.[35]

It would seem therefore simplistic to assume – on the basis of rapid cemetery company foundation – that pre- and early- Victorian communities were satisfied to see the market respond to the demand to meet need for burial space. Compared with other types of cemetery company, the speculative cemetery company had a significantly higher failure rate in terms of being unable to attract sufficient capital to open a cemetery: for example, nearly 70 per cent of profit-oriented companies failed, compared with fewer than 10 per cent of companies affiliated to a particular religious denomination.[36] Overt speculation in cemeteries was not acceptable since it indicated an unacceptable shift in control of burial land to entrepreneurs, who were almost always from outside the town or city.

Local ownership and management of burial space

The success of the cemetery company is best understood in terms of its ability to ensure local ownership and management of burial space. The 1840s in particular were marked by cemetery company establishment where directorates were dominated by past and present mayors, town councillors, clergymen, Nonconformist ministers and leading businessmen, all of whom were overtly rooted in the locale. For example, the City of Canterbury Cemetery Company prospectus of 1845 listed 49 members of a provisional committee. Forty-three members of the committee were indicated as coming from Canterbury: ten of these were listed as 'Magistrate of the City of Canterbury'; the mayor, an alderman and a handful of councillors made up a further half dozen.[37] Similarly, Glasgow's City Burial Grounds Institute and Père Lachaise of Sighthill listed ten directors on its interim, all of whom had strong local connections and were prominent in Glasgow society. The committee included two professors from the Glasgow College, the Lord Provost, a bailie, a town councillor, and three directors of local banks.[38] A strong connection was also evident between the Newcastle General Cemetery Company and the town council. Aside from having the mayor as one of its directors, the company's acceptability was also made evident through the council's sale of land to the company in exchange for shares.[39] This action can be contrasted with Stirling Town Council's determined non-co-operation with a speculative cemetery company. The local newspaper carried notice of the Stirling Cemetery Company in February 1845.[40] The enterprise was effectively opposed by the town council, which blocked all attempts by the company to buy land, even though it was aware of the need for extra burial space in the town.[41]

Shareholding in the cemetery companies was dominated by people from the locality. For example, the shareholders list of the Westgate Hill General Cemetery of Newcastle gives 149 names. Only six of these shareholders are from outside Newcastle, and three of these six are from either Gateshead or Durham. The City Burial Grounds Institute and Père Lachaise of Sighthill was unusual in taking this degree of control a step further, in giving all lair (grave) owners a vote at company meetings. In Ipswich, the purchase of shares in the local cemetery was exhorted by the local newspaper as 'a duty': the company had been formed by a burials subcommittee of the town council in 1849 following discussion of the need for new burial ground.

The principle of local control of burial space was underlined by burial legislation that has, since the mid-nineteenth century, regulated interment in Britain. Allusion has already been made to the failure of the Chadwick-inspired Metropolitan Interment Bill. The bill was replaced by the Metropolitan Interment Act which was, in part, based on McKinnon's recommendations and looked to London vestries to deal with the problem of interment in the capital. Although the legislation was extended to the provinces a year later, a further flurry of legislation meant that, by 1857, the Church's success in taking back control of burial space had been short-lived. The additional legislation had extended responsibility for cemetery establishment to a whole range of local agencies. Town councils, Improvement Commissioners and local Boards of Health were all empowered to establish burial boards which were able to finance the laying out of cemetery land through the levying of a special rate. Brooks comments that success of the new legislation rested in its return of burial responsibility to the parish.[42] It is perhaps more accurate to say that the success of the Burial Acts of 1850 rested in their ensuring that ownership and management of burial space remained generally with the local community, following on from the successful precedent of cemetery company establishment.

Conclusion

This chapter has addressed a key urban governance issue: deciding which agency is best placed to provide a service essential to the well-being of the community. Cemeteries constitute an amenity with significance beyond their apparently basic remit of providing land for burial. Even aside from the obvious religious political dimensions of the issue, there remains a much more basic imperative for a community to protect and control the final resting place of its dead. Changing styles of governance in the first half of the nineteenth century meant that – more than at any other time in Britain's recent history – this issue was the subject of open debate and conflict as communities came to decide which agencies could best be trusted with this task. Despite the incursion of big business interests from the USA, Britain remains a country in which burial of the dead rests for the most part with democratically accountable local authorities. It may be that in the ever-shifting patterns of urban service provision, a single constant has been discovered.

Notes

1. See, for example, D. Eastwood, *Government and the Community in the English Provinces, 1700–1870* (Basingstoke: Macmillan, 1997).
2. See, for example, D. Fraser (ed.), *Municipal Reform and the Industrial City* (Leicester: Leicester University Press, 1982).
3. One notable exception is C. Brooks, et al., *Mortal Remains* (Exeter: Wheaton, 1989).
4. J. Rugg, '"A Few Remarks on Modern Sepulture": Current Trends and New Directions in Cemetery Research', *Mortality*, 3 (1998), pp. 111–28.

5. S. French, 'The Cemetery as a Cultural Institution: The Establishment of Mount Auburn and the "Rural Cemetery" Movement', in D.E. Stannard (ed.), *Death in America* (Philadelphia: University of Pennsylvania Press, 1975); D.C. Sloane, *The Last Great Necessity: Cemeteries in American History* (Baltimore: Johns Hopkins University Press, 1995).

6. S.S. Nicieja, 'Cemeteries – Pantheons of Distinguished Poles', in O. Czerner and I. Juszkiewicz (eds), *Cemetery Art* (Warsaw: ICOMOS, 1995).

7. M.C. Kearl, *Endings: A Sociology of Death and Dying* (New York: Oxford University Press, 1989); B.S.A. Yeoh and T.B. Hui, 'The Politics of Space: Changing Discourses on Chinese Burial Grounds in Post-War Singapore', *Journal of Historical Geography*, 21 (1995), pp. 184–201.

8. J. Rugg, 'The Rise of Cemetery Companies in Britain, 1820–53', unpublished PhD thesis, University of Stirling, 1982. See also J. Rugg, 'Researching early nineteenth-century cemeteries', *The Local Historian*, 28, (1998), pp. 130–44.

9. MS 'The personal narrative of George Hadfield', (1860), p. 81, Manchester Archive Office.

10. *Copy of the Deed of Settlement of the Public Cemetery Company established at Newport, Monmouthshire* (1842), 5, Newport Central Library; Unidentified newspaper clipping dated 18 Dec. 1844, pasted into the MS Minute Book of the Wisbech Cemetery Company, Wisbech and Fenland Museum.

11. See, for example, E.A. Wrigley and R.S. Schofield, *The Population History of England: A Reconstruction* (London: Edward Arnold, 1981).

12. See, for example, A. Brundage, *England's 'Prussian Minister': Edwin Chadwick and the Politics of Government Growth* (London: Pennsylvania State University Press, 1988); S.E. Finer, *The Life and Times of Sir Edwin Chadwick* (London: Methuen, 1952); R.A. Lewis, *Edwin Chadwick and the Public Health Movement* (London: Longman, Green, 1952).

13. General Board of Health, *Report on a General Scheme of Extramural Sepulture for Country Towns*, PP (1851) XXIII, p. 18.

14. *Report from the Select Committee on Improvement of the Health of Towns: Effect of Interment of Bodies in Towns* (1842), p. 186.

15. *Health of Towns: an Examination of the Report and Evidence of the Select Committee of Mr McKinnon's Bill; and of the Acts for Establishing Cemeteries around the Metropolis* (London: 1843), p. 21. This pamphlet reproduces articles on the issue of burials from the Nonconformist *Patriot* newspaper.

16. Ibid., pp. 6 and 9.

17. *Hansard*, 13 Jun. 1843, c. 1445.

18. *Health of Towns*, p. 123; see also G. Collison, *Cemetery Interment* (London: 1840).

19. Untitled circular dated 8 Jan. 1844, Bodleian Library, GA Oxon b112 (207).

20. D. Watts to James Rawson, 9 Feb. 1844, MS Leeds General Cemetery Company miscellaneous correspondence, Brotherton Library, University of Leeds.

21. W. Collins, *Modern Hereford* (Hereford: 1911), p. 41.

22. *The Times*, 22 Dec. 1843.

23. Brundage, *England's 'Prussian Minister'*, p. 90.

24. *Hansard*, 3 Jun. 1850, c678.

25. *Health of Towns*, p. 115.

26. *Hansard*, 8 Apr. 1845, c342.

27. See Rugg, 'The rise of cemetery companies', ch. 4.

28. *Manchester Guardian*, 23 Apr. 1836.

29. *Manchester Guardian*, 2 Apr. 1836.

30. *Manchester Guardian*, 30 Apr. 1836.

31. Ibid.
32. Ibid.
33. *Renfrewshire Advertiser*, 15 Feb. 1845.
34. *Glasgow Herald*, 17 Feb. 1845.
35. *The Post Office Greenock Directory for 1849–50* (Greenock: 1849), p. 69.
36. Rugg, 'The Rise of Cemetery Companies', p. 225.
37. *Kentish Gazette*, 9 Sep. 1845.
38. MS Minute Book of the City Burial Grounds Institute and Père Lachaise of Sighthill, Glasgow Archive Office, Mitchell Library. See also *Glasgow Courier*, 25 Feb. 1840.
39. *Prospectus of the Newcastle-upon-Tyne General Cemetery Company* (1834), Tyne and Wear Archives Office, Newcastle-upon-Tyne.
40. *Stirling Observer*, 20 Feb. 1845.
41. *Stirling Journal and Advertiser*, 10 Jul. 1846.
42. Brooks, *Mortal Remains*, pp. 47–50.

CHAPTER FIFTEEN

Ritual and civic culture in the English industrial city, *c.* 1835–1914

Simon Gunn

In 1882 the Birmingham Liberal J.T. Bunce argued that municipal government should be carried out with 'such stateliness of manner as to dignify the corporate life'. In making this point, Bunce echoed Walter Bagehot's celebrated division of the constitution into its 'efficient' and 'dignified' parts, the former designating the day-to-day process of decision-making and rule, the latter the ceremonial trappings of state.[1] While Bagehot was concerned with Westminster and national government, and Bunce with Birmingham and municipal government, both recognised in different ways the importance of the symbolic aspects of political power to its exercise and legitimation. Governance, in the larger sense, involves a mode of symbolic representation which is integral not merely to the co-ordination of its multiple functions, but also to the projection of its authority and the continuity of its rule. In mid- and later nineteenth-century England these precepts were well understood by the 'political' classes. At national level, the public prestige of the monarchy was reinvigorated from the 1870s and used, with considerable effect, to lend ceremonial dignity to the British state.[2] Locally, the decades after 1850 saw an efflorescence of ceremonial carried out in the name of civic pride. Implicit in both instances was the idea of the visualisation of power. In order for power to be realised it required to be made visible, to be given visual and symbolic form.

The subject of civic ritual in nineteenth-century towns and cities has been interpreted variously over the last 20 years. It has been seen as part of the 'invention of tradition' in the late nineteenth century, in which urban élites sought to construct a largely factitious version of the past for the town and its government.[3] More recently, the growth of civic ritual between the parliamentary reforms of 1832 and 1867 has been analysed in the context of the political culture of these years and of the shifting boundaries between the 'official' and the 'popular' polity.[4] These studies have been important in illuminating what remains a relatively neglected area of the history of urban governance, but they also have limitations. First, they indicate uncertainty about the periodisation of a distinct civic culture, the key moments being located variously in either the mid- or the late nineteenth century. Second, they have focused on towns – Boston, Oldham, Colchester – rather than on large provincial cities. While this is a useful corrective to the view from the metropolis, it overlooks the significance of civic ritual in the larger urban context. The size and anonymity of the large industrial city in the second half of the nineteenth century raised in particularly acute form the problems of order, authority and identity to which the rituals of civic culture were at least partly an antidote.

This chapter analyses the development and meanings of civic ritual in Birmingham, Leeds and Manchester between municipal reform in 1835 and the First World War. With populations rapidly expanding to half a million or more by 1914, these cities took on the characteristic spatial forms of urban modernity in the second half of the nineteenth century, exhibiting a significant degree of social and functional segregation. Serving as the industrial hubs of more extended 'manufacturing districts', it became increasingly difficult to define their boundaries, to say precisely what 'Birmingham' or 'Manchester' was.[5] The purpose of this chapter, therefore, is to examine civic ritual in these novel and amorphous urban centres. The first section charts the development of a repertoire of civic ceremonial and symbolic practice, reaching a highpoint in the 1870s. In the second section, the specific form and composition of civic and other parades are analysed, emphasising the connections between visibility, authority and identity within a larger politics of public performance. The third section examines the evidence for the decline of civic ritual before the First World War, pointing to changes in the visual representation of authority as well as to wider shifts in the social and political landscape. In conclusion, I shall draw out some of the implications of the analysis for the study of urban governance in England in the period between 1850 and 1914.

The efflorescence of civic ritual in English industrial cities after 1850 was not a novel invention; nor did it represent a simple continuation of traditional forms of urban pageantry. Civic ceremonial in older towns like Norwich, Coventry and Ipswich appears to have been in decline by the early nineteenth century, alongside the guild festivals with which it was closely associated. In London, the Lord Mayor's Show, which had flourished in the 1730s, atrophied to the point where it required to be actively revived in the 1880s.[6] Where such ceremonies did survive they were often exclusive to members of the corporation; according to David Cannadine, the Colchester Oyster Feast in the early Victorian period was 'not a public pageant, but a private party'.[7] In Birmingham, Leeds and Manchester there existed a tradition of public ceremonial, but it too showed signs of decay. In Birmingham a public procession was arranged to mark Victoria's coronation in July 1838, allowing the pre-reform local authorities to parade for one last time. But as the *Birmingham Gazette* confessed, whether from 'the shortness of the notice ... the previous engagements of many of the inhabitants, or from some other cause, the attendance was by no means such as was expected'.[8]

One reason for the lack of concern with these public events was the degree of interparty strife over control of local authority in industrial cities prior to municipal reform in 1835. Even so, urban Liberalism was notably slow to develop a repertoire of civic ritual, despite the importance of municipal reform for Liberal élites and their sweeping victory in Birmingham, Leeds and Manchester at the first municipal elections.[9] In Manchester the first elections in December 1838, after a protracted political and legal struggle over incorporation, passed 'without the slightest degree of excitement' according to the *Manchester Guardian*. Liberals were handicapped by inexperience in the etiquette of power as much as by any radical hostility to ritual, exemplified by the confusion at the first meeting of the Birmingham Council regarding the procedures appropriate to the election of the Mayor and aldermen.[10] For all these reasons, civic authorities could not match the symbolic vitality of popular radicalism in the first half of the nineteenth century, the display of banners and emblems which transformed mass demonstrations from Peterloo to Chartism into what James Epstein has termed 'highly stylised rituals of collective solidarity'.[11]

The event which did most to stimulate large-scale civic pageantry in the industrial cities was the visit of Queen Victoria in the 1850s. Paradoxically it was the symbol of the aristocratic hereditary principle which acted as the catalyst for provincial, bourgeois civic pride. While royal visits had previously been made to Leeds and Birmingham, the prototypical event was that staged for Queen Victoria in Manchester in 1851. From the outset the event was conceived very differently by the two parties involved. For the royal party it represented a stage on the Queen's journey south from Balmoral to London; for the Manchester Corporation, on the other hand, it represented the opportunity to project the city to the nation at large. The event itself was designed as a mass pageant, enacted in front of vast crowds, the leading parts in the drama being taken by the corporation and a largely unwitting monarch. Following the royal visit to Salford, the Manchester Town Council processed to the newly named Victoria Bridge in robes of scarlet and purple, the first time ceremonial dress had been worn. Italianate triumphal arches had been constructed to mark the passage through the city, on which were 'blazoned in high relief the arms of the incorporated borough'.[12] The royal party, led by the carriages of the Mayor and High Sheriff, then processed around the central streets, the warehouses festooned with flags and crowded with spectators. At the Exchange, converted for the occasion by the Borough Surveyor, the Queen was seated on a throne surrounded by the town council in front of an audience of 2,000 notables, evoking the coronation ceremony. Here she was presented with addresses from the Mayor and corporation which carefully matched respect for the royal office with the promotion of Liberal causes: free trade, the advancement of industry, civil and religious freedom. In return, the Queen knighted the Mayor, John Potter.

As a spectacle, the royal visit to Manchester worked on multiple levels. Symbolically, it involved a series of reciprocal gestures between the monarchy and the bourgeois representatives of urban industrial society. Each of the events involved a mutual act of recognition; both parties were enhanced by the other's approbation. But the royal dimension can obscure the extent to which this was constructed as a civic occasion to which the urban community at large was witness. Press reports of the crowds noted not only their size and orderliness, but also their precise social composition at different stages of the route. The procession was thus seen as incorporating the diverse sections of the urban population within the event. It also had its commercial aspect, the triumphal arches and raised platforms being paid for by local firms in return for publicity. Nor was the national significance of the event overlooked. The *Manchester Guardian* used the occasion to project Manchester as a 'community based upon the orderly, sober and peaceful industry of the middle classes' and to claim that 'social importance and political power have passed into the hands of those classes upon whose shoulders the burden of maintaining the national edifice has shifted'.[13]

Events such as this did not meet with universal approval even among leading Liberals. Cobden, in particular, was vocal in his condemnation of Manchester's civic 'junketing', and four councillors refused to wear the new ceremonial robes as a mark of their radicalism, including two future mayors.[14] But the Manchester visit was influential in promoting similar events in other cities. The Leeds Corporation sought guidance on ceremonial practice from its Manchester counterpart before the Queen's opening of the town hall in 1858, while reports of the royal visit to Birmingham were couched in the terms of civic rivalry, the council being 'confidently informed ... that Manchester never turned out anything so fine'.[15] More generally, the royal visits of the 1850s paved the way for an upsurge of civic pageantry in the industrial cities, which reached its zenith in the 1870s. It encompassed not only the most highly publicised occasions, such as royal celebrations and the opening of town halls, but also a host of less noted events: the unveiling of memorials and statues, the inauguration of parks and public buildings, Mayor's Sunday and the opening of the assizes. In the north, older customs such as the Whit Walks in Lancashire, the Bishop Blaize celebrations in the West Riding, and the 20-yearly Preston Guild Merchant festivities were incorporated into the civic calendar. As this suggests, the trend from the 1860s was for pageantry to become more socially inclusive, drawing in friendly and trade societies as well as the regional aristocracy in honorific roles.[16]

In Birmingham, Leeds and Manchester the ideological framework of civic ritual was provided by urban Liberalism. Between 1838 and the 1890s the councils remained predominantly, and for much of the period overwhelmingly, Liberal in composition; in Manchester there were only three Tory mayors before 1870.[17] The Liberal inflexion of civic pride was evident, first, in the assertion of a specific identity for the city, represented by its principal trades and its most prominent 'public' buildings. Corporation addresses on ceremonial occasions never failed to highlight the city's character and significance: 'this ancient and enterprising town, the centre of so much of our manufacturing industry', 'the most democratic town in England', as Birmingham was described at the Queen's visit in 1858.[18] By the 1880s important visitors to Manchester were taken on a tour of the city's 'official institutions' by the Mayor and senior corporation members, including the Free Trade Hall, Owens College, the Royal Exchange and the town hall.[19] Like the town histories of the period, these rhetorical and visual strategies were used to associate the corporation with civic and economic progress. At the same time, they served to stamp a symbolic 'image' on what were increasingly distended and amorphous cityscapes, the city being identified with a particular municipal history and with its official buildings and monuments.

Liberalism also infused urban ritual with a radical obduracy, in defence of municipal autonomy against the perceived threat from a centralising state and an aristocratic county. At a specially convened gathering in York in 1873, the mayors of England and Wales paraded through the streets in ceremonial dress to protest at the interventionist tendencies of the newly established Local Government Board, characteristically combining political demonstration with civic display.[20] Despite the incorporation of the regional aristocracy in civic occasions, relations with the county hierarchy remained edgy, often taking symbolic form in struggles over custom and precedent. One notably tetchy and protracted encounter took place in the 1880s and 1890s, in which the precedence of the Mayor of Manchester over the High Sheriff of Lancashire within the borough, or indeed of any personage short of royalty, was successfully upheld.[21] Likewise, events such as the transfer of the assizes to industrial cities and the appointment of members of the urban élite to county offices were moments of civic triumph, celebrated with full pomp and show.[22] What such episodes demonstrated was not only the growing power of urban authorities, but also their increasing adeptness in handling a symbolic register. By the 1870s urban Liberalism had developed a new symbolic language for civic ritual centred on the identification of the corporation with the city, as the preserver of its dignity and defender of its interests.

While ritual was important in negotiating relations with the State and the county, it also had a central role in ordering relations within the urban community. Civic pageantry and processions were a principal means by which an 'urban community' was evoked, the presence of particular groups . in a procession signalling both the diversity of identities within the city and a public recognition of the legitimacy of those identities. The meanings of these events were multiple, depending fundamentally on who viewed them (by class and gender) and in what capacity (as participant or spectator). Moreover, they were enacted in a specific context, defined by the mid- and later nineteenth-century city which was itself a shifting physical and cultural construct. Cities such as Birmingham, Manchester and Leeds were extensively remodelled in the period between the 1840s and the 1880s, as populations and manufacturing industry were displaced from the centre and moved to locations on the periphery or in distinct suburbs. The city centre was thus increasingly reserved for business, warehousing, consumption and civic administration, these functions themselves occupying different zones within the centre. In particular, a distinct 'civic' space was carved out, focusing on the municipal buildings, squares and statues.[23]

The monumental character of later Victorian cities provided a theatrical backdrop for ceremonial of all kinds, especially the processions and parades which accompanied the more important civic occasions. Marching in rank order through the main city streets with banners and costume dress became an important part of the social experience of a significant section of the urban population. As voluntary, friendly and trade societies were drawn into the public arena by the 1860s, so a processional culture took shape in industrial cities, centred on civic ritual though not limited to it. Civic processions embodied ideas of authority and identity in a symbolic yet highly visible fashion. Thus, a fundamental aspect of such events was their gender-specific character. While women had been active in radical demonstrations in the first half of the century, civic pageants were essentially all-male affairs. Civic space was male space, women's role in events being confined to spectating, organising private parties and supervising charitable functions.

Civic pageants embodied notions of authority and hierarchy in other specific ways. First, they assembled and presented the most powerful individuals and institutions in the city in a single public space. At the opening of the Birmingham and Midland Institute by Prince Albert in 1855, the great and the good were convened on the ceremonial platform: mayor and town council, magistrates, governors of the Grammar School, clergy and ministers, together with the neighbouring 'nobility and gentry', in a singular display of civic solidarity.[24] It was customary for the city's largest employers to be invited as 'gentlemen' on such occasions, even where they were not council members, thus adding economic to political weight. At the reception for the assize judges in Leeds in 1865, the Mayor and the corporation were accompanied on the town hall steps by what were described as 'leading public men', Crossley, Forster, Denison and Lupton, who were also major employers in Leeds or the region.[25] Civic events thus gave the representatives of urban authority opportunity to display themselves, not only to the assembled crowds, but also to those who read the voluminous, highly detailed reports in the local press.

Second, the order of the procession itself signified degrees of authority and prestige. The elevation of the importance of the mayoralty after 1835 was demonstrated in Birmingham by the tendency to place the Mayor at the end of the procession, rather than in its midst. In Leeds and Manchester, on the other hand, the same principle dictated that the Mayor should head any procession.[26] Every procession had its own social logic, however. That this was apparent to participants is indicated by the refusal of groups to participate if they were not assigned what they deemed an appropriate place in the rank order.[27] Yet the issues were complex since the parade was a fluid entity whose composition changed over time. In Liberal-dominated cities, for example, the regular units of the army which had accompanied processions prior to municipal reform were replaced by volunteers. From the late 1830s the more important and respectable voluntary associations, such as temperance societies, began to be incorporated in events, though participation was only established on a widespread and regular basis after 1850. Similarly, while artisan trades had long been involved in civic festivities, by the 1860s they were joined by other groups of urban workers and participated on different terms. Corporation sub-committees were now required to negotiate with local associations over their involvement, and trade and friendly societies used the events to assert a collective identity independent of employers as well as to demonstrate local patriotism.[28]

The entry of working-class groups into the civic arena was an inherently ambiguous enterprise, open to diverse interpretations. The act of marching in an orderly fashion through the city represented a public claim to social and political identity. Thus a *Manchester Guardian* editorial commented on the significance of a Manchester trades demonstration in support of the strike of agricultural labourers in 1874:

> The lengthy procession of Saturday, important enough in itself, was more important still in the representative character of the bodies of which it was composed. Nearly every group in the line belonged to some larger combination of workmen.

The demonstration spoke, in the Guardian's words, of the 'newly-recognised brotherhood of labour'.[29] Where demonstrators marched was also significant: by processing around the central streets and major civic buildings organised labour asserted its rights to public space, and to a voice within the city and the larger political nation.

The meanings of processions organised under civic auspices were more complex, however. They represented social order in the double sense of the term. By participating, working-class groups rendered themselves visible to the urban public and staked their claim to a place in the urban polity. At the same time, the hierarchical ordering of civic processions framed the event and gave physical form to the concept of social authority. Within the procession, the sequential order in which groups were placed meant that they did not come face to face with one another; they appeared before the urban public in a linked but separate manner. In the Liberal conception of the social order represented in civic parades, therefore, the notions of dependence and independence were held in mutual tension. Improvisatory, fluid and voluntaristic, civic processions encompassed the representation of different social identities within a framework of hierarchy and stability.[30]

The idea of processions and parades as expressive of order was widespread in the industrial cities. The extent to which bourgeois attitudes to marching workers, evinced in the press, shifted between the two halves of the nineteenth century is indeed striking. Whereas the quasi-military processions of workers were regularly seen as threatening in the Peterloo and Chartist periods, by the 1860s they were represented as evidence of the orderliness and loyalty of workers. A Manchester periodical in 1870 contrasted the violent events occurring in Paris with the peaceable character of the several parades held the previous weekend:

> Probably not less than 40,000 people were gathered together in these ... localities, without taking into account the vast throng who lined the streets through which different processions passed. Flags were flying, bands play-ing, and all was harmony, rejoicing and peace.[31]

By this period, therefore, processions were taken to be an index of civility. The bodily self-discipline of the marchers, the degree of organisation apparent in the procession as a whole, and the ritualistic nature of the events rendered them inherently respectable, a model of collective behaviour in public. They contrasted not only with earlier forms of popular protest, and with events abroad, but also with the disorderly character of city streets and slums and the continuing fears of crime and violence which these aroused. The voluntarism of the parade and its public visibility served in this context as an ideal of the self-regulating urban community, which policed itself through its own intrinsic codes of conduct.

However, as a widening number of institutions and social groups participated in the public processional culture, so the opportunities for bourgeois display were reduced. From the 1870s civic processions were rivalled as public spectacles by the great demonstrations of Conservative and Liberal parties, and of organised labour. In Birmingham the inauguration of the assizes in 1884 might have been expected to be celebrated with considerable civic panache, as had earlier been the case at both Leeds and Manchester. In fact, it was poorly attended, overshadowed by the great Liberal demonstration in favour of franchise extension, addressed by Chamberlain, Bright and many city councillors, and involving an estimated 100,000 people in the procession.[32] The very success of the processional culture inititiated in the 1850s diluted the appeal of civic ceremonial in the longer term.

As a result, the ritual which came to represent civic and bourgeois authority most publicly in the late nineteenth century was the 'centipedic funeral' of large employers and municipal dignitaries. There was nothing wholly new in such obsequies. The extravagance of funerals of both national and local notables was the source of much criticism in the early nineteenth century, and after 1850 the trend was for simpler events among the upper echelons of society.[33] Yet this did not preclude a magisterial 'send-off'. Julian Litten has described the 1890s as 'the golden age of the Victorian funeral', culminating in the sober yet massive state funeral of Gladstone in 1898.[34] In the industrial centres, the decades after 1880 were notable for the number and scale of funerals of local worthies, conducted in the public gaze with full civic pomp.

The funeral of Sir Edward Baines, owner of the *Leeds Mercury*, in 1890 was characteristic. The cortège left the Baines mansion on the edge of Leeds, to be joined by the carriages of the region's leading employer families, the Illingworths, Kitsons and Luptons, and wound its way through streets lined with spectators to East Parade Chapel, seat of worship of the Baines dynasty for several generations. Mills were closed and the 160 staff of the *Leeds Mercury* marched as a body to the chapel. After the funeral service, the procession – now half a mile in length – headed northwards, led by the representatives of 26 public institutions and followed by the carriages of the city's civic and business élite. 'All the way there was evidence of mourning', the *Leeds Mercury* reported. 'Most of the shops were closed. Blinds were drawn at the Town Hall and Municipal Buildings.'[35] The town hall bell tolled and flags were hung at half-mast. The cortege was met at Woodhouse Cemetery by the Mayor and town council, though Baines had never been a member. As a 'public man', however, he was given a civic burial.

Rites of this type were customarily enacted on the death of urban notables in industrial towns and cities until 1914. They reflected the status of such men as public figures, closely identified with the city. This association was symbolised in the route adopted by the funeral procession, taking in locations specific to the life of the deceased – home, workplace, church or chapel – as well as the representative civic sites, the town hall, principal squares and streets. In this way the life of the individual notable was figuratively aligned with the life of the city, recreating simultaneously an ideal of urban community and of civic authority. By extension, what such rites signalled was both the death of the patriarch and the continuity of patriarchal authority. This was most explicit in the published funeral addresses, which sought to evoke a life devoted to the benificent exercise of power and to place the individual within a long line of patrimonial duty. Thomas Ashton, the cotton manufacturer of Manchester and Hyde, 'lived and died like a patriarch'; at his funeral in 1898, the congregation was reminded that he 'represented the third generation of Ashtons, who employed, to a very large extent, the third and fourth generations of workpeople'.[36] If a language of patriarchal continuity was most commonly applied to industrial employers, it was not confined to them. The funeral rites of leading clergymen and ministers similarly sought to embrace them within a tradition of religious piety and civic responsibility: in Birmingham, the Congregationalist minister R.W. Dale was depicted as an exemplar of English puritanism and 'a leading citizen'; at Manchester the Anglican James Fraser was located in the great tradition of reforming bishops, 'full of civic virtue'.[37]

The ceremonial rituals of the mid- and late nineteenth century thus offered rich resources for the display of authority, social order and identity. Their meanings were complex and frequently ambiguous. Yet in differing ways the civic parade and the 'centipedic funeral' served to symbolise a unity of leadership and authority in the industrial city more powerfully than any other event. That urban élites were so often perceived by workers, and by subsequent historians, as a unified group is perhaps partly testament to the capacity of public rituals to project an image of collective harmony and purpose.[38] It was possible on ceremonial occasions for political and sectarian strife to be transcended in the expression of elemental themes: community, solidarity, mourning. In bourgeois funeral rites, especially, civic virtues were sanctified and spiritual virtues enhanced by the secular glow of civic duty. Under the mantle of the civic, employers, clergy and municipal leaders shared modes of ritual expression which had the capacity to transform evanescent authority into something resembling the permanence of power.

The forms of power embodied in later Victorian civic ritual were, of course, transitory. While in many smaller industrial and county towns the years between 1880 and 1914 represented the highpoint of civic culture, in the industrial cities there is evidence that enthusiasm was waning in the same period.[39] The major civic occasions were described no less minutely in the local press, but reports bore signs of weariness at their formulaic character. At the opening of the Manchester Ship Canal by Queen Victoria in 1894, the *Manchester Guardian* confessed to a certain civic ennui: 'One tired of the decorations, about which there was, after all, a considerable degree of sameness'. At the opening of City Square in Leeds in 1903, it was reported that 'the display of enthusiasm was not so great as it might have been'. Meanwhile, Birmingham's principal municipal achievement of the early twentieth century, the Elan Water Valley Scheme, was celebrated away from the city, the Mayor and corporation being transported by train to mid-Wales for the opening by King Edward VII.[40] The sheer number of civic spectacles in the second half of the nineteenth century, it would seem, gradually satiated the appetite of observers for such events.

There were also other reasons for the appearance of decline. By the 1870s civic pageantry in the industrial city was forced to compete for public attention with other processional events, such as party demonstrations, and with the attractions of an increasingly commercialised popular culture, including department stores, music halls and professional sport. In short, the civic no longer occupied so unique a position in the repertoire of visual spectacle which the city had to offer. Wider social and political shifts also played a part in the declining appeal of civic ritual. Patrick Joyce has noted the 'passing of the old order' in the factory north around 1900, signalled by the advent of the limited liability company, the slow exodus of large employers, and the rise of socialism and militant trade unionism which challenged employer versions of the 'community of interest' on which the old order had rested.[41] Concomitant changes were occurring at the municipal level. From the mid-1870s there was a reduction in the number of large proprietors on many urban councils. The intervention of the Local Government Board and the growing number of interest groups in local affairs made municipal government itself more complex and onerous than at an earlier period. In addition, Liberalism, which had provided much of the political impetus for the creation of civic culture, was increasingly under challenge from Conservatives, Labour representatives and economy-minded elements in cities such as Leeds and Manchester by the 1890s. The decline in civic culture can thus be partly attributed to a series of shifts in the constellation of urban authority between 1880 and 1914.[42]

All these tendencies were slow-acting and uneven in effect; the extent and timing of change was registered differently in particular urban locales. At a political level, for example, the numbers of businessmen on municipal councils in Leeds and Birmingham actually increased in the last decades of the century.[43] Likewise, decline did not affect all aspects of civic ritual equally; it is integral to the definition of ritual that it retains an aura or mystique independent of the individuality of the persons participating in it. Significantly, while there was a steady stream of criticism of the declining social status of mayors and councillors from the 1850s, the prestige of the mayoralty and corporation as institutions was little affected. It was precisely this symbolic prestige which made the mayoralty, in the words of a recent historian, an 'embracing fixation' of the Labour party in the north during the interwar years.[44]

These themes of continuity and of decline in civic ritual were both in evidence at the funeral of Joseph Chamberlain in Birmingham on the eve of the First World War. Commemorated in Birmingham less as a national statesman than as a local patriarch, 'a pioneer [who] laid the foundations for Birmingham's civic greatness', Chamberlain's funeral was a testament to the power of provincial civic culture. Following his death in London in July 1914, the body was conveyed by train to Birmingham for burial. Birmingham itself was transformed into a 'city in mourning', in the words of the *Daily Post*: 'business was suspended so that all citizens might join in a last tribute to Birmingham's greatest citizen'. While the Mayor and corporation were prominent in the procession, in which every significant institution in the city was represented, the crowds lining the streets were depicted as a silent chorus, a community united in memory of a common struggle enacted under Chamberlain's leadership:

> The bulk of those who gathered there, young and old, artisan and clerk, were people who felt that they had been intimately associated with the man who was being borne to his last resting place. They were the rank-and-file who had responded to his call ... they, more than others, were his people.[45]

Yet if the funeral registered the still powerful pulse of civic culture, it also bore witness to its decline. Descriptions in the press consistently referred backwards to an already mythologised past associated with the highpoint of 'municipal socialism' in the 1870s and 1880s. It was this historical moment, above all, which was presented as the focal point of remembrance. In this sense Chamberlain's funeral represented a valediction for a whole civic culture. It marked the passing of an era characterised by the primacy of the local and the identification of authority with a bourgeois civic leadership. Henceforward, no civic leader in the provincial cities would receive a funeral of this scale or importance; nor would civic ritual itself be imbued with so potent a political and cultural resonance.

I have argued in this chapter that urban governance has important symbolic dimensions. In the context of the urban modernity of the later nineteenth century, in which the visual served as the predominant sense, this symbolic aspect required that power should be public, spectacular and performative in order to be effective. The pageantry and processions which characterised civic culture between 1850 and 1914 enabled the personal authority of employers and 'public men' to be transmuted into larger, more stable and more permanent symbols of urban leadership. They incarnated the idea of a distinct social order, incorporating a diversity of social interests and agencies, thus giving physical expression to the concept of urban community. In the process, they contributed to the reorganisation of urban space and of bodies in space. Ceremonial and processions affirmed the symbolic significance of certain streets, squares and buildings by virtue of their identification with the civic as a source of power. At the same time, processions embodied an idealised vision of urban order and sobriety set against the disorganisation of the city, its anonymous crowds, random streets and labyrinthine slums.

Such public rituals were intimately bound up with the historical moment of urban Liberalism. Liberalism provided the political creed which infused much of civic ritual, transcribing it into the familiar language of municipal pride and progress. It also shaped the larger vision of an urban social order characterised by a specific admixture of voluntarism and hierarchy, autonomy and authority. Within this political culture, identity was linked to visibility on public occasions. Participation in the rites of civic culture affirmed the rights of a group to recognition within the public life of the city. Those groups not represented in this way – women, the poor, ethnic minorities – were effectively denied recognition as independent entities, and with it, the right to public expression. The gradual decline of civic culture from the late nineteenth century was thus marked not simply by the weakening of Liberalism or by the withdrawal of élites, but also by the fragmentation of a politics of visual representation which had rested on a series of exclusions. Once the streets had been occupied by groups of unemployed workers and suffragettes, the claims of civic authority to represent urban community and social order were brought into question. As Lisa Tickner has pointed out, the sight of marching women, dressed in the suffragette colours and with banners held aloft, marked a turning-point in the politics of visual display in Britain.[46] From this perspective, the success of Liberal civic culture was partly its undoing in the longer term. By linking visibility, identity and power in explicit yet exclusive ways in the nineteenth century, it paved the way for the return of the repressed in the early twentieth.

Notes

1. E.P. Hennock, *Fit and Proper Persons: Ideal and Reality in Nineteenth-Century Urban Government* (London: Edward Arnold, 1973), pp. 321–2; W. Bagehot, *The English Constitution* (London: Watts, 1964), p. 61.
2. D. Cannadine, 'The Context, Performance and Meaning of Ritual: the British Monarchy and the "Invention of Tradition", c. 1820–1977' in E. Hobsbawm and T. Ranger (eds), *The Invention of Tradition* (Cambridge: Cambridge

University Press, 1984); W.M. Kuhn, 'Ceremony and Politics: The British Monarchy, 1871–2', *Journal of British Studies*, 26 (1987).

3. D. Cannadine, 'The Transformation of Civic Ritual in Modern Britain: The Colchester Oyster Feast', *Past and Present*, 94, (1982); Hobsbawm and Ranger, *Invention of Tradition* (see note 2).

4. J. Vernon, *Politics and the People: A Study in English Political Culture, c. 1815–1867* (Cambridge: Cambridge University Press, 1993), ch. 2; F. O'Gorman, 'Campaign Rituals and Ceremonies: The Social Meaning of Elections in England 1780–1860', *Past and Present*, 135 (1992).

5. P. Deane and B. Mitchell, *Abstract of British Historical Statistics* (Cambridge: Cambridge University Press, 1962), pp. 24–7; M. Savage and A. Warde, *Urban Sociology, Capitalism and Modernity* (London: Macmillan, 1993), chs 2 and 5; A. Redford, *A History of Local Government in Manchester*, vol. 2 (London: Longmans, 1940), ch. 24.

6. S. and B. Webb, 'The Manor and the Borough', *English Local Government*, vol. 2 (London: Frank Cass, 1963), pp. 424, 441, 537–8, 565, 583; Cannadine, 'Context, Performance and Meaning of Ritual', p. 138.

7. Cannadine, 'Transformation of civic ritual', p. 113.

8. *Aris's Birmingham Gazette*, 2 July 1838.

9. Whigs and Liberals won all 48 seats in Birmingham and Manchester in 1838, and all but six in Leeds in 1835. D. Fraser, *Urban Politics in Victorian England* (London: Macmillan, 1979), p. 124.

10. *Manchester Guardian*, 15 December 1838; *Aris's Birmingham Gazette*, 31 December 1838.

11. J. Epstein, *Radical Expression: Political Language, Ritual and Symbol in England, 1790–1850* (Oxford: Oxford University Press, 1994), p. 89.

12. *Manchester Guardian*, 11 October 1851, p. 5.

13. *Manchester Guardian*, 11 October 1851, p. 8.

14. N. McCord, 'Cobden and Bright in Politics, 1846–57' in R. Robson (ed.), *Ideas and Institutions of Victorian Britain* (London: G. Bell, 1967), pp. 112–14; *Manchester Guardian*, 11 October 1851, p. 7.

15. A. Briggs, *Victorian Cities* (London: Penguin, 1963), p. 171; *Birmingham Daily Post*, 16 June 1858, p. 4.

16. P. Joyce, *Visions of the People: Industrial England and the Question of Class, 1840–1914* (Cambridge: Cambridge University Press, 1991), pp. 183–5. For a wider discussion of aristocratic involvement in civic ritual in the period see R. Trainor, 'Peers on an Industrial Frontier: The Earls of Dartmouth and of Dudley in the Black Country, c.1810–1914', in D. Cannadine (ed.), *Patricians, Power and Politics in Nineteenth-Century Towns* (Leicester: Leicester University Press, 1982), pp. 103–13.

17. Fraser, *Urban Politics*, ch. 6; Hennock, *Fit and Proper Persons*.

18. *Birmingham Daily Post*, 16 June 1858, p. 6.

19. *Manchester Examiner*, 14 December 1881.

20. *Leeds Mercury*, 26 September 1873, p. 3.

21. T. Baker, 'Reminiscences of my Own Life', MS, Manchester Central Reference Library Archives; 'The mayor's social status: a question of precedence', *Manchester Examiner*, 31 July and 1 August 1882; 'Precedence in public ceremonies', 1897, MSS, Manchester Central Reference Library Archives.

22. See for example *Leeds Mercury*, 13 August 1865, p. 12 for the opening of the assizes at Leeds; *Manchester Courier*, 16 April 1883 and Ashton papers, Manchester Central Library Archives, for a description of the events surrounding the elevation of Thomas Ashton, the Manchester cotton employer,

to the office of High Sheriff.

23. Vernon, *Politics and the People*, pp. 50–64; C. Cunningham, *Victorian and Edwardian Town Halls* (London: Routledge and Keegan Paul, 1981); S. Gunn, 'The Middle Class, Modernity and the City' in A. Kidd and D. Nicholls (eds), *Gender, Civic Culture and Consumerism* (Manchester: Manchester University Press, 1999).

24. *Aris's Birmingham Gazette*, 26 November 1855.

25. *Leeds Mercury*, 13 August 1865, p. 12.

26. The change in the processional order in Birmingham can be seen by comparing the coronation procession in 1838 with that for Prince Albert in 1835. See *Aris's Birmingham Gazette*, 2 July 1838 and 26 November 1855. For descriptions of civic processions in Leeds see J. Mayhall, *The Annals of Leeds* vols 1–3 (Leeds: 1860; 1866; 1875). For processional etiquette in Manchester see the letter from the Town Clerk, W.H. Talbot, of 16 January 1895 in 'Precedence in public ceremonies'.

27. This occurred with the freemasons at the coronation celebrations in Manchester in 1838, *Manchester Guardian*, 30 June 1838. Similar ideas structured the ordering of processions in electoral campaigns; see O'Gorman, 'Campaign Rituals and Ceremonies', p. 107.

28. J. Garrard, *Leadership and Power in Victorian Industrial Towns, 1830–80* (Manchester: Manchester University Press, 1983), pp. 27–8; P. Joyce, *Work, Society and Politics: The Culture of the Factory in Later Victorian England* (Brighton: Harvester, 1981), pp. 272–82.

29. *Manchester Guardian*, 22 June 1874, p. 5.

30. For a comparative perspective see the illuminating analysis by Mary Ryan, 'The American Parade: Representations of the Nineteenth-Century Social Order' in L. Hunt (ed.), *The New Cultural History* (Berkeley: University of California Press, 1989), pp. 131–53.

31. *The Freelance*, 16 August 1870.

32. *Birmingham Daily Post*, 5 August 1884. For party demonstrations in Manchester see Joyce, *Work, Society and Politics*, pp. 280–82.

33. For the scale of civic funerals in industrial cities in the first half of the nineteenth century see the example of Sir Thomas Potter, first Mayor of Manchester, in 1845, *Manchester Guardian*, 29 March 1845, p. 9. For national trends see P. Jalland, *Death in the Victorian Family* (Oxford: Oxford University Press, 1996), ch. 9.

34. J. Litten, *The English Way of Death: The Common Funeral Since 1450* (Cambridge: Cambridge University Press, 1991), p. 170.

35. *Leeds Mercury*, 7 March 1890, p. 8.

36. *Manchester Guardian*, 22 January 1898.

37. *Birmingham Daily Post*, 14 and 19 March 1895; T. Hughes, *James Fraser, Second Bishop of Manchester* (London: 1887), pp. 359–62.

38. For comments see Joyce, *Work, Society and Politics*, pp. 22–3; J. Seed and J. Wolff, 'Introduction', in J. Seed and J. Wolff, *The Culture of Capital: Art, Power and the Nineteenth-Century Middle Class* (Manchester: Manchester University Press, 1988), esp. pp. 1–7.

39. For descriptions of civic culture in smaller towns during this period see D. Cannadine, 'Transformation of Civic Ritual'; E. Hammerton and D. Cannadine, 'Conflict and Consensus on a Ceremonial Occasion: the Diamond Jubilee in Cambridge in 1897', *Historical Journal*, (1981); J. Garrard, 'Urban Elites, 1850–1914: The Rule and Decline of a New Squirearchy?', *Albion*, 27 (1995), pp. 603–15; R.H. Trainor, *Black Country Elites* (Oxford: Clarendon Press,

1993), pp. 280–81, 325, 349–51, 355, 368–70.

40. *Manchester Guardian*, 22 May 1894, p. 7; *Leeds Mercury*, 17 September 1903, p. 8; *Birmingham Daily Post*, special supplement, 21 July 1904.

41. Joyce, *Work, Society and Politics*, epilogue.

42. For a wider discussion of these themes see Garrard, 'Urban elites', pp. 603–21; T. Woodhouse, 'The Working Class', in D. Fraser (ed.), *A History of Modern Leeds* (Manchester: Manchester University Press, 1980), pp. 362–3; A. Kidd, *Manchester* (Keele: Ryburn Press, 1993), pp. 148–9.

43. Hennock, *Fit and Proper Persons*, pp. 214 ff.

44. J. Garrard, 'The Mayoralty since 1835', *Transactions of the Lancashire and Cheshire Antiquarian Society*, 90 (1994), p. 29.

45. *Birmingham Daily Post*, 7 July 1914.

46. For an interesting discussion of this issue see L. Tickner, *The Spectacle of Women: Images of the Suffrage Campaign, 1907–14* (London: Chatto and Windus, 1987).

CHAPTER SIXTEEN

The management of urban public spaces: Shahjahanabad, New Delhi, Greater Delhi, 1857–1997

Narayani Gupta

India has a long history of urban settlements, but urban governance has not been studied very much, not even for the two centuries of colonial rule, during which the discourse on urban questions was copious and can be culled from a range of official records. This year (1998) marks the centenary of British India's first Improvement Trust (in Bombay); to the Trusts and town planning Acts, modelled on those of Britain, the early years of Independence (1950s) saw the addition of the USSR's principle of a planned pattern of settlements and the USA's faith in planned settlements. Planning implies recognising public areas as distinct from private, and the last 100 years have seen attempts to subvert the planners' attempts to safeguard public spaces. All is not well in the governance of urban public areas, and perhaps we can understand this better if we try to appreciate the perceptions of urban-dwellers.

In Hindi/Urdu, the word *aam* does duty for 'public' as well as for 'generally'. In officialese, public is translated as *lokartha* (for the benefit of people) or *sarvjanik* (of all the people), both Sanskritic, or *sarkari* (of the government), derived from Persian. In referring to family/property, *niji/apna* translates as one's own. There is no word to mean privacy, but demarcation of areas within the house is clearly understood: the *zenana* refers to the women's quarters and *mardana* to the men's. Again, though there are no terms for it, the gradations from the public to the private are understood. The public street leads to the semi-public *gali* (lane) or *kucha* (dead-end road), then to the semi-private section of the house, which leads on to the private inner rooms. In the pre-automobile age the mental maps of most town-dwellers were fairly narrowly circumscribed, and those of women in most cases limited to their homes and those of their immediate neighbours, who usually included the extended family. Since goods and services came to the house, and worship could be conducted at home, nothing took them far afield.

Present day Delhi is a collage in which there are buildings going back to the thirteenth century, a seventeenth-century city and palace-complex, a twentieth-century British capital, and overlaps and extensions built in the last 50 years. Of the 13 million inhabitants of the city today, a large percentage are first-generation immigrants, and only a very small number can claim continuous residence in the city of more than four generations. To explain how this came about, a quick survey of the city's history for the last 350 years will be useful.

When the Mughal emperor Shah Jahan decided to build a capital at Delhi, he bought the land for a city, which accordingly became *Khalisa* (royal domain).[1]

Much of this was parcelled out to individuals or collectivities, with the understanding that the land could be reclaimed by the king.[2] Assigned plots of land were often converted to *auqaf* (land held in trust, for a shrine or a charitable institution); this then became inalienable.[3] Some plots were developed as orchards, thus earning exemption from the tax levied on agricultural land. The city wall spelt protection as well as serving as a tax barrier. Neighbourhoods grew around the nuclei of the aristocrats' or rich merchants' town houses, a lane of row houses, or an enclosed market.[4] These *mohullas* (neighbourhoods) were inward looking, and with a single point of entry which was guarded at night.[5] The palace complex of the emperor had a well laid-out network of gardens and low-rise buildings shading off from public to private.[6]

From 1803 to 1857 the British Resident, who shared political power with the Mughal emperor, helped control the public areas, with an army contingent in reserve. The undulating land north of the city was growing into a suburb which became the preferred living area for the Europeans.[7]

The Revolt of 1857 witnessed four months of the suspension of urban governance, while the city within the walls was ruled by a revolutionary council. After the British forces stormed into the city, and the emperor and his entourage fled to the southern suburbs, the imperial control of the city was ended. In the course of the next ten years, there were major changes in the morphology of the city and in rights over land. The army moved in to occupy the palace and a large segment of the town. The *mohulla* (gates) were pulled down so that troops could, if necessary, swiftly move into a neighbourhood. The buildings, gardens and villages (about 100) belonging to the emperor passed to the new municipality.[8] The latter also had power to control *auqaf* properties. In the 1920s, when many historic buildings, inside and outside the walled city, were taken under the protection of the Archaeological Survey, the symbiotic link between these public buildings and their custodians and users ended.

Land control henceforth was based on English common law norms, by which individuals leased land from the State. This was different from the Roman law concept of giving individuals outright ownership and rights in land, as was done in the colonies of France, the Netherlands and Spain.[9] It was also different, of course, from the precarious private control that had existed under the Mughals. In Delhi, British policy led to two changes.

The symbiotic relationship between the city and the palace complex was ended; and the city was sliced in two, as the east–west railway line was cut through it, displacing many neighbourhoods.

If there were many individuals who rejoiced at becoming undisputed owners of urban land, there were many more who were shell-shocked by the sudden imposition, in the wake of brutal military conquest, of those two Victorian institutions: impersonal municipal government and the railways. Apart from all the buildings that were torn down, something else was destroyed – the gradation of public to private spaces. This was replaced by a stark public/private contradistinction.

The British New Delhi (the last of many New Delhis) was built on land which the government, like the Mughal emperor 300 years earlier, bought and laid out – the first example in India of a colonial town where the land was completely under public control.[10] The subsequent history of Delhi was as unexpected as the 1857 Revolt and its sequel had been. In 1947 Delhi was swamped with refugees from West Pakistan; in the staggeringly vast task of providing for them, the reserves of land owned by the government came in useful. Ten years later the Delhi Development Authority (DDA) was constituted – yet another landlord which would control the further use of land in and around the twin capital cities.[11]

Delhi's area has expanded in quantum terms, and in this century its population has increased from 200,000 to 13 million. The control of public spaces by a powerful government is constantly challenged by the inhabitants who treat the city in predatory fashion, taking what they can. The mental baggage of first-generation immigrants has images of living in villages and small towns. The sense of neighbourhood/*mohulla* comes easily to them, but the sense of the sanctity of public spaces has to be *learned*. The second generation has acquired this, together with concern for the future of the city which they see as theirs. In this chapter, we shall see how public areas streets, gardens, buildings and official housing estates have been regulated and used. This may lead us to the conclusion that urban governance can be more effective not by literal adherence to printed rules but by sympathetically understanding popular perceptions.

In Mughal Delhi the street was the most democratic element. The climate conspires to direct much activity and social interaction between men out of doors. 'We are sitting on the public street/Who dares dislodge us' is a popular line by Delhi's favourite nineteenth-century poet Ghalib. The street was a moving feast, with shops and cafés, a contrast to the quieter *galis* where the blank frontages of inward-turned houses discouraged people from observing them/looking in. The street was on a human scale; even if it was wide and long, it had frequent pauses, in the form of *chowks* (a widening of the street, in the form of a circle or octagon). In the absence of an agora, a *chowk* was often the locale for informal meetings, debates and performances.

The use of the street for formal processions was the privilege of the ruler. After 1858, following the Queen's Proclamation promising neutrality towards Indians, every denomination was allowed the right to use the street. On occasion this led to clashes between different groups. Processions and demonstrations continue to be a device to mobilise people, with the concomitant use of loudspeakers fixed on trees/poles, and with the extravagant use of visual propaganda material, all adding up to an aural and visual appropriation of the street. It has also become a common practice, with nominal sanction, to cordon off secondary streets for weddings/prayer-meetings where, again, the overkill in terms of illumination and heightened decibels is tolerated by a people with a history of treating the street as informal space.

The long tradition of not delineating pavements along streets has meant that pavements on the miles of road laid out in Greater Delhi are not respected. Right of way is taken to mean vehicle way, and pavements are narrowed and, increasingly, eliminated, to carve out yet another traffic lane. In the behaviour of road-users, blatant class-consciousness is evident as between vehicles, and between vehicles and pedestrians. The pavements are used to set up kiosks and shops, to store material and even for shanty houses. As the number of cars on Delhi roads increases exponentially, streets are becoming traffic corridors. Ghalib would find it difficult to use them as places of social intercourse. Local government, clearly on the side of the private driver, has decided to ignore pedestrians and not make the effort at upgrading public transport so as to minimise the number of private vehicles on the road. The assumption is that every city is an incipient Los Angeles; to the citizens pavements are not corridors for pedestrian movement but areas to be appropriated where possible.

In pre-colonial Delhi, enclosed gardens or orchards were popular areas for outings; wooded areas (like the spine of the ridge running west of the city) were associated with shrines and ascetics. To the colonial regime, open areas of meadow or woodland were a measure of security, separating the civilians from the army, the Indians from the Europeans. This belief was continued into the design of New Delhi, where a dauntingly open expanse two miles long fronted the Viceroy's palace, and designated gardens serve as buffers between the new capital and future suburbs.[12] Later, the Master Plan of 1962 incorporated the currently fashionable 'green belt' as well as other 'green areas'. In mapping colonies (housing estates) the planners prescribed 'green areas' in proportion to their estimated populations.[13] There was an escape clause – which the citizens were not aware of – that the DDA could change the prescribed land use of any area whenever it chose to. Over time, many 'green areas' have been sacrificed for car parks or shopping precincts. In the last decade, however, as the built area increased, the small neighbourhood parks became more prized, carefully tended and enthusiastically used, by the local Residents' Associations. Larger parks (district parks) are more impersonal and are looked after to the extent that funds permit. There is a strong conviction that picturesque (model) parks need to be protected from people; this explains why there are some parks with exquisite lawns and well designed beds of flowers where the custodians (the DDA Horticulture Department) clearly discourage visits from children, and in some cases bar the gate for many hours a day. The park culture is growing, together with the awareness that Delhi is very generously provided with these, in contrast to other Indian cities, thanks to its Mughal and British heritage.

The counter-colonisation of sections of streets, parks and gardens has been happening since the 1860s. Shops and houses encroached on roads, and poor immigrants built shanty towns on public land. In the 1950s the poorer refugees, and the many construction workers requisitioned to build new government offices also built their own neighbourhoods. In 1959 a count indicated that there were 85 distinct shanty towns, each a miniature village with its own diminutive public space.[14] Squatter settlements are officially illegal, but deals struck with political parties just before elections ensure that political patronage and populist policies will win them a reprieve. The occupants have even learned to negotiate the periodic aggressive measures taken by the government to 'resettle' them elsewhere. They do this by subletting the new flats and moving back to the centre.[15] Another form of defiance is by more exalted beings. An 'unauthorised' religious shrine is almost impossible to demolish. Confident of immunity, the neo-religious begin with a small mound or a ruin and gradually enlarge it into a large-sized shelter. Another form of defiance is the cows and buffaloes that roam comfortably on the streets and neighbourhoods which were built on the pasture or farmland of villages which had been purchased by the DDA. Public areas thus became covert battlegrounds, not between rival neighbours but between a distant government and a people who feel they can equally stake a claim to these areas. There is no agency which is committed to safeguarding public areas. The inconvenience is borne by that most anonymous of town-users, the pedestrians. Arguments based on aesthetics carry little weight; buildings are read critically but not streetscapes.

The Mughals had been great builders, but impersonal public buildings were a British innovation. Libraries and museums, built often on a monumental scale, could overawe, but their interiors tended to depress rather than exalt. They did not generate the sense of affinity that their equivalents in Britain did. Was it to do with the climate? In grey Britain a library was a warm shelter from the rain, in Delhi dreary exile from a sun-soaked outdoors. In offices, a sense of belonging was minimal because of the strong adherence to the principle of hierarchy, a principle translated from the military cantonments. There is a sad contrast between the love and care lavished on private territories and the glaring absence of these in public buildings, a sense of alienation and of lack of responsibility which almost seems to give a sense of satisfaction.[16]

Housing has played a major part in Delhi's landscape in the last 150 years. Like the cantonment, New Delhi and 'colonies' built later hived off much land to provide 'official accommodation' for a burgeoning bureaucracy.[17] About 10 per cent of Delhi's built area is covered with housing conjured up by the Public Works Department (second only to that of the Roman Empire, British officials had said with pride). The DDA's tally of flats built to be sold (by drawing lots) has been an awesome one, too. The flats are divided in nomenclature on the basis of income. This has meant that the ethnocentric city of the colonial period has given place to a strongly class-centric one. As land within the boundaries of Delhi becomes scarce, in space-intensive co-operative housing projects the vertical *mohulla* has become the answer to housing needs. The class basis here is less strident, as are the attendant snobberies. Cosmopolitan Delhi is seen at its best in these apartments, which are the index of Delhi's modernity. They also mark a point of departure in civic management particularly in the business of garbage management. Here they offer a telling contrast to more affluent neighbourhoods, where the rich can retreat into their private territories, ignoring the public areas, and bearing out the truth of Galbraith's comments about private affluence and public squalor.

The colonial and post-colonial city was wasteful of space, where the pre-colonial one had been economical. The latter scored in the sense of *mohulla*/community, the ensuring of security, the willingness to share open spaces. At the time that New Delhi was being built, Patrick Geddes expressed his admiration for the way Indians organised urban space.[18] Today there are very good reasons why it would be useful to revert to these values. 'If land is a primary resource, its intensive and efficient utilisation is an essential requirement of any appropriate planning framework' wrote Geoffrey Payne 20 years ago.[19] It is still valid. Urban problems will remain, as long as planners and people are seen as antagonistic, as long as urban land is viewed in terms of rival colonisations. Official control could be made minimal and intelligible; instead of attempting to adhere to printed laws, one could give the neighbourhoods/*mohullas* a greater share in town governance.

The class segregation created by the colonial government and reinforced by the zoning principles of the DDA breaks down in the face of common threats, of epidemic disease and of crime. The straws in the wind are the voluntary association of three adjacent neighbourhoods in Okhla, in South Delhi – one affluent upper class, one lately rural, one a university campus – in the face of politically generated communitarian tension after 1992. Interneighbourhood and intraneighbourhood interaction on issues can soften the rampant individualism that has characterised modern Delhi, and raise urban living beyond the level of land control to that of living as communities.

Such an outcome – the result of governance from below as well as from above – could help recover not only the gradation from private to semi-public to public which got lost after 1857 but also something of the beautiful city that Delhi once was.

Notes

1. Irfan Habib, *The Agrarian System of Mughal India* (2nd edn, Delhi: Oxford University Press, 1999).
2. Inayat Khan, *Shahjahan-nama*, in A.R. Fuller's translation, by W.E. Begley and Z.A. Desai (eds), (Delhi: Oxford University Press, 1990).
3. Jamal Malik, 'Islamic Institutions and Infrastructure in Shahjahanabad', in E. Ehlers and T. Krafft (eds), *Shahjahanabad/Old Delhi* (Stuttgart: Steiner, 1993).
4. Dargah Q. Khan, *Seir-e-Delhi*, translated from Persian to Urdu by N. Ahmed, (Delhi: Oxford University Press, 1981).
5. T. Krafft, 'Contemporary Old Delhi', in E. Ehlers and T. Krafft (eds), *Shahjahanabad/Old Delhi* (Stuttgart: Steiner, 1993).
6. Stephen Blake, *Shahjahanabad, the Sovereign City in Mughal India* (Cambridge: Cambridge University Press, 1991).
7. Anthony D. King, *Colonial Urban Development* (London: Routledge and Keegan Paul, 1976).
8. Narayani Gupta, *Delhi Between Two Empires (1803–1931)* (Delhi: Oxford University Press, 1981, 1998).
9. P. McAuslan, *Urban Land and Shelter for the Poor* (London: Earthscan, 1985).
10. R.G. Irving, *Indian Summer* (Bombay: Oxford University Press, 1982).
11. Albert Mayer papers, Regenstein Library, Chicago.
12. W.Y. Wolff, *Open Space Planning in India* (Hanover: self-published, 1988).
13. Delhi Development Authority, *Master Plan for Delhi* (Delhi: Delhi Development Authority, 1962).
14. Geoffrey K. Payne, *Urban Housing in the Third World* (London: Routledge and Keegan Paul, 1977).
15. Sabir Ali, *Environment and Resettlement Colonies of Delhi* (Delhi: Har-Anand, 1995).
16. Norma Evenson, *The Indian Metropolis* (Delhi: Oxford University Press, 1989); J. Lang, and M. Desai, *Architecture and Independence: The Search for Identity, India 1880–1980* (Delhi: Oxford University Press, 1997).
17. Anthony D. King, *The Bungalow* (London: Routledge and Kegan Paul, 1984).
18. Patrick Geddes's papers, National Library of Scotland, Edinburgh.
19. Payne, *Urban Housing*.

Index

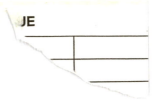